W

Streetsmart Guide to

Valuing a Stock

Other Books in the Streetsmart Series

Streetsmart Guide to Managing Your Portfolio
Streetsmart Guide to Short Selling
Streetsmart Guide to Timing the Stock Market

Streetsmart Guide to Valuing a Stock

The Savvy Investor's Key to Beating the Market

Second Edition

Gary Gray, Patrick J. Cusatis,
and J. Randall Woolridge

McGraw-Hill

New York   Chicago   San Francisco   Lisbon
London   Madrid   Mexico City   Milan   New Delhi
San Juan   Seoul   Singapore   Sydney   Toronto

The **McGraw·Hill** Companies

1 2 3 4 5 6 7 8 9 0 DOC/DOC   0 9 8 7 6 5 4 3

ISBN 0-07-141666-8

McGraw-Hill books are available at special quantity discounts to use as premiums and sales promotions, or for use in corporate training programs. For more information, please write to the Director of Special Sales, McGraw-Hill, Professional Publishing, Two Penn Plaza, New York, NY 10121-2298. Or contact your local bookstore.

 This book is printed on recycled, acid-free paper containing a minimum of 50% recycled de-inked fiber.

Library of Congress Cataloging-in-Publication Data
Gray, Gary
Streetsmart guide to valuing a stock : the savvy investors key to beating the market / by Gary Gray, Patrick J. Cusatis, J. Randall Woolridge.—2nd ed.
    p. cm.
ISBN 0-07-141666-8 (handcover : alk. paper)
1. Corporations—Valuation. 2. Stocks—Prices. I. Cusatis, Patrick.
II. Woolridge, J. Randall. III. Title.
HG4028. V3G696 2003
332.63'221—dc21
    2003003682

To Katie O'Toole, a great writer, a terrific editor,
and a wonderful wife and mother.

G.G.

To my wife, Deborah, my children,
Jacob and Julia, and my parents.

P.J.C.

To my daughters, Jillian, Ainsley, and Ginger.

J.R.W.

Contents

Preface

Streetsmart Guide to Valuing a Stock is a how-to book that provides you with the tools to make money in the stock market. The book's focus is on *stock valuation*—an area of great interest to many investors, but understood by very few.

When you've finished this hands-on, easy-to-use guide, you will have learned how to:

- Value stocks of general market and high-tech companies, such as Microsoft and Cisco Systems;

- Value stocks of financial companies and real estate investment trusts, such as Citigroup, Merrill Lynch, Berkshire Hathaway, and Washington REIT;

- Spot undervalued or overvalued stocks for buying and selling opportunities;

- Estimate important valuation inputs such as growth, operating margin, and cost of capital;

- Find valuation inputs on free Internet Web sites;

- Develop a spreadsheet to value a stock;

- Combine stocks in an efficiently structured investment portfolio;

- Manage your risk; and

- Use the 10 principles of finance to your advantage.

This book is a complete revision of *Streetsmart Guide to Valuing a Stock* (1999). In the four years since the publication of *Streetsmart*, the stock market has crashed, managers of many corporations such as Enron, WorldCom, and Adelphia have been indicted for fraud, and certain Wall Street stock analysts have been discredited and have attained a business stature below that of used car salesmen. We feel that it is time to place stock valuation within the context of some general rules and concepts that are at the core of finance theory. This book explains in simple terms the 10 principles of finance and describes how you can use them to make better investment decisions and to estimate a stock's value.

This book is for all of you who *mistakenly* think you have to be a stock market guru to value stocks like a pro. All the tools you need to value stocks are outlined in the chapters that follow. All that is required is a bit of patience, practice, and persistence.

You don't need an MBA to understand the book's concepts or the 10 principles. The goal of the book is to give all stock market participants—*individual investors, investment club members, stockbrokers, SEC staffers, corporate managers, directors of corporate boards, and ordinary people who want to learn about stock valuation*—a simple quantitative approach for estimating stock values. Our model is a recipe for correctly and conservatively valuing common stock and increasing investment profits.

In this book we describe how you can use Excel to write a spreadsheet to value stocks with a minimum number of inputs. If you don't want to write a spreadsheet program, we show you how and where you can purchase the computer software, which we have developed and use in the book. Finally, we provide a free online stock valuation service on our Web site, *www.valuepro.net/*.

If you're technologically challenged, not to worry. You don't need a computer or an Internet connection to use the discounted free cash flow method to value a stock. In Chapters 5 and 6 we describe how to calculate and estimate, *long-hand,* a company's free cash flow and cost of capital—these are the essential ingredients of stock valuation. In Chapter 7 we show you how and where to get the information that you need for serious valuations. In Chapter 8 we value Citigroup, Merrill Lynch, Berkshire Hathaway, and Washington REIT. This book will help you to learn a lot about valuing stock even if spreadsheets and computers are too intimidating for your personal tastes.

Our goal is to teach you about stock valuation by using a simple and powerful valuation model. This book will make you a better informed, more intelligent, more profitable investor and will help you to understand why stocks such as Cisco trade at $14.45 and Berkshire Hathaway trades at $72,000 per share. Our valuation approach revolves around some very simple calculations that use only addition, subtraction, multiplication and division—no calculus, differential equations, or advanced math. So let's begin by taking our initial plunge into stock valuation.

Good luck, tight lines, and happy valuations!

Gary Gray
Patrick J. Cusatis
J. Randall Woolridge

Acknowledgments

The original *Streetsmart Guide to Valuing a Stock* was conceived and outlined on a trip to Spain. The concepts underlying stock valuation crystallized only as real livestock (6 fighting bulls and 8 steers) attempted to run over us on the narrow, crowded streets of Pamplona.

Integral to the book's progress were the discussions, over many fine meals with our friends in Navarra, of its structure and international appeal. Ana Vizcay and Eduardo Iriso, María Jesus Ruiz Ciordía and Emilio Goicoechea, Luis Arguelles and Merche Amezgaray, José Marí Marco and Carmela Garraleta, Fefa Vizcay and Héctor Ortiz, and Manolo Asiain: We thank you for your hospitality and friendship over the years.

Many readers reviewed various parts of the book. We'd like to thank finance Professor Russ Ezzell and management Professor Charles Snow for peer review and helpful suggestions, and Blake Hallinan for his research efforts. We'd also like to thank merchant bankers—Scott Perper of Wachovia Capital Partners and Rusty Lewis of Verisign; derivatives specialists—Patrick Mooney of Calibre Capital, Mark Hattier of Newman Financial Services, and Dave Eckhart of IMAGE; investment bankers—Gerry Fallon (retired) and Buck Landry of Morgan Keegan; securities law expert Steve Huff of Kutak Rock; Web masters Joe and Jen Cusatis of Intelligent Data Management; and noted Washington bureaucrat—David Seltzer, for their professional and careful review and assistance.

Especially helpful to us were the review and comments from our friends from investment clubs and the general investing public—Lassie MacDonald, Ann Barton, Sarah Ezzell, Barbara Snow, and John Nichols.

The input of the members of the Spruce Creek Rod & Investment Club is appreciated. Those members include: John Wilson, Nick Rozsman, Manny Puello, Rick Simonsen, Kevin Dunphy, Constantin Nelson, Charlie Barkman, Bill Cusatis, Gary Evans, Dean Nelson and the late Uncle Bob.

As always, the input of the members of the Aspen Ski Institute has always been helpful. Those members include: John H. Foote V, Tom Carroll, Bob Jones, Alec Arader and Bill McLucas, among others.

Many thanks to all of the professionals at McGraw-Hill who brought this book to publication, particularly: Stephen Isaacs, acquisition editor; Sally Glover, senior editing supervisor; and Ruth Mannino, production supervisor.

A special thank you to Deb Cusatis and Katie O'Toole, whose writing and editing skills are greatly appreciated.

CHAPTER 1

Introduction and Overview

Financial Flameout

Even the creations of brilliant rocket scientists sometime flame out of control. The financial equivalent of incineration occurred during September 1998, at Long Term Capital Management (LTCM), a multi-billion-dollar hedge fund[1] that was owned by some of Wall Street's greatest intellects. After several years of spectacular returns (43 percent in 1995, 41 percent in 1996, and 17 percent in 1997) for its owners and investors, LTCM suffered a massive collapse and was rescued from bankruptcy by a consortium of its creditors.

Ironically, in 1997 two of LTCM's general partners shared the Nobel Prize in Economics for their breakthrough academic research relating to risk management techniques and the valuation and pricing of stock options. The writings of Dr. Robert C. Merton and Dr. Myron Scholes laid the groundwork for the creation and growth of the financial derivatives (options, forwards, and swaps) markets. Scholes collaborated with the late Fischer Black in developing the famous Black-Scholes Option Pricing Model.

Merton, along with Dr. Zvi Bodie, coauthored the excellent college textbook, *Finance*, published in 1997. The text is structured around three analytical pillars of finance—the time value of money, the valuation of assets, and the management of risk. At the foundation of these pillars are the basic principles, rules and theories of finance that should guide investors to make intelligent financial decisions.

LTCM apparently did not practice properly the risk management strategies that its Nobel Laureates carefully formulated. Nor did LTCM adhere to the financial principles that Bodie and Merton articulated so well in *Finance*. The collapse of LTCM is evidence that even very smart people sometimes employ questionable investment strategies. It also shows that the financial marketplace exacts a heavy toll on those who stray too far from shore. We all can learn from the mistakes of LTCM as well as from more recent examples of carnage—WorldCom, Xerox, Adelphia, Tyco, and Enron among others—in corporate finance and the stock market.

Good Companies—Hot Stocks—Ridiculous Prices

The long bull market of the 1990s spoiled investors and made us overconfident in our stock picking abilities. We did not understand risk. Now that the bubble has burst and we have seen that the stock market moves in more than one direction, we realize that it's not easy to be a successful investor, to beat the averages, or to outperform the indices consistently. The stock market was manic during the late 1990s. Exhibit 1-1 shows the blastoff and then the plummet of the stock market averages over the past five years.

When the stock market soars, cocktail party chatter centers on hot tips and inside information. As Martha Stewart can attest, that information is sometimes true—and in the end, incredibly costly! Stock market touts hype dozens of once-in-a-lifetime opportunities. Every business day on CNNfn and CNBC, promoters and analysts push the current new, new thing—the next Starbucks or Krispy Kreme. Beware, place a hand on your wallet, and hold on! The hype associated with former hot stocks (such as Internet Capital Group once at $200.94—at $0.36 at the end of 2002, Corning down from a high of $75 to $3.31 per share, and JDS Uniphase once at $140.50, now $2.47) propelled their prices to such high levels that they were grossly overvalued. As an ex-

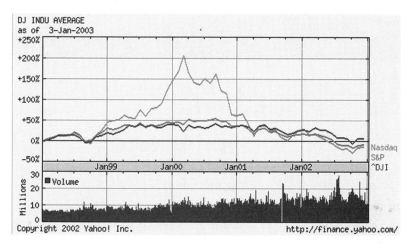

EXHIBIT 1-1   S&P 500, DJIA, and NASDAQ: Five-Year Stock Index Chart

ample, look at Exhibit 1-2 to see the five-year performance of the stock of ICGE.

The prices of many stocks during the late 1990s defied the laws of gravity. It's important that you understand that what goes up without reason eventually must come down. At one point in 2000, the market equity (shares outstanding times stock price) of ICGE was more than $50 billion, even though its book value was negative, and JDSU had a

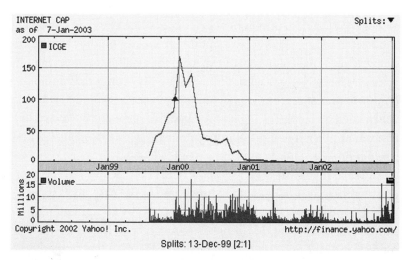

EXHIBIT 1-2   ICGE: Five-Year Stock Price Chart

market equity of over $200 billion—more than 200 times its revenue. Even if God were the CEO of these companies, they could never have generated profits from operations sufficient to support their lofty stock price levels.

Don't be fooled by Jack the Promoter praising a stock, a sector, an industry, or the market in general. Jack is paid to put a positive spin on a story and sell his optimistic tales to the masses. You must educate yourself so that you can ignore Jack and make your own informed decisions. You decide which stocks are undervalued or overvalued and whether to buy or sell. No one should do it for you unless you have hired him or her to manage your assets. If you are unwilling to invest the time and energy necessary to understand the stock market and stock valuation, keep your money in a conservative savings account or in a no-load stock index fund.

The Investment Decision

This book focuses on the *investment decision*—what to do with your excess income and wealth. When you *invest,* you use today's dollars to purchase assets that generate future cash flows in the form of annual income (dividends, interest, rental payments) and price appreciation over time.

We assume that you have fulfilled your consumption needs, however extravagant or spartan they may be; have purchased sufficient insurance to take care of potential catastrophes; have saved enough in a money market or savings account to take care of financial emergencies; and now must allocate your wealth among different investments. We consider only passive financial investments—ones that do not require you to make operating decisions, such as a personal business in which you control the hiring and firing of personnel, or the ownership of a rental property where you may contend with late-night calls regarding broken water heaters or leaking toilets.

Finance is the study of why, how, and whether to invest in projects, ventures, or stocks that have uncertain (*risky*) cash flows to be received in the future. The decision to buy or sell any investment or stock should be based upon three cash-flow-related criteria: a conservative projection of the amount (*rate of return*) of the cash flows, the probable *timing* of the cash flows, and a reasonable assessment of the probability or *risk* associated with receiving the cash flows. Once you estimate the amount, timing, and risk, you use financial techniques to determine the true value of the investment or stock.

When you consider an investment in real estate, each property's location makes it a unique asset. This is not so in the stock market. Shares of common stock of a company are identical[2] and plentiful. Cisco has over seven billion shares outstanding, and after a stock split in January of 2003, Microsoft has over ten billion shares. When Sarah buys 100 shares of Cisco through her online broker, it doesn't matter if the seller is Lehman Brothers, the Christian Brothers, or the Blues Brothers—the shares are identical from an ownership perspective. The world's major stock markets are extremely liquid. Shares of thousands of companies trade on a day-to-day, minute-to-minute basis, with prices reported for all to see.

In this book we teach you how to value a stock. Your buy or sell decision should be driven by the stock's *valuation ratio*—equal to the stock's *value* divided by its *price*. If the valuation ratio is greater than 1.0, the stock's value is greater than its price by some margin, and you should consider buying it. For example, if the value of stock A is $20 and its price is $10, the valuation ratio is $20/$10 = 2.0—a serious buy! If a stock's value is less than its price and the valuation ratio is less than 1.0, you should sell the stock, or at least wait until the price drops before you buy. If the value of stock B is $5 and its price is $10, the valuation ratio is $5/$10 = 0.5—sell it or don't buy the stock at this price.

The 10 Principles of Finance

This book explains the 10 principles of finance and how *you* can use them to help you to make better investment decisions. The 10 principles and our valuation approach apply to investment decisions for all asset classes—*real*, such as real estate, small business ownership, coins and stamps, art and antiques, and other hard assets; and *financial*, such as bonds, other debt instruments, and equities. An important aspect of the book is the valuation of common stocks, an area that we focused on originally in *Streetsmart Guide to Valuing a Stock* (1999). In this book, we dig even deeper into valuation. We show you how to:

- Value stocks of general market and high-tech companies, such as Microsoft and Cisco Systems;

- Value stocks of financial companies and real estate investment trusts, such as Citigroup, Merrill Lynch, Berkshire Hathaway, and Washington REIT;

- Combine stocks in an efficiently structured investment portfolio;

- Manage your risk; and

- Use the 10 principles of finance to your advantage.

We keep the book simple, and we explain the concepts of modern finance using easy-to-understand examples. Our approach revolves around the same three analytical building blocks described by Professors Bodie and Merton:

1. Valuation of assets, which affects the *amount* or the expected rate of return (*rate of returns*);

2. Time value of money, which affects the timing of returns (*timing*); and

3. Management of risk, which affects the probability of receiving returns (*risk management*).

Too frequently, investors have short memories and lose sight of this amount-timing-risk relationship. "Greed run amok,"[3] is Burton Malkiel's description of speculators who caused history's investment manias and the inevitable market collapses that followed. The boom and bust cycle occurred in Holland in the seventeenth century. During the period from 1634 to 1636, prices for tulip bulbs climbed steadily and beyond reason. Then, in the month of January, 1637, prices increased twenty-fold. In February, the market collapsed and tulip bulb prices dropped by more than the amount they gained in January. Many investors lost fortunes and drove Holland's economy into a severe and prolonged depression.

Speculation ran wild in the late 1920s when stocks soared in the United States and then crashed causing the Great Depression. According to Malkiel,[4] most blue-chip stocks fell over 90 percent by the time the stock market bottomed out in 1932. The same inflate-crash-burn scene unfolded in the bursting of the high-tech bubble of 2000, as the NASDAQ Index fell more than 75 percent from its record high.

We could quote dozens of additional examples of investment manias and the inevitable corrections that followed to show how nearsighted and gullible investors can be. An investor should always be skeptical when someone justifies an outrageous price for a risky asset with the phrase, *this time it's different.* It is *never different*! In all economies, in all markets, in all time periods, the principles of investment valuation are the same. If you follow our recommendations, you won't succumb to the irrational exuberance associated with investment manias.

The principles that underlie finance theory cut across and incorporate the three analytic building blocks of *return-timing-risk.* The 10 principles are:

1. Higher Returns Require Taking More Risk
2. Efficient Capital Markets Are Tough to Beat
3. Rational Investors Are Risk Averse
4. Supply and Demand Drive Stock Prices in the Short Run
5. When Analyzing Returns, Simple Averages Are Never Simple
6. Transaction Costs, Taxes, and Inflation Are Your Enemies
7. Time and the Value of Money Are Closely Related
8. Asset Allocation Is a Very Important Decision
9. Asset Diversification Will Reduce Risk
10. An Asset Pricing Model Should Be Used to Value Your Investments

Overview of the Book

In Chapter 2, we examine the 10 principles of finance and lay the groundwork for all that follows. As we describe each principle, we also recommend how you can use it to make better investment decisions. The principles range from common-sense suggestions, such as minimizing transactions costs, to concepts that may be new for nonfinance types, such as understanding and using a pricing model to value a stock.

In Chapter 3, we provide definitions relating to valuation, describe the stock valuation process, and introduce you to the discounted cash flow (*DCF*) valuation method. We discuss the role that all investors played in inflating the high-tech bubble. We describe the different types of stock valuation approaches and examine the importance of expectations, emotions, and analyst recommendations in determining a stock's price. We also differentiate between a stock's price and its value.

In Chapter 4, we describe the discounted cash flow approach. We use Microsoft, the company that at the end of 2002 had the largest market capitalization in the world, as our first valuation example. In Chapters 5 and 6, we show you how to value the common stock of most corporations by using a small set of cash flow and interest rate inputs. Our goals are to demystify the stock valuation process, make stock valuation easier to understand, and show you how to make money in the stock market by purchasing *undervalued* stocks and selling *overvalued* stocks.

How do we do it? In Chapter 5, using Cisco Systems as our example, we explain which corporate cash flow measures are important, how they are related, and how they influence a stock's value. In Chapter 6, we look at the simple capital structure of Cisco and the more complex capital structure of Consolidated Edison, and we examine the effect of a firm's capital structure and interest rates on its stock value. This book helps you put into perspective the various pieces of the stock valuation puzzle to see the big picture. It makes the seemingly complex world of Wall Street easier to understand.

If you're familiar with the stock market, using the DCF valuation approach should be relatively easy, and a lot of previously confusing concepts will fall into place. If you're a relative newcomer to the stock market and are unfamiliar with investing concepts and jargon (a Glossary and List of Acronyms are included in the book), you may need to read certain sections twice to understand them. Hang in there! It will be worth your investment of time and should compound quickly into investment profits.

The approach for valuing stocks that we favor and use throughout the book is a discounted cash flow method. The DCF approach is a technique that is employed by investors and traders to value all types of financial instruments, such as U.S. Government bonds, preferred stocks, corporate bonds, and mortgage-backed securities. Investment bankers use DCF models to value merger and acquisition targets, leveraged buyout transactions and initial public offerings of stock. Domestic and international corporations use DCF techniques to analyze virtually all of their capital budgeting and investment decisions. Corporate managers who read this book will immediately understand how their operating and financing decisions affect their company's stock price. DCF is the preferred valuation approach of both Wall Street and Main Street.

The DCF method has four steps:

1. Develop a set of future cash flows (*rates of return*) for a corporation based on expectations about the company's growth, net operating profit margin, income tax rates, and fixed and working capital requirements.

2. Estimate a discount rate for the corporation that takes into account the *timing* and potential *risks* of receiving those cash flows.

3. Discount the resulting cash flow estimates and total them to determine an enterprise value for the corporation as a whole.

4. Reduce the enterprise value by the amount of debt, preferred stock, and other claims of the corporation, and divide that amount by the number of shares outstanding. This gives us the per-share intrinsic value of the corporation's common stock.

We can then compare the intrinsic value to the price of the stock to determine which stocks are undervalued or overvalued, and which stocks to buy, sell, or hold.

If the valuation procedure sounds complicated, trust us, it's not. We show you how you perform these calculations easily—using simple addition, multiplication, subtraction, and division. If you have a computer, you can use our valuation approach to write a simple stock valuation spreadsheet program. If you don't want to write a spreadsheet program, we show you how and where you can purchase the ValuePro 2002 computer software, which we have developed and use in the book. Finally, we provide a free online stock valuation service on our Web site, *www.valuepro.net/*.

Chapter 7 points and clicks you to the information you will need to value a stock. Most of the inputs come from corporate annual and quarterly reports that are found easily on the Internet or in the corporation's published financial statements. In today's data-friendly environment, financial information flows quickly. Most companies post their annual and quarterly reports and earnings releases on their own Internet Web sites. Also, the Securities and Exchange Commission (SEC) allows users to download various corporate financial reports through its EDGAR database, available at its Internet Web site address *www.sec.gov/*.

Reams of corporate financial information are accessible through computer information services like America Online and the Microsoft Network. These services, which charge a monthly fee to subscribers, allow free access to some Web sites that you otherwise might have to pay for. Investment information is available through online financial information Web sites such as Morningstar, Hoover's, Value Line, the Motley Fool, Wall Street Research Net, and Standard & Poor's Information Service. Some of these services are free or partially free, and some involve subscription and payment of fees.

In Chapter 8, we value the stock of four companies. Three are financial companies: Citigroup, the world's largest commercial banking conglomerate; Merrill Lynch, a leading investment bank and securities brokerage firm; and Berkshire Hathaway, the principal business of which is property and casualty insurance. We discuss aspects of valuation that are particularly important when valuing highly levered companies in the finance industry. We also value a small-cap REIT, Washington Real Estate Investment Trust, and discuss adjustments that we make to the DCF valuation when we value REITs.

The book gives you the concepts and information that you need to buy low and sell high. Our valuation approach allows you to play different what-if games to see how a change in growth, profits, or interest rates affects a stock's value.

So exactly what went wrong at Long Term Capital Management? Some market pros think that the bets that LTCM made were too big for the market segments in which they were playing. Others believe they had strayed into asset classes that they didn't understand. Based on available information, we believe that their hedging strategy may have been too concentrated. LTCM's assets were broadly diversified, but its hedges were not—a serious mismatch. We discuss the importance of diversification in Principle 9 of Chapter 2. Many of LTCM's hedges depended in some way on the U.S. Treasury bond market, either directly through futures contracts, or indirectly through derivative contracts such as interest rate swaps.

The Russian debt crisis that occurred in mid-1998 spurred a flight to quality by investors, who sold risky assets and purchased safe U.S. government bonds. Treasury bond yields dropped sharply, bond prices rallied significantly, and the value of LTCM's hedge liabilities (what it owed) increased much more rapidly than the value of its assets (what it owned) increased. These unequal price movements and LTCM's highly levered position resulted in an asset/liability imbalance that wiped out LTCM's capital and placed it in violation of its lending agreements—de facto bankruptcy.

Robert Merton and Myron Scholes were unable to convince their partners at Long Term Capital Management to follow their Nobel Prize winning risk management strategies to the letter. As a result, LTCM exploded. Similarly, many investors who owned the red-hot Internet stocks at the end of the high-tech bubble were scorched. If you had followed the advice contained in this book, you would not have bought ICGE at $200.94, or JDSU at $140.50 per share. You would have insulated your portfolio from irrational exuberance and avoided these financial flameouts.

Notes

1. A *hedge fund* is a sophisticated investment partnership that borrows money, purchases financial assets, and simultaneously hedges the risks associated with owning the assets by selling offsetting hedge liabilities.

2. A number of companies have dual classes of common stock. One class of stock usually has preferential voting rights over the other class of stock.

3. See Burton Malkiel, *A Random Walk Down Wall Street*, W.W. Norton, (1999) page 35.

4. Malkiel, page 51.

CHAPTER 2

The 10 Principles of Finance and How to Use Them

During the inflating of the high-tech bubble in the 1990s, investors believed that stock prices moved only upward and that the Dow would climb to 36,000. Investors subscribed to the *greater fool theory*—if they bought Internet Capital Group (ICGE) at $200.94 per share, they thought they could sell it to someone tomorrow for $225. Many investors did not understand risk or the trade-off between risk and expected return. Nor did they realize how quickly stock prices plummet in response to bad news, or how interest rates and profits affect stock values.

The bubble imploded. At the end of 2002, the NASDAQ index closed at 1,335.51—down 75 percent from its high; ICGE traded at $0.36 per share; and investors desperately needed a rational and informed approach for investing in stocks. This book fills that need.

This chapter introduces the 10 principles of finance, which anchor the stock valuation process. Some principles are obvious. Others are subtle, such as efficient capital markets, and are based upon the results of academic research and testing. Some of the research that we discuss may use terms that are unfamiliar to readers who don't possess a finance or statistics background. Not to worry! When we describe a new term, concept, or principle, we use simple examples to illustrate its importance. If a section is initially unclear, please reread it. It will be worth your investment of time because ultimately, we will show you how to use the 10 principles to increase your wealth and make better investment decisions.

Principle 1: Higher Returns Require Taking More Risk

Return versus Risk

A rational investor favors a higher return on a stock over a lower return, and prefers to take less risk rather than more risk. Unfortunately, there is no free lunch in the world of finance. A trade-off exists between higher expected return on an investment and greater risk. Safe investments have low returns. High returns require investors to take big risks.

Some Definitions Relating to Return and Risk

It's important that we all start on the same page when discussing expected returns and risk. In this section, we define some important terms that relate to the calculation of returns on an asset. We then tackle the thorny problem of understanding risk.

Definitions Relating to Return:

Expected Return on a Risky Asset—$E(R_i)$ is the rate of return an investor expects to receive on a risky asset over a period of time. The expected return consists of regular cash flow payments, such as dividends on a stock or interest on a bond, plus or minus any changes in the price of the asset. When we discuss a pricing model in Principle 10, we describe how to estimate the expected return on a risky asset using a simple equation.

Expected Return on a Portfolio of Risky Assets is the expected rate of return on each risky asset in a portfolio, multiplied by its portfolio weight. The portfolio weight is the percentage of the total portfolio's value that is invested in each risky asset.

Expected Return on the Market—$E(R_m)$ is the rate of return that an investor expects to receive on a diversified portfolio of common stock. The expected return on the market is usually measured by the recent average return on the stock market. Many investors use the rate of return on the S&P 500 Index as a measure of market performance.

Return on the Risk-Free Asset—R_f is the rate of return that an investor receives on a safe asset—free from credit risk. Obligations of the U.S. Treasury are assumed to be risk free because it is believed that the U.S. government will always meet its financial obligations. To meet those payments, the government has powers that companies and individuals don't have—it can borrow money, increase taxes, or print more money. For the rate of return on the risk-free asset, we use the current yield on a 10-year U.S. Treasury bond.

Definitions Relating to Risk:

Risk reflects the uncertainty associated with the expected returns of an asset. Buying Treasury bills is a low-risk investment. You are assured of receiving your money with interest when the T-bill matures. On the other hand, the risk of investing in a volatile biotech stock is high. The actual return that you receive depends upon the future price of the company's stock. Often the stock price depends on the company's receiving FDA approval of a new drug, or on a set of other uncertain events. Many things could go wrong and torpedo the stock's price. Or the planets may align and the stock price could multiply. *Risk* is the part of an asset's price movement that is caused by a surprise or an unexpected event. It is measured by a statistic known as the *standard deviation* of the return on the asset, which we discuss below. The risk of a stock is subdivided into two categories: unsystematic risk and systematic risk.

Unsystematic risk is the risk caused by a surprise event that affects only one company, such as an accounting irregularity, new drug discovery, or a patent expiration; or it could be caused by an event that affects a small group of companies, such as a steel workers' strike. Unsystematic risk is unique to a stock or industry. The effects of unsystematic risks for an investor are reduced significantly by proper diversification of the assets in a portfolio.

Systematic risk is the risk caused by a surprise event that affects the entire economy and all assets to some degree, such as an increase in interest rates, a terrorist attack, or the declaration of war. The level of systematic risk for an asset is not reduced by diversification.

The stock market does not reward investors with a higher return for accepting greater unsystematic risk because it can be minimized or eliminated through proper diversification. In the valuation approach that we use, the expected return on a stock depends only on its systematic risk.

Beta—(β_i) is a measure of the systematic risk of an asset. The total stock market as measured by the S&P 500 Index has a beta of 1.0. The beta of a stock with the same price movement as the market also has a beta of 1.0. A stock that has a price movement that is generally greater than the price movement of the S&P 500, such as a technology or Internet stock, has a beta greater than 1.0. A stock with a below-average price movement, such as a public utility, has a beta less than 1.0.

Market Risk Premium—$[E(R_m) - R_f]$ is equal to the expected return on the stock market, the expected return on the S&P 500 Index, minus the rate of return on the risk-free asset, R_f. It is a measure of the increased return that you expect to receive when you buy a stock with average risk in excess of the return on a Treasury bond. Assume that McDonald's stock has a beta equal to the market beta of 1.0. If investors expect an 8 percent return on McDonald's stock, and 10-year Treasury yields are 5 percent, the market risk premium is 3 percent. Market risk premiums increase when investors become more risk averse, and decrease when investors become less risk averse.

Standard Deviation of Return—(σ): The overall risk of an asset is measured by the variability of its returns. The standard deviation is the statistic that is used to measure how wildly or tightly the actual observed stock returns cluster around the average. Higher standard deviation means wilder fluctuations, more volatility, and greater risk.

Although the term sounds intimidating, standard deviation is not difficult to calculate. We measure the standard deviation of a group of returns by taking each observed return, subtracting the average return, squaring the resulting difference, and adding the squares. This gives us the sum of the squares. Next, we divide the sum of the squares by the number of observations minus 1 (one). The result is the variance. Finally, we take the square root of the variance to get the standard deviation of the returns. While this may seem complicated to explain, it is easy to compute using any standard spreadsheet program like Excel, or a handheld calculator with financial functions built in. Furthermore, the interpretation of the standard deviation is much simpler than the calculation.

An example may be helpful. Assume that ABC stock has the four yearly returns shown in column 2 of Table 2-1.

TABLE 2-1 Standard Deviation of ABC's Stock Return

Year	Observed Return	Average Return	Deviation of Return	Squared Deviation
1	9.00%	10.50%	−1.50%	0.000225
2	15.00%	10.50%	4.50%	0.002025
3	−3.00%	10.50%	−13.50%	0.018225
4	21.00%	10.50%	10.50%	0.011025
Totals	42.00%		0.00%	0.0315

The average annual return over the four years is 10.5 percent as shown in column 3. The sum of the deviations around an average is always equal to zero, as shown at the bottom of column 4. The sum of the squares of the deviations divided by (n − 1) yields the *variance* of the returns—in this case it is equal to [.0315/(4 − 1)] = 0.0105. The square root of the variance is the *standard deviation* of the distribution, in this case $(0.0105)^{(\frac{1}{2})}$ = 10.25 percent.

The standard deviation measures the spread of the observations around the average of the returns. A high standard deviation means a big spread of returns and a high risk that the actual return will not equal the expected return. In finance and economics, risk has both positive and negative implications.

Normal Distribution: You may remember the grading curve that turned your high school Ds into Bs. The curve is called a *bell curve* and is a classic example of a *normal distribution.* Most theories regarding the pricing of financial assets assume that the distribution of returns for an asset follows a normal distribution. The normal distribution is a bell-shaped symmetrical curve. The shape of the curve is determined by two key variables: the average of the observations, and the standard deviation of the observations.

In a normal distribution, about two-thirds of the observations will be in a range of plus and minus one standard deviation around the average, and 95 percent of the observations will be in a range of plus or minus two standard deviations around the average. In the case of the stock of ABC, the average return is 10.5 percent and the standard deviation is 10.25 percent. We expect that two-thirds of the observations will be in the range between 10.5 percent plus or minus 10.25 per-

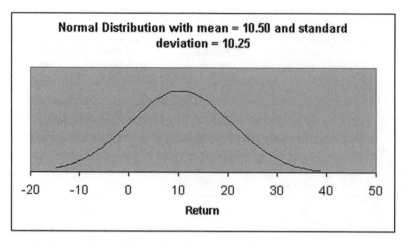

Normal Distribution with mean = 10.50 and standard deviation = 10.25

Return

EXHIBIT 2-1   Normal Distribution

cent—or 20.75 percent to 0.25 percent. We also expect that 95 percent of the observations will be between 10.5 percent plus or minus (2 * 10.25 percent), or 31 percent to −10.0 percent.

If the distribution of the returns of ABC stock over time is normal, it would appear as in Exhibit 2-1.

Congratulations! If you made it through the preceding discussion of variance and standard deviation and you're still reading, you've already survived the densest material you will encounter in this book. These concepts are to modern finance what Newton's laws of motion are to black holes—both are theories that are crucial to understanding some very dense matter. Now, let's review a study that examines the relationship between the expected rate of return of an asset and the risk of receiving that return.

The Ibbotson and Sinquefield Study

Professors Roger Ibbotson and Rex Sinquefield[1] calculated historical annual rates and distributions of returns from 1925 until 2001 on the following classes of investments:

1. U.S. Treasury bills with a three-month maturity

2. U.S. government bonds with an average 20-year maturity

3. High-quality corporate bonds with an average 20-year maturity

TABLE 2-2   Ibbotson and Sinquefield Study

Asset Class	Compound Annual Return	Simple Average Annual Return	Std. Dev. of Return
Inflation	—	3.10%	—
U.S. Treasury Bills	3.80%	3.90%	3.20%
U.S. Treasury Bonds	5.30%	5.70%	9.40%
Corporate Bonds	5.80%	6.10%	8.60%
Large Company Stocks	10.70%	12.70%	20.20%
Small Company Stocks	12.50%	17.30%	33.20%

4. Large cap common stocks as represented by 500 of the largest companies in the United States

5. Small cap common stocks as represented by the smallest twenty percent of the companies listed on the NYSE

The results of the study are important and show the direct relationship between the expected return of an asset and the risk associated with receiving that return. Table 2-2 presents the summary statistics for returns on the five asset classes. The average return is calculated on a compound average and simple average basis, the difference between which we describe in Principle 5. Risk is measured by the standard deviation of returns.

The I&S Study demonstrates the direct trade-off between return and risk. An investment in a Treasury bill with no default risk and little price volatility has a lower expected average return (3.8 percent) than a large cap stock (10.7 percent). The Treasury bill also has a lower risk measure—3.2 percent relative to a portfolio of large company stocks with a standard deviation of 20.2 percent. Returns on individual stocks can swing more wildly than the portfolios shown in Table 2-2. For example, we showed how the price of Internet Capital Group fell from $200.94 per share to $0.36 per share in a brief period of time. As shown below in Exhibit 2-2, on average, investing in common stocks and accepting risk have increased returns significantly.

When we think about risk, most of us focus only on negative outcomes—losing a job, breaking a leg while skiing a double black dia-

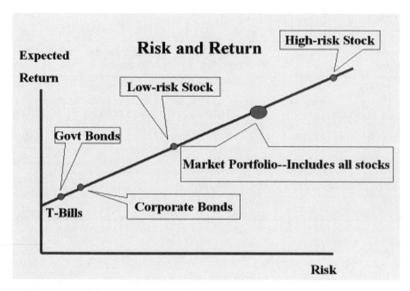

EXHIBIT 2-2   Risk versus Return Line

mond on Ajax Mountain, or being gored while running with the bulls in Pamplona. In economics and finance, risk is measured by assigning *equal probability to both negative and positive outcomes.* As we discussed, we typically calculate the risk of an investment by its standard deviation. The measure of risk is the same if the observed return exceeds the average return by 10 percent or if it is 10 percent below the average return.

Return versus Risk: Our Recommendation

When deciding whether to buy or sell a stock, we assess whether the probabilities of positive or negative surprises are equal, or whether the probabilities of reward or risk are skewed in a particular direction. Over time, there is a tendency for the return and risk of the markets to revert to their average levels, a concept known as *reversion to the mean.*

For example, the returns on the S&P 500 over the 1995-1999 period were as follows: 37.4 percent, 23.1 percent, 33.3 percent, 28.6 percent and 21 percent. The average annual return over this five-year period was 28.7 percent—the best five-year run in the history of the stock market! However, the average annual return for large company stocks over the long run, as we can see from Table 2-2, has been about 12 percent.

Mean reversion suggests that the stock market run of the late 1990s could not be sustained indefinitely, and that much lower or negative returns were on the horizon to bring stock prices back into line with their long-term trend.

When stock prices are at relatively low levels as measured by price-to-sales, price-to-book value, or price-to-earnings ratios, the probability of a very good stock return has the market screaming *buy*, and we buy. Conversely, when price-to-book values and price-to-earnings ratios approach levels of irrational exuberance, we sell overvalued stocks, flee to the sidelines, and invest in bonds or money markets. For instance, during the late 1990s the prices of technology stocks were at levels far higher than their operating profits could ever support. The downside risk of tech stocks appeared to be significantly higher than the upside potential. Consequently, we reduced our exposure to the equity market. Likewise, at the end of 2002, with the economy slowing and prices of many goods falling, a major concern among investors is the prospect of deflation. The 10-year U.S. Treasury rate was 3.82 percent—near a 40-year low, and not a great time to buy long-term bonds. Because of the historically low yields, we were light in the bond market.

Be prepared to take on additional risks to earn increased returns, but first make sure that the odds are in your favor. This is part of the asset allocation decision that we discuss in Principle 8.

Principle 2: Efficient Capital Markets Are Tough to Beat

Efficient Capital Markets

According to finance theory, this is the short story on *efficient capital markets* (ECM). The stock market is brutally efficient; current stock prices reflect all publicly available information; and stock prices react completely, correctly, and almost instantaneously to incorporate the receipt of new information. Sound realistic?

If the stock market is efficient, it would be useless to analyze patterns of past stock prices and trading volume to forecast future prices—which are what market technicians do in technical analysis. It also would be useless to analyze the economy, industries, and companies, and to study financial statements in an effort to find stocks that are undervalued or overvalued—which are what most research analysts do in fundamental analysis.

Many of Wall Street's investment professionals think that the concept of efficient capital markets is just the musing of some ivory tower academics and that the theory doesn't properly describe the real life action of the stock market. Many academics disagree and point to studies that support the notion that the stock market is efficient. The good news for Wall Street professionals is that serious chinks exist in the armor of proponents of efficient capital markets.

Efficient capital markets, along with the *random walk hypothesis* of stock prices and the *capital asset pricing model*, form the cornerstone of modern portfolio theory (*MPT*). The development and championing of efficient capital markets is identified closely with the finance faculty at the University of Chicago, particularly Dr. Eugene F. Fama.

In simple terms, an *efficient capital market* (ECM) is a market that efficiently processes information. Prices of securities fully reflect available information and are based on an accurate evaluation of all available information.

A *random walk* is a path that a variable takes, such as the observed price of a stock, where the future direction of the path (up or down) can't be predicted solely on the basis of past movements. As far as the stock market is concerned, a random walk means that it is impossible to predict short-run changes in stock prices by looking at past price patterns and trading volume. In short, successive price changes are independent of each other, so the best estimate of tomorrow's stock price is today's stock price. In the long-run, researchers have found that most stock prices move in tandem with a stock's long-term growth of earnings and dividends. After adjusting for this growth trend, the random walk hypothesis assumes that the paths of stock prices are, in fact, *random*.

The *capital asset pricing model* (CAPM) is a theory about the pricing of assets and the trade-off between the risk of the asset and the expected returns associated with the asset. In the CAPM, two types of risk are associated with a stock: unsystematic or firm-specific risk; and market or systematic risk, measured by a firm's beta. (We discuss CAPM and beta in greater detail at the end of this chapter and in Chapter 6.)

Hundreds of doctoral dissertations and academic papers are based on various *event studies*[2] that test the efficient capital market hypothesis. These studies are designed to find exceptions, or anomalies, to the predictions associated with efficiency. The goal of many of the studies has been to find an investment strategy or trading rule that consistently produces investment returns, adjusted for risk, that are greater than the returns associated with a long-term buy-and-hold the general stock market strategy.

Some of the studies found that certain trading rules produced higher returns than a buy-and-hold strategy, but when trading costs were incorporated, the excess returns vanished. Other studies found that a certain investment approach (the January effect, small cap stocks, Dogs of the Dow) worked for a period of time and generated excess returns. However, once the strategy was touted and known by the general public, the excess returns disappeared due to too many investors playing the same game. The majority of studies have shown that new information is quickly incorporated into stock prices and the excess returns that are associated with certain stock-selection strategies are arbitraged away. In market lore, there is empirical evidence that the stock market is relatively efficient, or at least semiefficient.

A number of assumptions about investor behavior and the structure of capital markets underlie modern portfolio theory and the efficient capital market hypothesis. Investors are assumed to be rational and calculating, to have identical beliefs and expectations of how the market works, and to have equal access to new information. Investors are assumed to be intelligent and so well informed that the prices they establish, based on new information, are correct (equilibrium) prices. Sound like the real world?

If the stock market is truly efficient, stock prices will react quickly to new information. Let's assume that at 11 a.m., XYZ Company releases positive-earnings news that should increase the value of its stock by \$10 to \$60 per share. If the efficient capital markets theory holds, we would expect the type of price reaction shown in Exhibit 2-3 as the Immediate Adjustment example. If markets are not efficient, we would expect the market to adjust to new information over time, as shown by the Gradual Adjustment example.

Enter Behavioral Finance

In recent years, the assumptions underlying MPT have been challenged by academicians who specialize in the field of behavioral finance, a branch of finance that examines human decision-making and

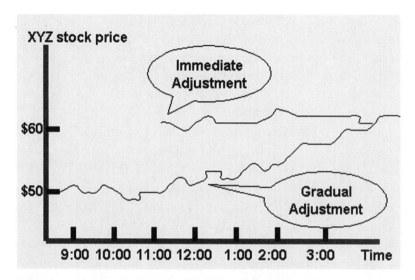

EXHIBIT 2-3   How Stock Prices Adjust to New Information

behavioral patterns and interjects sociology and psychology into the mix. MPT assumes rational, calculating, intelligent investors who focus solely on stock prices. Behavioral theorists have conducted studies that show that investors are not like that at all.

The 2002 Nobel Prize in Economics was awarded to behavioral finance specialists, Dr. Daniel Kahneman, a professor of psychology at Princeton University, and Dr. Vernon Smith of George Mason University. Kahneman, in collaborating with the late Dr. Amos Tversky, challenged the assumption that consumers are rational and markets behave rationally. He showed that individuals make errors in judgment that can be accurately predicted. Smith in the late 1980s conducted mock stock market experiments with students and showed that stock markets were not efficient. He found that people and markets, at times, behave irrationally. Sound like the high-tech bubble?

Today's younger proponents of behavioral finance, notably Professors Richard Thaler, Robert Shiller, and Robert Haugen, have published studies and books[3] that also call into question the assumptions of rational investor behavior that underlie efficient capital markets and modern portfolio theory. They find that investors hate to lose, which causes them to hold on to losing stocks much longer than they should.

They find that investors often are ill informed and tend to overreact or underreact to new information, and that investors love patterns (technical analysis) and tend to find them, even where they don't exist. They also find that investors are overconfident in their abilities and tend to be overoptimistic. Overconfidence causes investors to think that they are smarter than they are, and leads them to underestimate risk.

In short, they find that investors are human exhibiting all of the associated flaws of humanity. Investors are not the cold, calculating, completely rational automatons that are assumed in MPT.

The Fama and French Study

One set of anomalies, however, has been identified as very promising. We have designed our investment program and valuation approach around this research. Dr. Eugene F. Fama, the leading proponent of ECMs, and Dr. Kenneth R. French designed and conducted the breakthrough study.[4] The study was published in the June 1992 issue of the *Journal of Finance*, the world's most prestigious academic finance publication.

The study compares the performance of portfolios of stocks with certain similar characteristics. For example, Fama and French grouped stocks by book-value-to-market value ratios (BV/MV) and studied their return performance over time. They also grouped stocks by earnings-to-price (E/P) ratios, and by the size of stock market capitalization.

The study showed, among other things, that portfolios of stocks with a high ratio of book value of equity (BE) to market value of equity (ME), consistently outperformed portfolios with low BE/ME ratios. The study also found that stocks with high earnings-to-price ratios (low price to earnings ratios) consistently outperformed portfolios of stocks with low earnings-to-price ratios (high price-to-earnings ratios) and that stocks with small market capitalization outperformed stocks with large market capitalization. This study called to question the validity of efficient capital markets and was a very troubling result for Professors Fama and French.

The F&F study examines monthly stock returns during the period from July of 1963 until December of 1990 and includes nearly all of the nonfinancial stocks traded on the New York Stock Exchange, American Stock Exchange, and NASDAQ. The portion of the study that examines BE/ME ratios was designed so that, at the beginning of July of each year, stocks are divided into 10 portfolios based on their BE/ME ratios. Portfolio 1 consists of the stocks with the lowest BE/ME ratios, portfolio 2, 3, 4 . . . consist of groups of stocks with increasing BE/ME ratios, with portfolio 10 consisting of the stocks with the highest BE/ME ratios.

The monthly returns for each of the 10 portfolios are measured over 12 months. The following July, each stock's BE/ME ratio is recomputed and stocks are reassigned to the ten portfolios based on their new BE/ME ratios ranging from lowest to highest. Stocks may move from one portfolio to another. The returns for the portfolios are again measured over the ensuing twelve months. The return calculation and sorting process occurs again and again over the 26-year period, and an average return of each of the 10 portfolios is computed. Fama and French further subdivide portfolios 1 and 10 into two portfolios each, resulting in a total of twelve portfolios. Table 2-3 and Exhibit 2-4 present summaries of their findings:

TABLE 2-3 1992 Fama and French Stock Return Study
Portfolios Based on Ascending Book Equity/Market Equity Ratios

Portfolio	Monthly Return	Annualized Return	Avg. Number of Stocks	Weighted Avg. Return	Difference in Return
1A	0.30%	3.60%	89	14.99%	−11.39%
1B	0.67%	8.04%	98	14.99%	−6.95%
2	0.87%	10.44%	209	14.99%	−4.55%
3	0.97%	11.64%	222	14.99%	−3.35%
4	1.04%	12.48%	226	14.99%	−2.51%
5	1.17%	14.04%	230	14.99%	−0.95%
6	1.30%	15.60%	235	14.99%	0.61%
7	1.44%	17.28%	237	14.99%	2.29%
8	1.50%	18.00%	239	14.99%	3.01%
9	1.59%	19.08%	239	14.99%	4.09%
10A	1.92%	23.04%	120	14.99%	8.05%
10B	1.83%	21.96%	117	14.99%	6.97%
			2261		

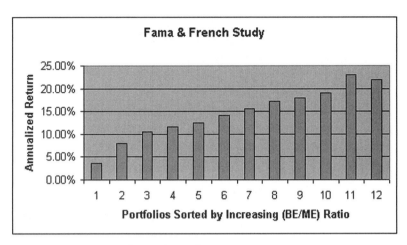

EXHIBIT 2-4 Fama and French Study

The study's results are eye popping. The efficient capital market hypothesis predicts that the returns of each of the portfolios should be about equal to the average stock return in the sample, approximately 15 percent. This certainly is not the case when the size of BE/ME ratios acts as the basis for the formulation of portfolios. As we move from portfolios with stocks that have lower BE/ME ratios to higher BE/ME ratios, we observe an almost uniform increase in monthly and annualized returns. The investment strategy, which purchases stocks with the highest BE/ME ratios, would have a return that exceeded the average annualized return (14.99 percent) of the 2261 stocks in the study by approximately 7 percent per year. The strategy would have a return that exceeded the average return of stocks in the lowest (BE/ME) portfolio by almost 20 percent per year. These results rock!

The F&F study also examines the relationship between earnings/price ratios and finds a similar result. Portfolios of stocks that have high E/P ratios (low P/E ratios) have consistently higher actual returns than portfolios of stocks with low E/P ratios (high P/E ratios).

Other researchers have conducted studies based upon the F&F study with roughly the same results. In 1997, Fama & French studied stocks that were traded in 13 international stock markets and found similar results. Stocks with high BE/ME ratios significantly outperformed stocks with lower ratios in 12 of the international markets. The Italian stock market was the lone exception.

In their 1992 study, Fama and French never use the words *growth stock, value stock, undervalued,* or *overvalued.* Conversely, Dr. Robert Haugen uses these words often in his book, *The New Finance: the Case Against Efficient Markets.* He uses the F&F study as the basis for much of his criticism of MPT. He equates stocks with high BE/ME ratios or high E/P ratios to *value stocks,* and low BE/ME ratios or low E/P ratios to *growth stocks.* He presents the typical behavioral finance arguments to suggest that fallible human participants in inefficient markets are guilty of being overly optimistic about profit levels for growth firms for periods far into the future, causing *growth stocks* to be *overvalued.* Likewise, market participants tend to be too pessimistic about the prospects for the stocks of recently unsuccessful firms that have low growth rates and small net operating profit margins. These stocks become *value stocks* and are *undervalued* in the stock market. In the long run, the returns on growth stocks drift downward to the average market return, and the returns on value stocks float upward to the average, reverting to the mean.

Although the results did not please them, Fama and French uncovered a good way to optimize the expected returns from investing in stock. Robert Haugen makes some strong arguments to follow the recommendations implied by the F&F study—purchase *undervalued* stocks and sell *overvalued* stocks. This is the investment approach that we advocate.

Efficient Capital Markets: Our Recommendation

Even if some anomalies exist, we believe that the U.S. capital markets are reasonably efficient. Stock prices react quickly to new information, and it is very difficult for an investor to beat consistently the investment returns associated with a buy-and-hold strategy.

Opportunities that produce excess returns still exist, such as investing in low P/E or high book-value-to-market-value stocks. We love to take advantage of these opportunities. However, following this strategy is not always for the faint of heart, particularly if the ratio is attractive because of a recent decline in stock price due to an accounting scandal (Enron or WorldCom) or corporate governance fiasco (Adelphia). A stock's price can go to zero, and bankruptcy proceedings frequently leave stockholders with worthless stock certificates—suitable only for the recycling bin.

We use the results of our own fundamental research of a stock, such as its book-to-market value and price-earnings ratios, as an initial signal to attract us to a company the stock of which may be undervalued or overvalued. We run the company through our valuation model and determine its intrinsic stock value. If the intrinsic value is greater than the stock's price, and the value/price ratio is greater than 1.0, the stock is undervalued and a buying opportunity may exist. If intrinsic value is less than the stock's price and the value/price ratio is less than 1.0, the stock is overvalued and we would sell it or avoid buying it.

We then assess the cause of the favorable value/price relationship. If the cause of the positive ratio is due to extreme financial distress, we would not purchase the stock. If the cause is due to a temporary problem or concern, it may be a buying opportunity. Once we're comfortable that the company will remain viable, we then determine if the value/price relationship indicates a purchase. If the odds are in our favor, we pull the trigger and buy!

Principle 3: Rational Investors Are Risk Averse

Risk aversion means that a rational investor prefers less risk to more risk. "A bird in the hand is worth two in the bush." This common expression along with, "A safe dollar is worth more than a risky dollar," reflects *risk aversion.* Finance theory is based upon the assumption that investors exhibit risk-averse behavior. To a risk-averse investor, the pain of losing a dollar is greater than the pleasure of winning a dollar.

A risk-averse investor does not avoid risk at all cost. She may gamble with small percentages of her wealth in hopes of attaining a significant but unlikely payoff. She can make the occasional trip to Las Vegas or Atlantic City and feed the quarter slot machines or take a seat at the two-dollar blackjack table. She also may participate in the Power Ball lottery in hopes of striking it big, even though she knows that the odds are greatly against her. With a small portion of her assets, she even may have purchased Internet stocks at their height in hopes of latching onto the next Microsoft or Dell.

For the principle of risk aversion to hold, it's not necessary for all investors to make intelligent risk/return decisions at all times—only

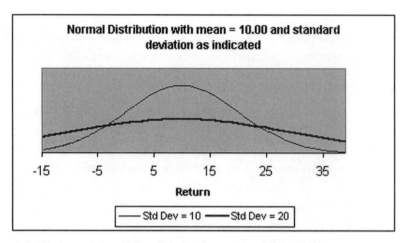

EXHIBIT 2-5   Return/Risk Bell Curve for Stock of ABC versus XYZ

when they are deciding how to invest a significant amount of their assets.

Let's assume that an investor has decided to buy one of the following two hypothetical stocks: stock ABC that has an expected return of 10 percent, and a risk measure—the standard deviation of return—of 10 percent, or stock XYZ that has an expected return of 10 percent, and a standard deviation of 20 percent. (See Exhibit 2-5.)

Both stocks have the same expected return of 10 percent. The dispersion of the returns of stock ABC is much more concentrated around the average, and the probability of ABC's return being closer to the average return is much higher than the returns for stock XYZ. A risk-averse investor, given the symmetric nature of the returns, would always prefer to buy stock ABC because of the lower risk associated with the same expected return.

What does risk aversion mean in real life? Risk averse investors approach investments with caution. When they value an investment, they use conservative assumptions and try to determine what is the most likely outcome. They examine the downside and ask a lot of "what if" questions. If the odds don't appear to be in their favor, they don't invest.

Risk Aversion: Our Recommendation

Risk aversion is a good thing—we are very risk averse—we enjoy winning money but we really despise losing it. It's important that you realize what type of investor you are and how much risk you can stomach in the way of investment losses. Make sure that you understand the risks involved in the asset in which you are investing. If the odds aren't in your favor or the extra return isn't sufficient to compensate you for the additional risk, take a pass and find an investment with more favorable risk/return characteristics. We always require an expected margin of safety before buying a stock. We recommend that you do likewise.

Principle 4: Supply and Demand Drive Stock Prices in the Short Run

The Law of Supply and Demand

The stock market performs like all markets in a competitive economy. The market price of a stock is determined by the interaction of the supply of stock by sellers and the demand for stock by buyers. Current price is where the supply of stock intersects with the demand for stock.

On the demand side, a substantial reduction in transaction costs helped to fuel the bull market of the 1990s. Lower costs greatly increased demand for stocks, thereby driving up prices. Investors, who during the 1980s had to pay a full-service broker several hundred dollars in commissions to buy 100 shares of Microsoft, can now buy 1000 shares for an $8 Internet brokerage fee. These low costs make it possible for day-traders to buy and sell stocks and garner substantial net profits from small moves in a stock's price.

Additionally, the price performance of Internet stocks in the late 1990s spurred an almost insatiable demand by investors for stock of companies in the Internet space. This excess demand drove price-to-sales (P/S) and price-to-earnings (P/E) ratios to levels that were unprecedented in the history of the U.S. stock markets. On the supply side during the Internet heyday, investment bankers and corporate issuers moved quickly to create new companies that could sell initial public offerings (*IPOs*) to investors to help satisfy demand. Supply during the Internet bubble followed demand with a slight lag.

The performance of Internet IPOs in the late 1990s was extraordinary—V.A. Linux Systems soared 733 percent on the day it was issued. FreeMarkets, Webmethods, Akamai, and CacheFlow all had first-day closing prices over 400 percent above their IPO offering prices. CEOs of Internet companies didn't worry about revenues, products or employees. As long as they had catchy business models and Internet stock analyst Henry Blodget's or Mary Meeker's endorsements, they would be billionaires the minute the IPO was priced. Rest assured, if investor demand for the stock of a type of company exists, investment bankers will team with entrepreneurs to create the companies to fill the demand. Eventually, supply will exceed demand. When that occurs, demand and price inevitably fall.

What Does the Current Stock Price Tell the Market?

A stock's current price multiplied by the number of shares outstanding determines the market equity of a company. Think about that statement! Does the fact that a share of ICGE traded at $200.94 on January 3, 2000 mean that Internet Capital Group with 287.7 million shares outstanding was truly worth $57 billion? Would some investor or group of investors have ever paid $57 billion for an Internet incubator whose underlying portfolio of assets was not worth one-tenth that amount? It's doubtful!

Current stock price indicates the amount that the marginal investor, given supply and demand considerations, is willing to pay to acquire a share of a particular stock. In the short run, this price may or may not have anything to do with the true long-term value of a company. The current price may be heavily influenced by a very temporary supply-and-demand imbalance or by the stock market's reaction to the receipt of new information.

An extreme example of a temporary supply-and-demand imbalance occurred for the stock of EntreMed (ENMD), a biotech firm that specializes in cancer research. The short-term demand for the stock drove the price to unsustainable levels. On Friday, May 1, 1998, a total of 19,100 shares of ENMD stock changed hands, and the price closed at $12-1/16. On May 3, the company was the subject of a very favorable front-page article in the *New York Times*. The article contained no new information regarding the company, but described its cancer research in glowing terms. It also gave the company exposure to potential new investors who read the NYT and wanted to be owners of the next Microsoft of biotech. The article significantly influenced the short-term demand for EntreMed's stock.

On Monday, May 4, faced with a tremendous increase in demand, the stock opened at $84.87—a jump of over $72—six times the closing stock price on the previous trading day. ENMD closed at $51.87, down $33 from its opening price. ENMD's trading volume on May 4 was 23,432,500 shares—an increase from the 19,100 shares traded on May 1. On December 31, 2002, ENMD closed at $0.86 per share.

Most publicly traded companies have an investor relations department that is responsible for distributing information about the company to investors and to the media. We have noticed the tendency for good news, such as a patent award or a new oil discovery, to gush freely and in great detail from the company's investor relations department. The IR department spins the positive news that increases the demand for the company's stock and drives up its price. Conversely, IR departments downplay negative news regarding a company, such as accounting irregularities and SEC investigations (Enron, Adelphia, WorldCom, Computer Associates, Tyco). Bad news dribbles out slowly over time and in very sketchy detail.

Supply and Demand: Our Recommendation

The short-term supply and demand trading techniques are the arena for technical analysis, which we describe in Chapter 3. We tend not to be momentum purchasers, buying a stock simply because its price has risen due to excess short-term demand. When we buy a stock, we buy it because we believe it's undervalued.

If a company releases a piece of bad news, we give it a smell test. If it smells funny, like rotting fish or a piece of bad chicken, we unload the stock. When a company announces negative information that is not fully explained, such as a weakly worded resignation of a CFO or CEO (such as, I want to spend more time with the wife and kids, inferred Jeff Skilling of Enron), or a brief announcement of an SEC inquiry, that's a very bad signal. We expect that more bad news will dribble out and depress the company's stock price over a longer period of time.

It is our opinion that the best thing to do is sell a stock on the first bad piece of news of this type that doesn't pass your smell test. You can then see how the stock price performs and how the market reacts, and you can reassess the desirability and wisdom of owning that stock again.

Principle 5: When Analyzing Returns, Simple Averages Are Never Simple

Simple Averages versus Compound Averages

The fifth principle deals with the math underlying investment returns. We examine the somewhat perverse math that computes investment gains more favorably than comparable investment losses. For example, Martha the portfolio manager tells you that she has good historical investment performance. Two years ago, her portfolio skyrocketed 100 percent. This year things haven't gone as well—her stocks lost 80 percent. She states that her average annual return over the past two years is 10 percent—a good showing in a tough stock market.

Is she correct, or is she a pathological liar? Her average yearly return over the past two years is: (100 percent − 80 percent)/2 = 10 percent, as she alleges. Let's check her boast by injecting some real numbers into the analysis. We'll keep the example simple. Let's assume her portfolio consists of one stock, Stock A, which she bought two years ago for $10. Her timing and analysis were impeccable, and Stock A went up to $20 at the end of the first year—a return of 100 percent. The next year the stock market tanked, and Stock A dropped 80 percent to $4.

When we look at real dollars as opposed to the annual averages, her actual two-year return is negative 60 percent—a $10 portfolio shrinking to $4. This is a far worse outcome than one would suspect from the 10-percent average annual performance that Martha is touting. How can this be?

The problem is embedded in the calculation of simple averages. In fact, if there is a negative percentage in the group, the calculation of a simple average return is biased upward. For example, look again at Table 2-2, which shows the returns and risks for the five asset classes. In each case, the compound annual return, also known as a geometric rate of return, is lower than the simple average return. The compound average return is the correct measure of what you would have received from holding an investment over time. Sometimes, as in the case of Martha's investment performance, the differences between simple and compound averages are substantial.

Table 2-4 shows how Martha's investments performed over the past two years. The simple average annual return, or arithmetic mean,

TABLE 2-4 Martha's Investment Performance Simple & Compound
Average Returns

Year	Beginning Value	Ending Value	Annual Return
1	$10	$20	100%
2	20	4	−80%
			20%
Simple Average Return			10%
Compound Average Return			−36.75%

is easy to calculate and is equal to the sum of the annual returns (20
percent) divided by the number of returns (2).

The compound average return is calculated by (1) dividing the most
recent value—(A) ($4 at the end of Year 2) by the beginning value—(B)
($10 at the beginning of Year 1); (2) taking the resulting ratio to the
(1/T) power, where T is the number of years in the compounding period; and (3) subtracting 1.0 to bring it into percentage terms. In math
terms, the previous sentence looks like this: $[(A/B)^{(1/T)} - 1.0]$. The
calculation of the compound annual return above is:

$$[(\$4/\$10)^{(1/2)} - 1.0] = [(.4)^{(1/2)} - 1.0] =$$
$$[0.6325 - 1.0] = -36.75\%$$

**Many Investment Professionals Use Simple Averages to
Tout Performance**

Many investment managers and advisors use simple averages to por-
tray their historic performance. Simple averages are a misleading way
to assess investment returns—compound or geometric averages are
far more representative of actual investment performance. Be careful
when you read advertising material that bases performance records
upon simple average returns. John Brennan, Chairman of the Van-
guard Group, calls simple averages " . . . the insidious math . . ." of investing. Mr. Brennan says that, "Once you lose big, it is very hard to
catch up."[5]

With simple averages, a larger percentage gain is required to offset
a given percentage loss. For example, *The Wall Street Journal* reports

that, between the NASDAQ high in March of 2000 and April 4, 2001, the Pro-Funds Ultra OTC Fund incurred a drop of 94.71 percent. So if Jim had an investment of $1000 in the Ultra OTC Fund in March of 2000, 13 months later it would have dropped to $52.90.[6] A turnaround occurred between April 4, 2001 and May 2, 2001, and the Ultra OTC Fund rose an enormous 95.6 percent. Jim's $52.90 investment increased by 95.6 percent to $103.50—still down 89.65 percent below its March, 2000 high. The average return for these two unequal time periods is: (−94.71 percent + 95.6 percent) / 2 = 0.45 percent. The true return for Jim's 15-month holding period is −89.65 percent. In this example, we would guess that the difference in the calculation of average and actual returns qualifies as *insidious*.

The following equation yields the percentage gain required to make an investment whole again after suffering a loss:

$$\text{Percentage Gain to Break Even} = 1 \; / \; (100\% - \% \text{ drop})$$

In Jim's example above, the equation looks like this:

$$1 \; / \; (100\% - 94.71\%) = 1 \; / \; (.0529) = 1890\%$$

The likelihood of Jim's ever breaking even on this investment appears somewhat remote.

Analyzing Performance: Our Recommendation

We strongly believe that investment advisers and fund managers should measure their performance by using compound (geometric) averages rather than simple averages. Compound returns tell you what's really happening to your money. If you are analyzing the performance of fund managers or mutual funds, we suggest that you make sure that they provide you with compound returns or the raw underlying yearly returns so that you can calculate the compound average returns. Otherwise, the historic returns they are touting could be overstated—perhaps grossly overstated.

Principle 6: Transaction Costs, Taxes, and Inflation Are Your Enemies

Transaction costs and the effects of taxes and inflation can greatly reduce the real returns on your investments. Transaction cost comes in many forms: brokerage commissions when you execute a trade; sales loads, 12b-1 fees, and redemption fees when you purchase or sell a mutual fund; and yearly asset management fees paid to a mutual fund, stockbroker, or investment adviser. Transaction costs can significantly decrease the returns on your investment portfolio.

It should be every investor's mission to reduce her transaction costs to the lowest possible level. A stockbroker or financial planner can tell you what stocks to buy, how to allocate your investments among asset classes, and how to make your investment program tax efficient. If you benefit from his advice and services, be prepared to pay a reasonable commission or fee. However, if you purchase a mutual fund and pay a 5.25-percent commission to an investment advisor, you have wasted a huge chunk of your money. You have paid far too much for handholding. You can purchase a similarly managed no-load fund with no sales charge.

If you make your own investment and asset allocation decisions, you should search for the lowest brokerage fees or investment management charges available from reputable financial institutions. We own individual stocks. When we buy a stock based on our own analysis, we execute the trade through a well-known online broker at a low fixed fee. When we purchase a stock based on a recommendation from a full-service broker, we execute the trade through his firm at a negotiated fixed commission.

We own no-load domestic index funds and international stock mutual funds, no-load REIT funds, and no-load intermediate bond funds. We also invest in a hedge fund with a very specialized market niche and pay the manager of the hedge fund a substantial management fee for his expertise. We understand the difference in experience, services provided, and fees charged, and are willing to pay for performance. However, we despise paying any unnecessary costs. You should also. Make it your goal to minimize transactions costs!

Taxes and inflation are also enemies. Exhibit 2-6 shows the long-term effect of taxes and inflation on investment returns for common stocks, long-term government bonds, Treasury bills, and municipal bonds over 1926-1999. The results are dramatic. Common stocks provided a 5.0 percent compounded annual return after taxes and inflation. However, taxes and inflation wiped out the returns on Government bonds and Treasury bills. Given their exemption from federal

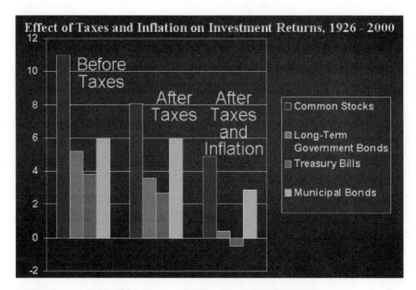

EXHIBIT 2-6   Returns Before and After Taxes and Inflation

income taxes, municipal bonds provided a 2.5-percent positive return after inflation.

As shown in Exhibit 2-6, taxes can have a negative effect on investment performance. Each year when you receive dividends, interest income, and short-term capital gains, you pay a portion of that income to Uncle Sam at current Federal income tax rates of up to 39.9 percent. Long-term capital gains are taxed at rates up to 20 percent. Tax payments greatly decrease the after-tax return on your investments, if they are held in a taxable account. Investors can establish tax-advantaged accounts to accumulate retirement assets. Three types of accounts are individual retirement accounts (IRAs), Roth IRAs, and 401(k) retirement accounts.

An investor's annual contribution to an IRA is tax deductible, if the investor's taxable income does not exceed a certain level. The current maximum tax-deductible contribution to an IRA is $2000 (which is scheduled to increase to $5000 over time). Tax on the income received on the IRA is deferred until money is withdrawn. Such moneys are then taxed as current income.

Contributions to a Roth IRA are not tax deductible, but the Roth IRA allows dividend, interest, and capital gains on the investments to compound on a tax-exempt basis. If the investor is at least 59½ and has invested for at least 5 years, he may withdraw money on a tax-free basis. This is similar to the treatment of interest on a municipal bond, which is generally exempt from federal income taxes and often exempt from state income taxes as well.

Many employers establish 401(k) plans for their employees, allowing them to make tax-deferred investments to a retirement account. The contributions can be matched by the employer. As with IRAs, tax on the 401(k) is deferred until the money is withdrawn and then is taxed as ordinary income. Self-employed professionals may have substantial pension programs that allow taxes to be deferred until distributions are made to the pensioners.

Inflation decreases the real rate of return on the investment. Needless to say, inflation is beyond the control of the investor. However, she should understand how inflation affects her resources and her future consumption requirements. In an inflationary environment, all financial assets become less valuable.

Transactions Costs, Taxes, and Inflation: Our Recommendations

Our recommendation on transactions costs is brief. Cut all transactions costs to the lowest level possible!

Our recommendation on inflation is also brief. Other than investing in a special type of bond called Treasury inflation-protected securities (*TIPS*), there is little that you can do about it. Be prepared to invest in riskier asset classes to help overcome the negative effect that inflation has on fixed-income assets.

Taxes are complex. Investors should take full advantage of the tax laws and establish tax-advantaged accounts for retirement. Investors should fund tax-advantaged accounts to the maximum that the law and income will permit.

At the time of this writing, financial reform that gives preferential tax treatment to certain dividend payments is being pushed by President George W. Bush and is receiving serious consideration in Congress. Exempting dividend payments from taxes would give a major boost to stocks of dividend-paying companies. On January 16, 2003, Microsoft announced that it would begin to pay a dividend. Other companies that have not paid dividends may follow.

Given a choice of tax class, an investor should hold tax-advantaged assets such as municipal bonds or stocks that earn tax-sheltered income (such as master limited partnerships, for example) in fully tax-able accounts, and use tax-advantaged accounts to trade stocks or to own assets that have substantial dividend or interest payments.

After you've finished this book, you should be well on the way to making your own investment decisions, and be able to reduce the amount of your annual transactions costs greatly.

Principle 7: Time and the Value of Money Are Closely Related

A basic idea underlying finance theory is that a dollar today is worth more than a dollar tomorrow. We invest today's dollars to purchase the greater cash flows of tomorrow. In fact, any financial or investment decision involves spending money today and receiving cash payments in the future. To assess whether an investment is a diamond or a dog, you must be able to compare the value of money that you invest to-day with the value of the money that you expect to receive in the fu-ture. To make this comparison effectively, you must understand the simple math that underlies the time value of money—compounding and discounting.

When we value a company, we first estimate the future profits that we expect the company to earn. The projection of profits involves mul-tiplying earnings by a series of inputs that estimate growth over a pe-riod of time—a process that's known as *compounding*. Once we esti-mate future profits, we use another math concept to bring those future dollars back to today's values—a process known as *discounting*.

Compounding and Future Value

A key to the pricing of any investment is to understand the concepts of discounting and compounding. Compounding is the process of go-ing from today's value, or present value (PV), to some expected but unknown future value (FV). Compounding also means to multiply by a number greater than 1.0, over a number of time periods. You'll soon see what we mean by this statement.

Future value is the amount of money that an investment will grow to at some future date by earning interest at a certain rate. Let's look at an example to see how compounding and future value works.

TABLE 2-5 GHI Steady Growth Company
Compounding and Future Value Schedule

Year	Beginning Stock Value	Growth in Value	Ending Stock Value
1	$10.00	$0.80	$10.80
2	$10.80	$0.86	$11.66
3	$11.66	$0.93	$12.60
4	$12.60	$1.01	$13.60
5	$13.60	$1.09	$14.69
Total Growth in Value		$4.69	

Suppose that Jane buys stock for $10 per share in GHI Steady Growth Company (which pays no dividend), and the shares increase in value (exactly and miraculously) at the rate of 8 percent per year. If Jane holds the stock for five years, what is the ending value of a share? Table 2-5 shows how the stock price of GHI will grow over time, compounding by 8 percent per year over the five-year period. The future value of the GHI compounded at a rate of 8 percent is $14.69.

In this example, when we compound we multiply the beginning stock value of $10 by 1.08 over five periods:

$$\$10 * (1.08) * (1.08) * (1.08) * (1.08) * (1.08) = \$14.69$$

When we compound, if r is the compounding rate (also called a *growth rate, interest rate* or *yield*), n is the number of years, PV is the present value of a single payment investment, then the future value (FV) of the investment is:

$$FV = PV \times (1.0 + r)^{\wedge}n$$

In math terms, this says that when you compound the number PV at a rate r for n periods, the future value is equal to the present value times (1.0 plus the compounding rate), raised to the nth power. Jane's GHI Steady Growth Stock example looks like this:

$$\$14.69 = \$10 * (1.0 + .08)^{\wedge}5$$

Discounting and Present Value

The math underlying discounting and the calculation of present value is the exact flip side to compounding and future value. Discounting is the process of going from an expected future value to a present value. Discounting also means to multiply by a number less than 1.0, over a number of time periods. Present value is what an investment is worth today, if an expected future value is discounted at a certain rate and for a period of time. Let's look at an example to see how discounting and present value works.

Today's your birthday, and Uncle Larry promises you a present—$100 to be given to you at some time in the next five years. What is the present value of Uncle Larry's $100 promise? This is a tough one. Uncle Larry is usually reliable, but he's a tad overweight and is not in great health. There's a slight chance that he may die before he pays off, so risk is involved. You're also not sure exactly when that $100 is going to flow to you. With the uncertainty of both risk and timing, this sounds like a problem for a present value table. In Table 2-6 we lay out the possibilities, with the number of years, n, ranging from 0 to 5, and the discounting rates ranging from 6 percent to 8 percent to 10 percent.

The numbers listed in Table 2-6 are known as *discount factors*. These factors give the present value of a dollar that you expect to receive at some time, n, in the future, discounted at a rate, r. As you can see in Table 2-6, as n increases and the payment is expected further into the future, the present value factor decreases—meaning that the

TABLE 2-6 Uncle Larry's $100 Gift

	Present Value Discount Factors		
Year (*n*)	*r* = 6%	*r* = 8%	*r* = 10%
0	1.0000	1.0000	1.0000
1	0.9434	0.9259	0.9091
2	0.8890	0.8573	0.8264
3	0.8396	0.7938	0.7513
4	0.7921	0.7350	0.6830
5	0.7473	0.6806	0.6209

future payment is worth less today. For example, if Uncle Larry pays today, it doesn't matter what the discount rate is—the value is $100. If Uncle Larry's health risk increases to the 10-percent level and you do not expect the $100 for five years, the present value factor is where row $n = 5$, intersects with column $r = 10$ percent—equal to 0.6269. The $100 promise is worth $62.69 today. Likewise, as the discounting rate, r, increases, the present value discount factor decreases—meaning that the future payment is worth even less today. If time to payment increases or risk increases, the present value of an investment decreases.

The equation for a discount factor for the payment of $1 to be received n years from now with a discounting rate of r is:

$$\text{Discount Factor} = 1/(1 + r)^{\wedge}n$$

Let's see what happens when $r = 8$ percent, and $n = 3$. The number $1/(1 + .08) = .9259$. And $(.9259) * (.9259) * (.9259) = 0.7938$—just as Uncle Larry's present value factor table promised.

The Time Value of Money: Our Recommendation

If you are serious about investing, it is essential that you understand how to value stocks and bonds properly. This requires that you know the basics regarding the time value of money—the math underlying compounding and discounting.

The math is not difficult but does require you to understand the relationship between present and future values, how to use exponents, and how to compound to future value and discount to present value. Inexpensive calculators have built-in financial programs that quickly churn out future and present values. We strongly recommend that you take the time necessary to understand compounding and discounting and learn how to use a financial calculator for those functions.

Principle 8: Asset Allocation Is a Very Important Decision

It's important to examine your assets and investment policy periodically to determine the best way to invest to meet your life's goals— putting children through college, taking vacation trips to foreign countries, earning a pilot's license, learning how to hang glide, or owning a home in Key West for the winter and a ranch on the Madison River for the summer. Along with your goals, you may also have some constraints, such as liquidity needs, tax considerations, or unique health concerns.

In short order, the volatile markets of the new millennium have demonstrated some valuable lessons about risk and return in managing a portfolio of assets. Modern finance theory teaches us that if we are to achieve the highest level of return for the amount of risk we can stomach, we should diversify our investment holdings over an array of asset classes.

The diversification process begins with asset allocation—dividing investment funds among different asset classes. The most basic classes are cash and short maturity deposits, bonds and fixed income securities, and common stock. Conservative investors tend to put more of their funds in cash and fixed income securities, while more aggressive investors will have a larger portion of their wealth invested in common stock.

Within the asset classes are subclasses. Bonds include subclasses related to security type (Treasury, corporate, municipal, and foreign) and maturity (short-term, medium-term, and long-term). For common stock, there are many different subclasses. The most general relate to market value: large cap—over $5 billion, mid cap—$1 to $5 billion, and small cap—under $1 billion; and investment style—value versus growth.

The trade-off of risk and return that we discuss in Principle 1 also applies to asset classes, as illustrated in Exhibit 2-7 below. Fixed income asset classes have less risk (as measured by the standard deviation of returns) and provide lower expected returns than equity asset classes. Among equity asset classes, large cap stocks tend to be less risky than small cap stocks, and value stocks generally tend to be less risky than growth stocks. International equities over time have exhibited greater risk and return than domestic stocks.

Typical Asset Allocation Mixes

Some investors maintain a fixed percentage of their funds in asset classes (say 20 percent cash, 30 percent bonds, and 50 percent stocks), and others prefer to change their asset allocations based on their expectations of risk and return. Wall Street firms employ market strategists who recommend an asset allocation mix for clients. *The Wall*

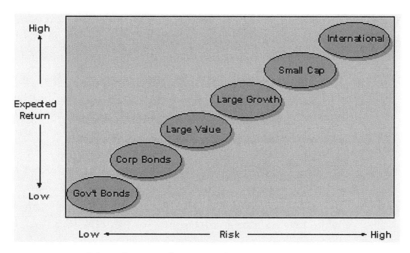

EXHIBIT 2-7   Risk and Return by Asset Class

Street Journal periodically polls the brokerage firms to determine their preferred asset allocation levels. Recommended allocations in a recent poll ranged from 80 percent stocks, 10 percent bonds, and 10 percent cash for one firm, to 40 percent stocks, 55 percent bonds, and 5 percent cash for another. The standard Wall Street benchmark for asset allocation is 10 percent cash, 35 percent bonds, and 55 percent common stocks.

Your asset allocation levels should reflect your beliefs about the anticipated risk and return of asset classes. If you believe that the stock market is going to crash, you should lower your stock allocation, shifting moneys to bonds or cash. If you believe that long-term interest rates are going to rise substantially, you should shift money from bonds into cash. In this way, there may be an element of *market timing* involved in your asset allocation. Market timing—moving into and out of different asset classes because of beliefs about their expected performance—is frowned upon by followers of modern portfolio theory. Nonetheless, it is a practice that many Wall Street professionals embrace.

Asset allocations should be tailored to an investor's particular circumstances and risk preferences. For example, a friend who fervently believes in modern portfolio theory is a tenured professor and has 100 percent of his investments in stock index funds. He views the expected earnings from his stable academic career, which other than illness or death are protected through the tenure process, as secure and filling the role of bonds and cash reserves in his portfolio.

At the other extreme is a semiretired writer friend with moderate wealth, who under no circumstances wants to go back to full-time employment in the real world. He suffers pain and panic if he sees the value of his stock portfolio drop when he pulls up the *My Portfolios* link on the AOL Web site. He dislikes the risk/return profile associated with today's stock market and believes that long-term interest rates will rise significantly from their current level of about 4 percent. His asset allocation is 20 percent stocks, 20 percent bonds and 60 percent cash. As you can see from these two real life examples, asset allocation is a personal and very important decision. (See Exhibit 2-8.)

Studies of Asset Allocation

The importance of asset allocation in explaining the investment performance of mutual funds and pension funds was highlighted a decade ago in two studies[7] by Dr. Gary Brinson and his colleagues. Their research showed that more than 90 percent of the variability in fund performance over time was attributable to asset allocation, as shown in Exhibit 2-8. This means that from a total rate of return perspective the decision of the asset classes in which to invest is more important than the specific securities that are selected for investment.

Asset Allocation: Our Recommendation

Your investment portfolio should be divided between stocks, bonds, and cash reserves. We recognize that risky stocks have a higher expected return than bonds, which have a higher expected return than cash reserves. Let's assume that you are 50 years old, have been successful in business, have significant funds to invest, and have decided on the consensus Wall Street asset allocation recommendation—55 percent stocks, 35 percent bonds, and 10 percent cash. How should you assemble these asset classes?

Your *cash reserves* should be readily available when you need them, so we assume that you'll invest them in an unrestricted taxable account. You can invest cash reserves in money market mutual funds, either on a tax-exempt basis or a taxable basis, depending on relative yields and your tax bracket. As yields and your tax bracket change, those cash reserves can be easily switched back and forth—usually by

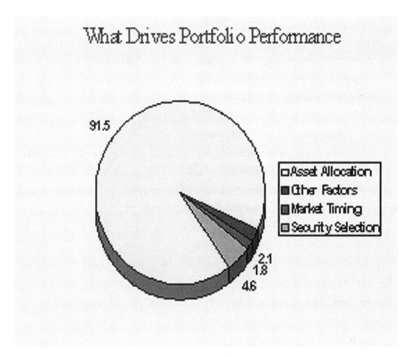

EXHIBIT 2-8 The Importance of Asset Allocation

telephone or online within the same funds group—between taxable and tax-exempt accounts.

The decision to invest in tax-exempt or taxable *bonds* will also be dependent upon relative yields and tax brackets. An additional consideration will be the source of the funds that are being invested. For instance, if you are in the maximum marginal tax bracket and are investing monies in an IRA, 401(k), or self-funded pension fund, you probably would want to purchase taxable bonds, such as intermediate U.S. Treasury or Agency debt or GNMA mortgage-backed securities, or shares of a no-load mutual bond fund that invests in these securities or in corporate bonds. You will usually find it tax-effective to invest monies from your fully taxable investment accounts in tax-exempt bonds or in no-load tax-exempt bond funds.

Based on our preferences and investment expectations, our *stock* allocation as of December, 2002 is divided among large cap value, small cap value, large cap growth, international, and stocks with exposure to domestic real estate, such as REITs. We have a strong preference for value stocks over growth stocks. Our largest allocations are in large cap value at 35 percent, and small cap value at 25 percent. Our allocation for large cap growth is 20 percent, REITs at 10 percent, and international stocks at 10 percent.

You must decide your desired asset allocation and in what asset classes you want to focus. Your allocation will be a function of your risk/return profile—how much risk you can stomach when it comes to volatility and potential losses in your stock allocation. Your risk/return profile should also be a function of where you are in your financial life cycle. As you approach retirement, you may want to lower your stock exposure and increase your bond allocation.

We always want to have some exposure to the stock market, but depending on our market perceptions, we reserve the right to increase or reduce that exposure. Sound like market timing here? As an example, when 9/11 occurred and anthrax scares dominated the news, a terrorist seemed to be lurking in every shadow. In response, we reduced the percentage of our assets allocated to the stock market and shifted into cash. With the ensuing U.S. offensive and its success in Afghanistan, international and stock market opinion turned positive. However, rumors of accounting scandals and trouble at Enron began to surface. WorldCom and Adelphia fiascos soon followed. At the end of 2002, the concern that other corporate governance debacles may be simmering, along with the threat of war with Iraq kept many investors underweighted in equities.

Principle 9: Asset Diversification Will Reduce Risk

As we discuss in Principle 3, rational investors are risk averse. As such, we require additional compensation in terms of expected return to take on more risk. We discuss the direct trade-off between expected return and risk in Principle 1. Over time, if you want to achieve a higher return, you are going to have to take on more risk.

How much risk can *you* deal with in your investment portfolio? Could you sleep at night knowing that your retirement nest egg could be cut in half due to any number of social, political, and economic factors that could rile the world's financial markets? This is a perplexing problem. We all want to earn a higher return. But, can we deal with the higher risk necessary to earn that expected return? What if disaster strikes? An assessment of your risk tolerance is an important first step in the investment process. A number of Internet online investment personality quizzes address the issue of Internet risk tolerance.

The first step in reducing the risk of your portfolio is to diversify your holdings. Diversification means to spread your wealth among a number of different investments. The goal of diversification is to invest in a group of assets that provides you with the best possible return given a level of risk. Your assets are everything that has value to you: your family, home, career, health, cars, furniture, clothing, and financial assets, such as insurance policies, stocks, bonds, and cash reserves.

When you make decisions affecting risk and return, consider the total amount of your assets—your career, house, and all of your tangible and financial assets as being held in one portfolio, one pool. Protect against having too much concentration of your assets in one financial institution that could conceivably fail. We suggest that you maintain financial accounts at different commercial banks, brokerage firms, and mutual fund companies. Within these accounts, allocate your assets efficiently to minimize taxes in the manner that we discuss in Principle 8.

First, take an inventory of your assets.

Your Career, Home, and Employer

If you are young and intend to work for a number of years, in all probability your biggest asset is your human capital—the ability to earn income by selling your skills or labor. A large portion of the cash flow that will finance your lifestyle and enable you to purchase investments will come from your job.

Since the goal of diversification is to reduce the downside risk of your asset base, you should avoid investing in the stock of the company for which you work. Also avoid investing in companies in related industries. For instance, if you work in the relatively volatile financial industry for an investment bank such as Merrill Lynch, you shouldn't invest a large portion of your assets in the stock of Goldman Sachs.

From a risk perspective, it usually is a bad idea for an employee to sink a significant portion of his investment portfolio in the stock of his employer, whether in a retirement account or through holdings in other accounts. We felt the pain for what happened to employees-pensioners-shareholders of Enron. Employers often make it financially attractive for employees to purchase shares of the company, sometimes at a steep discount. If the discount is significant enough, purchase the stock; but at your earliest opportunity, liquidate the shares and deploy the money into other assets.

Likewise, many American families, especially younger families, have a large percentage of their wealth tied up in a house. If you live in an area that is dependent upon one industry, such as high-tech in Silicon Valley, the entertainment industry in Los Angeles, or the finance industry in New York, avoid investing a large portion of your financial assets in that industry. You don't want an economic event that crushes your investments also to negatively affect the value of your house, giving you a double dose of pain.

If you are employed by a dominant company in your area, have a large investment in a home, and also have money invested in your employer's stock, a corporate-specific downturn could be catastrophic. Your net worth could take a triple whammy—the loss of your job, a steep drop in your investment and retirement accounts, and the collapsing value of your home. For instance, Adelphia's woes are triply troubling for employees who live in the small rural town of Coudersport, Pennsylvania, where the company is headquartered.

For a first shot at diversification, try to separate your career assets from your investment assets. Also, don't overinvest in a house if its value is closely tied to the well being of your employer.

Financial Assets

We assume that you have enough liquid assets to finance six months of expenses and some unforeseen emergencies, and that you have insurance coverage to cover tragedies. In Principle 8, we note that the diversification process begins with asset allocation. Spreading your funds over alternative asset classes reduces the overall risk of your portfolio. We now want to go one step further and get a better understanding of diversification and risk.

The key to diversification and risk reduction is the *correlation* of the returns of your assets. Correlation is a statistic which measures the degree to which the movements of two variables are related. Correlation is measured on a scale of −1.0 to +1.0. If two stocks have a correlation coefficient of +1.0, then when one stock is up 10 percent, the other stock is also up 10 percent. Conversely, a correlation coefficient of −1.0 means that when one stock is up, the other stock is down. A correlation coefficient of 0.0 indicates no meaningful relationship between the two assets. Assets that are highly correlated offer less risk reduction from diversification than assets that are less correlated.

Coke and Pepsi are examples of two individual stocks that are highly correlated. These two companies benefit and suffer from many of the same macro-economic forces. An oil company and an airline company may experience negative correlation. As oil prices go up the oil company benefits through increasing revenues, while the airline suffers because of fuel price increases and higher operating costs. It is important to consider the correlation of assets when constructing a portfolio.

Achieving the highest return for each level of risk is known as investing efficiently—investing on the *efficient frontier*. Efficient frontiers are portfolios that are designed with the help of computer modeling and are beyond the scope of this book. This type of investing is normally accomplished by investing in different asset classes. The most general asset classes for stocks are value and growth stocks, and large and small capitalization stocks. If you have decided to increase your expected return on your assets by investing a portion of your portfolio in common stock, how should you diversify to reduce your risk?

Stockholders face two types of risk: systematic risk and unsystematic risk. Systematic risk represents the risk of the stock market. Changes in stock prices are caused by changes in the economy, taxes, and other market factors. When these factors change, it affects the entire market. Although systematic changes in the market affect each stock to a different degree, all stocks are impacted. As discussed in Principle 1, we measure the systematic or market risk of a stock by its beta.

Unsystematic risk is specific to a company. It is risk inherent to a particular stock due to decisions made by a corporation relative to the industry in which it operates. While unsystematic risk is unique for all firms, it can be similar for firms in related industries.

Total Risk = Systematic Risk + Unsystematic Risk

Diversification reduces the unsystematic risk of a portfolio. Remember that on average, the negative stock-specific surprises affecting companies in a diversified portfolio will be offset by positive surprises.

TABLE 2-7   How Many Stocks Make a Diversified Portfolio?

Number of Stocks in Portfolio	Average Standard Deviation of Annual Portfolio Returns	Ratio of Portfolio Standard Deviation of a Single Stock
1	49.24%	100%
10	23.93%	49%
50	20.20%	41%
100	19.69%	40%
300	19.34%	39%
500	19.27%	39%
1000	19.21%	39%

Table 2-7 summarizes the results of a study[8] performed by Meir Statman in 1987. The study looked at randomly grouped portfolios of stocks of various sizes to determine the marginal amount of diversification achieved by adding additional stocks to a portfolio. Volatility of individual stocks is measured by the standard deviation of their returns. The average annual standard deviation for an individual stock was found to be 49.24 percent—a significant amount. According to the findings, if 10 randomly selected stocks are combined into a portfolio, its volatility dropped by more than 50 percent to an average of 23.93 percent. The volatility of a 10-stock portfolio was not significantly more than the volatility of a 1000 stock portfolio.

Based on these results, we see that diversification is easy to obtain in a portfolio. It does not require hundreds of stocks to diversify a portfolio adequately—most studies suggest that 20 to 25 stocks are sufficient. It does, however, require that stocks within a portfolio be selected from different industries to reduce the correlation among the assets. Diversification occurs in a portfolio only if the stocks selected have different types of unsystematic risk; that is, the prices of the stock do not move in lockstep because they are all in the same or highly related industries.

Diversification, while limiting your risk by spreading your investments over a larger number of securities, also limits the gains you would have received if you had concentrated your investments in a few stocks that turned out to be incredible winners. However, could you stomach investing the bulk of your fortune in a risky stock that may either climb to the moon or go bankrupt? What are the odds that you will identify very early in the life of a company the stock that in 2004 will perform similarly to Microsoft, Dell, or Cisco in the 1990s? Probably not great!

Diversifying your portfolio may not make you the next Bill Gates or Warren Buffet (both of whom became rich by focusing their investments), but if you're risk averse and feel more pain from losing than pleasure from winning, diversification is the way to go.

Diversification: Our Recommendation

We've made our recommendations regarding your career-oriented assets, house, and investments in your employer. Insulate the three as much as possible! We also have discussed how to invest your cash reserves and bonds in a tax-efficient manner through the use of no-load mutual funds and how to diversify your assets in these categories. Here is what we do to diversify our stock holdings. We divide the amount that we have allocated to our stock portfolio into twenty 5-percent increments and invest those increments in a combination of stocks and no-load mutual funds.

Let's assume that our investment analysis has turned up a number of screaming buy recommendations for undervalued stocks. If we are bullish on the stock and find the price attractive, we'll buy a 5-percent position for a portfolio. We'll do that for up to 20 individual stocks, making sure that none of the stocks is too closely correlated to another that we own. If we are extremely bullish on a particular stock that we own, we'll allow our relative portfolio percentage to increase, either through the appreciation in price of the stock over time or through an additional purchase, to a maximum of 10 percent of our equity portfolio. Any portion over 10 percent will be sold when we rebalance our equity portfolio, which we perform on an annual basis.

Let's assume that no individual stock tickles our fancy. We would have our entire stock allocation in no-load mutual funds. What types of funds? Since mutual funds themselves provide significant diversification, we would focus on just a few areas: domestic large cap and small cap value, domestic large cap growth, an international fund, and a domestic fund with exposure to the real estate market. A large cap no-load value, and a Russell 2000 or a BARRA value fund could each have a 25-percent to 35-percent allocation; an S&P 500 Index fund would effectively be a large cap growth allocation of up to 20 percent, and a managed international fund and an REIT fund each having 5-percent to 10-percent allocations.

We also combine the proportions of individual stocks and mutual funds to achieve our desired stock asset class allocation. Let's assume that we want to maintain the following stock allocation percentages: domestic large cap value—35 percent, domestic small cap value—25 percent, domestic large cap growth—20 percent, REIT—10 percent, international equity—10 percent. For instance, if we own a 5-percent position in an individual REIT stock, we would invest 5 percent in the no-load REIT fund. If we have 5-percent positions in the stocks of Cisco and Intel, we would invest only 10 percent in our S&P 500 Index Fund. Or if we own a 5 percent position in Telefonos de Mexico, we would reduce our investment to 5 percent in the international no-load fund.

Principle 10: An Asset Pricing Model Should Be Used to Value Investments

The anxiety level of some of the undergraduate business students that take the introductory finance class at Penn State rises dramatically when we mention the Capital Asset Pricing Model (CAPM). Students think that we'll pepper them with partial derivative equations or invoke the Black-Scholes Option Pricing Model to prove some obscure hypothesis. In reality, CAPM can be captured in a short equation that links the expected return on an asset to its risk.

CAPM—What Does It Do?

The Capital Asset Pricing Model is a simple model that estimates the rate of return that an investor should expect to receive on a risky asset. In valuation, its principal purpose is to determine the discount rate to use when valuing a stock. A lot of fancy academic finance theory underlies CAPM, and much of it is beyond the scope of this book. Chapter 6 explains the model, but here are the bare necessities so that you can use it to help to value a stock.

CAPM states that the expected return of a risky asset, $E(R_i)$, such as a common stock, is equal to the return on the risk-free asset (R_f) plus a risk premium. That's it! In equation form it looks like this:

Expected Return = Risk-Free Rate + Risk Premium

$$E(R_i = R + \beta_i \times [E(R_m) - R_f]$$

The risk-free rate (R_f) that we use for valuation is the rate on the long-term (10-year) Treasury bond. The risk premium is a function of two factors: the stock's beta (β_i), and the market risk premium, which is the expected return on the overall stock market (R_m) minus the risk free rate [$E(R_m) - R_f$].

When we value a risky asset, we assume that investors are risk averse and therefore prefer less risk to more risk; see Principle 3. Because of risk aversion, investors diversify their holdings and seek the greatest expected return for their chosen level of risk, see Principle 9. And since investors hold diversified portfolios, the measure of risk for any new investment is only its systematic risk as measured by beta.

So what does this mean in real life? It means that investors won't buy risky securities unless they are paid higher returns. How much higher depends on the risk of the stock, as measured by its beta, and the amount of the market risk premium. We represent the simple CAPM risk/return relationship in Exhibit 2-8. If the stock market prices stocks in the manner consistent with the Capital Asset Pricing Model, the expected return on each stock should fall on the risk/return line shown in Exhibit 2-9.

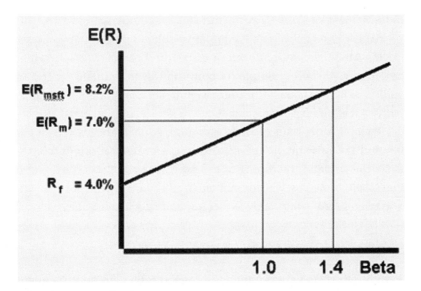

EXHIBIT 2-9 Graph of CAPM

If you can estimate an asset's beta and the market's risk premium, you can estimate the expected return for a particular stock. You can find betas for different stocks on Yahoo Finance and numerous other financial Web sites. (We discuss beta and the market risk premium in Chapter 6.) As an example, let's look at the expected return for Microsoft. We use a risk-free rate of 4 percent and an expected return on the stock market of 7 percent. If we go to the Yahoo Finance Web site on the Internet and type in the symbol MSFT for Microsoft, we find a beta estimate of 1.4. When we plug these numbers into the CAPM equation, we get:

$$E(msft) = 4\% + 1.4[\ 7\% - 4\%] = 4\% + 4.2\% = 8.2\%$$

This means that Microsoft's common stock is expected to generate a return of 8.2 percent this year.

CAPM: Our Recommendation

CAPM is the granddaddy of asset pricing models. It has been around since the mid-1960s, and provides an estimate of the return that the market requires for investing in risky stock. The CAPM has been the subject of hundreds of academic tests, most of which have found that it works reasonably well. Some academics have suggested that other models, such as an arbitrage pricing model and a multifactor asset pricing model, work better. But, the observed performance of these models does not seem to justify their added complexities.

We use the cost of equity capital calculated by the Capital Asset Pricing Model as an input for our discounted cash flow stock valuation model. It is a very simple yet powerful way to estimate the cost of equity, which is usually the most significant component of a company's weighted cost of capital.

Recall that the value of an investment is equal to the expected cash flows of the investment, discounted to the present at a rate that reflects the risk and the timing of the expected cash flows. We believe that CAPM is the best way to estimate the discount rate associated with a risky common stock, and we recommend that you use it as well.

Summary

A trade-off exists between higher expected return on an investment and greater risk. Safe investments have low returns. High returns require investors to take big risks. Most investors do not understand risk, the trade-off between risk and return, or the tendency for stock returns to revert to their average levels, a concept known as *reversion to the mean*. It's important to understand these concepts, and to recognize when a stock's price becomes too high for the operations of the company to support. When that situation occurs, it is overvalued—sell the stock!

The Fama and French study shows that investors can consistently make money by buying stocks with high book-value-to-market-value ratios—*value stocks*, and by selling stocks with low book-value-to-market-value ratios—*growth stocks*. This is the type of investment strategy that we follow in the book.

To a risk-averse investor, the pain of losing a dollar outweighs the pleasure of winning a dollar. Be sure that you understand the risks involved in the asset in which you are investing. If the odds aren't in your favor or the return isn't sufficient to compensate for the risk, take a pass and find an investment with more favorable risk/return characteristics.

Current stock price indicates the amount that the marginal investor, given supply and demand considerations, is willing to pay to acquire a share of that particular stock. In the short run, price may or may not have anything to do with the true long-term value of a company. Over time, price and value should align. Don't be afraid to sell on the first piece of bad news that doesn't pass your smell test.

Be skeptical when you see investment professionals tout their historical performance. Remember Martha's investment performance. The simple average of her returns was 10 percent per year versus the compound average return of −36.75 percent, which showed what really happened to her portfolio.

Cut all transactions costs to the lowest level possible! Establish tax advantaged retirement accounts and fund them to the maximum that the law and your income allow.

If you are serious about investing, you should understand how to value stocks and bonds. To do this properly, you need to know the basics regarding the time value of money—the math underlying compounding and discounting. The math is not difficult but does require you to understand the relationship between present and future values, how to use exponents, and how to compound to future value and discount to present value.

If you are to achieve the highest level of return for the amount of risk you can tolerate, diversify our investment holdings over an array of assets classes. The diversification process begins with asset allocation—dividing investment funds among different asset classes. You must decide your desired asset allocation and in what asset classes you want to focus. Your allocation will be a function of your risk/return profile—how much risk you can stomach when it comes to volatility and potential losses in your stock allocation.

Diversification means to spread your wealth among a number of different investments. The goal of diversification is to invest in a group of assets that provides you with the best return possible given a level of risk. Diversification reduces the unsystematic risk of a portfolio. Remember that on average, the negative stock-specific surprises affecting companies in a diversified portfolio will be offset by positive surprises. Most studies suggest that 20 to 25 stocks are sufficient for adequate diversification. It does, however, require that stocks within a portfolio be selected from different industries to reduce the correlation among the assets.

The Capital Asset Pricing Model is a simple model that estimates the rate of return that an investor expects to receive on a risky asset. In valuation, its principal purpose is to determine the discount rate to use when valuing a stock. CAPM states that the expected return of a risky asset, $E(R_i)$, such as a common stock, is equal to the return on the risk-free asset (R_f) plus a risk premium. We use the cost of equity capital calculated by the Capital Asset Pricing Model as an input for our discounted cash flow stock valuation model. It is a very simple yet powerful way to estimate the cost of equity, which is usually the most significant component of a company's weighted cost of capital.

That's it for finance theory. Now we show you how to use the 10 principles to value a stock.

Notes

1. See Ibbotson Associates, *The Stocks, Bonds, Bills and Inflation 2002 Yearbook*, Chicago, 2002.

2. An *event study* examines the movement of stock prices for a certain number of days prior to an event, such as an earnings announcement, until a certain number of days after the event. The

goal is to understand and capture any unusual stock price reaction to the event and to determine how quickly and completely the market reacts. The stock returns typically are adjusted for the general movement of prices in the stock market.

3. See Robert A. Haugen, *The New Finance: The Case Against Efficient Markets*, Prentice Hall, Upper Saddle River, NJ, 1999; Robert J. Shiller, *Irrational Exuberance*, Broadway Books, New York, NY, 2000; and Werner DeBondt and Richard H. Thaler. "Does the Stock Market Overreact," *Journal of Finance*, 40 (3) (1985): 793–805.

4. Eugene F. Fama and Kenneth R. French. "The Cross Section of Expected Stock Returns," *Journal of Finance*, 47 (1992): 427–466.

5. See Karen Damato, "Doing the Math: Tech Investors' Road to Recovery is Long," *Wall Street Journal*, Friday, May 1, 2001, Page C1.

6. Ibid.

7. Gary P. Brinson, L. Randolph Hood, and Gilbert L. Beebower, "Determinants of Portfolio Performance," *Financial Analysts Journal*, (July/August 1986). And, "Gary P. Brinson, Brian D. Singer, and Gilbert L. Beebower, "Determinants of Portfolio Performance II: An Update," *Financial Analysts Journal*, (May/June 1991).

8. Meir Statman, "How Many Stocks Make a Diversified Portfolio?" *Journal of Financial and Quantitative Analysis* 22 (September 1987), pp. 353–64.

CHAPTER 3

Stock Valuation: Some Preliminaries

Introduction to Valuation

On July 29, 2002, in the midst of an ugly three-year bear market, the Dow Jones Industrial Average advanced 447 points. This performance capped a 1009-point rally that marked the Dow's best four-day percentage gain (13 percent) since 1933 and the largest four-day point gain in history. The rally followed a dismal early July, during which prices fell 1400 points, including a 324-point loss on July 5th and a 390-point loss on July 19th. The steep jolts and jumps associated with stock prices alarmed market veterans and newcomers alike. Risk-embracing investors, thrilled by the volatility associated with the upward trajectory of the market during the euphoric 1990s, turned risk averse and suffered through a death spiral of stock prices after the bubble burst.

Since the turn of the twenty-first century, business news has been bleak. The terrorist attacks of 9/11 crushed the general level of stock prices. Accounting scams at Enron and WorldCom prompted legislative hearings with circuslike atmospheres in Washington. Former

Bernie

CEOs and CFOs, such as 78-year old John Rigas of Adelphia, Dennis Kozlowski of Tyco, and WorldCom's Scott Sullivan, were handcuffed and carted off to jail for corporate fraud and mismanagement. Insider trading scandals, such as the sale of shares of Imclone by Sam Waskal and superstar stylist Martha Stewart, created drama more compelling than the afternoon soaps.

With the stock market on a bungee cord, you need to empower yourself with knowledge, information, and a rational investment program to survive. You also need to measure properly the risks and rewards of investing in stocks. You don't want to be the jumper whose cord is too long and gets smashed because he severely misjudged stock valuation levels.

Before taking the plunge, some of the questions you might want to ask are the following: Do underlying economic conditions justify the high current level of stock price volatility? Has the stock market become a vicarious thrill for those who aren't drunk enough to run with the bulls? Has the random throw of darts become investors' preferred approach for choosing stocks? Most importantly, now that you've seen that stock prices go down quicker than they go up, you may want to find out how much a stock is really worth before investing your hard-earned money.

Chances are, you already know that the company's growth rate, earnings, and interest rates influence a stock's price. But you might not understand how all of these factors are interrelated. You may be wondering:

- How does the market come up with a stock's price?
- What's driving today's stock market valuations?
- Why does a stock's price react so violently to small quarterly earnings surprises?
- Why and how do interest rate changes affect a stock's value?
- And how can you make money by reading this book?

We answer these questions, introduce you to an easy-to-use approach for stock valuation, and teach you how to value common stock without pain, anxiety, or astrology.

DCF Stock Valuation

Before investing in the stock of a company, do some research! Do you understand the company's business? What is the growth potential of the industry in which the company operates, and how is the company positioned? Who are its competitors? What is the quality and stability of the company's management?

Let's assume that you've answered these questions to your satisfaction. How does this book help you? What this book and the Value-Pro 2002 software give you are the tools and the guidance that you need to *estimate the intrinsic value of a stock*. If you like the company, its products, and prospects, you can use our valuation approach to help you decide if the company is undervalued, overvalued, or fairly valued. Stock of even the best-managed company is a poor investment if its price is too high.

Your investment decision should be based solely on *price versus value*. If your analysis shows that a stock is greatly undervalued—take the plunge and buy! If it's overvalued, you can sell the stock if you own it; you can sell the stock short (if you are a market pro and know what you're doing); or you can patiently follow its price and acquire it when and if it moves into a more attractive price range. The DCF approach empowers you with the information that you need to buy and sell carefully.

Definitions Relating to Valuation

The *value of a financial investment* (stock, bond, mortgage, money market account, etc.) equals the present value of its expected future cash flows, discounted (reduced) for the risk and timing of those cash flows. This basic relationship underlies the theory of finance. It's so basic and important that it warrants more description and some valuation-related definitions.

Expected cash flows are the *most likely* cash payments (dividends, interest, capital appreciation) that you can expect (not hope) to receive from a stock or investment that you own, or moneys that you are expected to pay under a debt that you owe, such as a loan or a mortgage.

To *discount* means to multiply a number by less than one. The *discount rate* that you should use in any valuation depends upon the timing of the expected cash flows and the risks associated with receiving the expected cash flows. The discount rate is a function of both time and risk: discount rate = f (time, risk). The discount rate should increase with increasing default risk (e.g., a WorldCom bond) and decrease with lower default risk (e.g., U.S. Treasury bonds) associated with the expected cash payment.

Similar to the discount rate, the *discount factor* takes into account both the discount rate and the timing of the expected cash flow. The discount factor is a function of both time and the discount rate: discount factor = f (time, discount rate). For example, the discount factor for a one-year cash flow, whose discount rate is 6 percent, is simply equal to one divided by (1.06) which in equation form looks like this: 1/(1.06) = .9434. The discount factor for a two-year cash flow, whose discount rate is also 6 percent, is equal to one divided by (1.06) = .9434, that amount divided again by (1.06) = .9434/(1.06) = .8900. This process for a three-year cash flow continues with a third division by (1.06). And so on, ad infinitum. As you can see from this example, the discount factor decreases with increasing time to the payment of a cash flow, and it also decreases with an increasing discount rate.

The value of an investment, known as the *present value (PV)*, is found by taking the sum of the expected cash flows multiplied by their respective discount factors. For example, using a 6 percent discount rate, a discount factor of (.9434), and an expected $100 cash flow in one year, the present value of that cash flow would be $100 times (.9434): $100 * (.9434) = $94.34. Using a 6 percent discount rate, a $100 cash flow expected in two years, and a discount factor of (.8900), the present value of that cash flow would be: $100 * (.8900) = $89.00. The value of an investment is the sum of the present values of all of the expected cash flows. The present value of the two cash flows described above is:

$$PV = \$94.34 + \$89.00 = \$183.34.$$

Mary's Mortgage: A DCF Example Valuation

To understand the DCF process better, consider a home mortgage. Mary wants to purchase a new house, so she borrows $100,000 from the bank and is the obligor on an 8-percent, 30-year mortgage. The

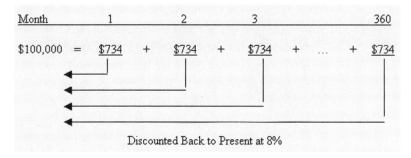

Month	1	2	3	360
$100,000 =	$734 +	$734 +	$734 +	... + $734

Discounted Back to Present at 8%

EXHIBIT 3-1   DCF Example for Mary's Mortgage

monthly mortgage payment is $734 for 360 months, as shown in Exhibit 3-1.

Mary's $734 monthly payments are the cash flows that she is obligated to pay under her mortgage agreement and that the bank expects to receive for lending her the money. Over the life of the mortgage (assuming that she doesn't prepay it), Mary will pay a total of $264,240 ($734 * 360 months) to the bank—$100,000 is the return of principal and $164,240 is the payment of interest. The initial mortgage amount of $100,000 represents the present value to the bank of the 360 monthly payments of $734—each discounted using a rate of 8 percent and the appropriate discount factor.

The 8-percent mortgage rate is the discount rate, or yield, that the bank requires to lend Mary the money. The discount rate is a function of the general level of interest rates in the economy, as represented by the yield on a U.S. Treasury bond with a similar maturity, plus a risk premium for the bank to compensate it for the possibility that Mary may not make her payments. U.S. Treasury bonds are risk free because Uncle Sam can always print more money to repay its loans!

The interest or discount rate that the bank requires on Mary's mortgage depends upon the market interest rate at the time she gets her loan. If interest rates change, the present value of the mortgage could increase or decrease. Consider these two scenarios:

1. If interest rates rise, the bank will increase its lending rates on new mortgage loans in order to cover the higher market interest rates that the bank offers to attract deposits. For example, if interest rates rise 1 percent (also known as 100 basis points), the

present value of Mary's 360 mortgage payments of $734 (discounted now @ 9 percent) decreases to only $91,223. Mary's 8 percent mortgage is now worth only $91,223. A new mortgage by the bank would have monthly payments increased to $805 (a monthly payment difference of $71) so that its present value, discounted at 9 percent, would equal $100,000.

2. If interest rates fall, the bank must decrease its lending rates in order to compete for new loans. Due to the declining interest rates, the bank's cost of deposits also drops. For example, if interest rates fall 1 percent, the present value of Mary's 360 mortgage payments of $734 (discounted now @ 7 percent) increases to $110,326. A new mortgage by the bank would have monthly payments decreased to $665 (a payment difference of $69) so that their present value, discounted at 7 percent, equals $100,000.

A Simple Stock: A DCF Example Valuation

The basic valuation calculation for a stock is the same as that used by the bank in making a fixed-rate mortgage loan, with an important exception. A mortgage has cash flows (the monthly payments) that are known with certainty. The range of future cash flows for a stock can be enormous. Let's use the DCF approach to value a stock.

We'll use a simple example. Assume that ABC Utility Company produces and distributes electric power to an urban rustbelt area that has no growth potential, and little competition. ABC has had revenue of $1 billion per year and profits and cash flows after taxes of $200 million per year for the last 20 years. ABC expects revenue and profits to remain exactly the same for the next 20 years. Further, the company pays out the entire $200 million per year in profits to its shareholders in the form of dividends. Also assume that ABC is financed solely with common stock, and that the yield required by common stockholders is 10 percent. What dollar amount of stock market equity can ABC's underlying business and operations support in today's market environment?

Our assumptions make this is an easy exercise. To calculate ABC's market equity, we *capitalize* (which means to divide an amount by a number between zero and one) ABC's expected annual profits at the yield required by the market. If ABC's profits are $200 million, its cost of capital is 10 percent, and there are no expectations of growth, the market capitalization that the operations can support is: [$200 million/(.10)] = $2 billion.

That $2 billion equity can be divided in many ways: 2 billion shares @ $1 per share; or 200 million shares @ $10 per share; or 20 million shares @ $100 per share; or 2 million shares @ $1000 per share—you get the idea. This price/share trade-off is similar to what happens when a stock splits (for example, the company issues two shares for every share that a shareholder owns—a two-for-one split). It's easy to change the number of shares and per-share intrinsic value, but the aggregate enterprise value should always equal $2 billion—the amount of market equity that ABC's profits of $200 million per year capitalized at 10 percent can support.

What if the unexpected happens on the upside, and as a result of growth in revenue or lower costs, ABC's profits and dividends increase by 50 percent to $300 million per year and are expected to stay at that amount for the next 20 years? The $300 million per year in profits and dividends, capitalized at a 10-percent yield, supports: [$300 million/(.10)] = $3 billion in market equity—an increase of 50 percent. Likewise, shareholders should experience an increase in their stock price of 50 percent—from $1 to $1.50 per share, or $10 to $15 per share, or $100 to $150 per share—depending on how many shares the company has outstanding.

What about the downside? What if a competitor enters the market or a new technology makes the pricing of ABC's power too expensive and reduces ABC's profits and dividends by 90 percent to $20 million per year, where it's expected to stay for the next 20 years? The $20 million in profits and dividends, capitalized at a 10 percent yield, supports: [$20 million/(.10)] = $200 million in market equity—a decrease of 90 percent from its $2 billion level. Shareholders also should experience a decrease in their stock price of 90 percent—from $1 to 10 cents per share, or $10 to $1 per share, or $100 to $10 per share. Sound like what's recently happened to high-tech stocks?

If profits and dividends go to zero and are expected to stay there for the next hundred years, the stock price should be zero (0), no matter how many shares are outstanding. Table 3-1 shows the direct relationship of a company's growth in earnings and market equity.

TABLE 3-1   ABC Stock Price

Changing Earnings–10% Capitalization Rate			
Earnings Scenario	**Earnings**	**Market Equity**	**Change in Market Equity**
No Growth	$200 million	$2 billion	
50% Growth	$300 million	$3 billion	Increase of 50%
90% Shrinkage	$20 million	$200 million	Decrease of 90%
No Earnings	0	0	Decrease of 100%

How about interest rates? Do changing interest rates affect ABC's stock value? YES! If interest rates change, the market equity that the profits of ABC Utility Company support also will change. If the required yield rises, e.g., to 12 percent, the market equity drops to: [$200 million/(.12)] = $1.667 billion. That's the amount that $200 million in profits and dividends, capitalized at 12 percent, can support. If the required yield falls, e.g., to 8 percent, the ABC's market equity rises to [$200 million/(.08)] = $2.5 billion. The inverse relationship between the change in a stock's price and a change in interest rates is shown in Table 3-2.

In this simple example we see that the market equity level of a stock is crucially dependent upon two variables: the amount of *future profits* that the firm is expected to generate—greater profits increase a stock's market value and lower profits decrease value, and the *interest rate* or required yield level that is expected from the investment—with lower yields and interest rates increasing market value, and higher yields and interest rates reducing market value.

TABLE 3-2   ABC Stock Price

Changing Interest Rate–Constant Earnings			
Interest Rate Scenario	**Earnings**	**Market Equity**	**Change in Market Equity**
10%	$200 million	$2 billion	—
12%	$200 million	$1.667 billion	Decreases 16.7%
8%	$200 million	$2.5 billion	Increases 25%

For the moment, let's forget the complexity of changing yields, and growth and contraction in profits and dividends. In our simple, static, no-growth stock valuation example, the operations of ABC Utility Company support a market equity value of $2 billion. The bells and whistles of stock splits, aggressive accounting practices, or fancy capital structure that complicate valuing a stock don't confuse us now, as they do in real life, and as they will when we value real companies in the examples that follow.

We Caused the High-Tech Bubble

In July of 2000, someone bought JDS Uniphase at $140.50 per share! Look at the price history of JDSU shown in Exhibit 3-2. The company had less than a billion dollars in sales and lost money by the hundreds of millions of dollars. Based on its 1.52 billion shares outstanding, JDSU had market equity of over $200 billion—more than 200 times revenue, and it had a price/earnings ratio of infinity. JDSU may have been a good company with bright prospects, but its underlying operations and business should never have justified $200 billion in market equity. How could we bid the price of a company with operating characteristics like JDSU to such a stupid level? JDSU closed 2002 at $2.47 per share.

How about an investment in Internet Capital Group? Someone paid $200.94 per share for ICGE. At that time, ICGE had negative book value

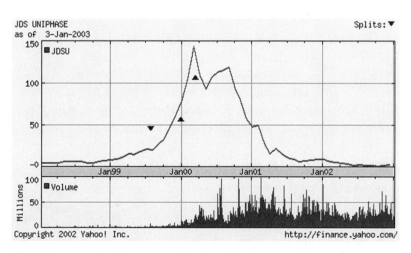

EXHIBIT 3-2 JDSU Five-Year Stock Price Chart

and $131 million in sales. Could these performance numbers ever justify its total market equity of over $50 billion in January 2000? Why buy stock in a risky company that is trading at a very high price? The shares trade now at $0.36 per share—that's 36 cents per share, and ICGE has market equity of about $100 million—down 99.9 percent from its high. We'd prefer buying shares in ABC Utility Company.

How about Lucent? This was a real company, one that had substantial revenues, thousands of employees, and billions in assets. One of the authors of this book owned a small amount (under 100 shares) of Lucent that he received in its 1996 spinoff from AT&T. He watched as LU hitched its fortune to the fiber optic cable craze, and its price increased to $64 per share—for a total equity value of over $200 billion on Lucent's 3.4 billion shares.

In September of 1999, he answered a posting regarding Lucent on the message board of the Web site, *www.valuepro.net/*, owned and administered by the authors of this book. The posting questioned the $64 price of Lucent and referenced a DCF valuation of Lucent, which was done by the postor and showed an intrinsic value of less than $10/share. The postor used an earlier version of the ValuePro 2002 software for his Lucent valuation. The author checked the assumptions underlying the lower valuation, found no holes or oversights in the valuation, emailed his thanks to the postor, and sold the shares at $64. A month later he was second-guessing himself as Lucent continued its rise to $75. Ultimately, the market realized that LU had no clothes. From that $75 peak, the stock price declined steadily (see Exhibit 3-3) to $1.26 per share on December 31, 2002.

The reality underlying the high-tech bubble is that all investors—individuals and institutions, domestic and foreign, women and men, workers and retirees—bid stock prices of companies up to unrealistic levels. The operating profits of the underlying businesses of the companies could never support the overvaluation by the market. We all participated in this stupid activity. We all are at fault. We all are guilty.

True, the stock analysts of Wall Street urged us to pay up to buy shares of these great companies. Henrico, the Internet analyst said, "No price is too high for a great company. The real risk is not buying, standing on the sideline, seeing your aggressive, risk-taking neighbor or coworker make bundles in the market, while conservative, cautious YOU owns bonds and money market funds and misses the upward

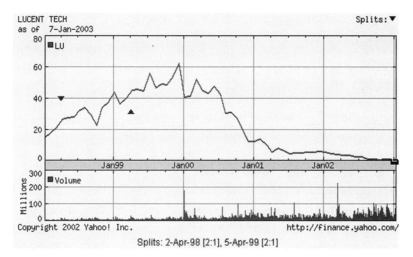

LUCENT TECH
as of 7-Jan-2003

Splits: ▼

Copyright 2002 Yahoo! Inc.   http://finance.yahoo.com/
Splits: 2-Apr-98 [2:1], 5-Apr-99 [2:1]

EXHIBIT 3-3 LU Five-Year Stock Price

surge in stock prices and all of its associated excitement." Unfortunately, many of us listened to Henrico's self-serving spiel and continued to inflate the bubble. And we have participated in the excitement—
on the downside.

How should you test your stock valuation insights or the plausibility of stock tips of others? You can pick up investment reports from
stock brokerage firms to see what conflict-laden stock analysts, such
as Henry Blodget, Jack Grubman, and Mary Meeker, are (or were) saying about these stocks. Or you can test these investments yourself with
the same valuation procedures employed by Wall Street investment
bankers and stock analysts—using the techniques described in this
book. Plus, with your own analysis you at least can be sure that your
assumptions are conservative and there are no unstated conflicts of
interest underlying a valuation or recommendation.

Investors should have cared enough to spend the small amount of
time that was necessary to see that the operations of ICGE, JDSU, LU,
and thousands of similar companies could not support the market equity levels that we were bidding them up to. The rise in stock prices
would have dampened, and the subsequent bursting of the bubble
could have been avoided. We contributed to the problem. We did not
have to invest in the stock market when it was at historic levels that
were ridiculously high. Read on and learn how you can properly value

stocks in the manner of our ABC Utility Company and avoid investing in grossly overpriced companies.

Return to Stockholders

Stock returns fluctuate enormously because they depend on random future events and states of the economy that are impossible to predict. Forecasting returns accurately is extremely difficult. Your principal concern with a stock should be your investment return or cash flows that you expect to receive. Does the stock pay dividends? Has the stock price gone up according to your expectations? What is your total rate of return? The bottom line is that you're interested in stock performance measures that relate to your pocketbook. We don't particularly care whether a company whose stock we own makes funeral caskets or Cabbage Patch Kids—as long as it generates free cash flows, has positive investment returns, and is fairly priced—that's what matters.

Calculation of Return to Stockholders

Return to stockholders includes any dividend payments plus the increase (or minus the decrease) in stock price that investors experience during an investment holding period. The market's focus is on yearly or annualized return to stockholders, as measured by percentage gains or losses, and usually uses the calendar year as the calculation period. Return to stockholders refers to an annual return, which is equal to the sum of the dividends paid plus the net change in a stock's price, divided by the beginning price of the stock.

$$\% \text{ Return to Stockholders} = \frac{(\text{Dividends} + \text{Change in Stock Price})}{\text{Beginning Stock Price}}$$

For example, if a stock's price started the year at $100, the stock paid $1 in dividends during the year, and it ended the year at $109, its percentage annual return to stockholders equals: ($1 + $9)/ $100 = 10 percent. This is not a complex calculation.

The stock market, however, sometimes acts in funny ways. The return on a stock may be negative even if the company had a successful year from an operations or earnings perspective. The stock market may have plummeted due to macroeconomic concerns like higher interest rates, lower earnings forecasts, inflation or deflation fears, or corporate governance or accounting scandals. Or the stock market could have fallen due to geopolitical concerns such as the 9/11 terrorist attacks, the war in Iraq, the perennial deterioration in Middle East relations, an economic and currency crisis in Argentina, or an improvement in Fidel Castro's health. The market downdraft may have pulled your stock with it, and there is nothing the company's management could have done to change the adverse stock price movement.

Conversely, the return to stockholders may be very positive, even though the company had mediocre or poor operating performance. The stock market may have skyrocketed due to positive economic events like the settlement of a major labor strike, the confirmation of the death of Osama bin Laden, or reduced inflation fears. Poor company performance or a legal scandal may put a company into the takeover candidate category and the increase in price may be the result of a tender offer for the company's stock.

Investor Expectations Regarding Stock Market Returns

What investment return should an investor expect from a diversified portfolio of common stocks? As a proxy for the market, let's use the rate of return associated with the S&P 500 Index and compare its performance with the change in operating earnings per share associated with the stocks that comprise the S&P 500 Index. During the 70-year period from 1928 to 1997, the S&P 500 had a compound average return of 10.6 percent. In more recent years, stock return performance has gone from spectacular to abysmal. Look at Table 3-3.

In calendar years 1997, 1998, and 1999, the total returns on the S&P 500 Index were 31 percent, 26.7 percent, and 19.5 percent respectively. But unless the companies are propelled by a similar percentage increase in profits or a general decrease in interest rates, general stock market performance that good can't last forever. It didn't—the market turned, the bubble burst, and the stock market has experienced three years of negative numbers. The S&P 500 was down (10.1 percent) in 2000, (13 percent) in 2001, and (23.4 percent) in 2002.

During the 1996–2002 period, overall stock market performance has been poor to anemic. Remember our discussion in Principle 5 about using compound average returns rather than simple averages? The differences between the two are shown at the bottom of

TABLE 3-3 1997–2002 S&P 500 and S&P Operating Earnings

Year	S&P 500 Index	% Change	S&P Earnings	% Change
2002	879.82	−23.37%	46.04	18.51%
2001	1,148.08	−13.04%	38.85	−30.79%
2000	1,320.28	−10.14%	56.13	8.61%
1999	1,469.25	19.53%	51.68	16.74%
1998	1,229.23	26.67%	44.27	1.23%
1997	970.43	31.01%	43.73	7.63%
1996	740.74	—	40.63	—
6-year simple avg.		5.11%		3.66%
6-year compound avg.		2.91%		2.11%

Table 3-3, and shows that simple averages overstate the performance of the S&P 500 Index. So we focus on compound averages. The compound average return on the S&P 500 for the six-year period was 2.91 percent—not too far from the 2.11 percent compound average growth rate of the operating earnings of the companies that make up the S&P 500 Index.

What are reasonable returns to be earned in the stock market over a long time period? Jeremy Siegel, in *Stocks for the Long Run*,[1] found that 7.13 percent was the average real yearly return, dividends plus appreciation after adjusting for inflation, from owning stock over the 50-year period from 1946 to 1996. This return is very close to the 6.96-percent median earnings yield, which he defines as corporate earnings per share divided by stock price, for the same time period. Historically, as a company's earnings have increased, its stock price also has increased proportionately to maintain this earnings yield. Siegel finds that real returns (after inflation) for common stock closely track real growth in corporate earnings, and stock prices in the long run are a very strong function of real growth in corporate earnings. For a first cut at expectations for stock returns from a diversified portfolio of stocks, investors should expect a real return that is roughly in line with the growth of corporate earnings.

The famous economist John Maynard Keynes scoffed at long time horizons, noting that in the long run, we are all dead. Then what about the short run? Stock prices exhibit an immediate and very strong inverse relationship to movements in interest rates. In general, as interest rates (and a corporation's financing costs) go down—stock prices go up, and as interest rates go up—stock prices go down.

Siegel believes and we agree that interest rates, in the short and intermediate time frame, are the single most important influence on stock prices. He analyzed Federal Reserve monetary policy over a 42-year period from 1955 to 1996. His results were quite striking.

Siegel found that the three-month average return for the stock market, after significant decreases in the Fed Funds rate (85 instances), was 5.6 percent. When the Fed increased the Fed Funds rate (92 instances), the three-month average return for the stock market was only 0.85 percent. The benchmark three-month average return during this period was 2.97 percent. The three-month return of 5.6 percent, after Fed Fund rate decreases, versus the three-month return of 0.85 percent, after Fed Fund rate increases, is a significant difference in stock market performance. Fed Funds rate movements have been a good predictor of short-term stock returns.[2]

During the 1997–2002 time period shown in Table 3-3, long-term interest rates, as measured by the 10-year U.S. Treasury yield, declined from 6.41 percent at the beginning of 1997, to 3.82 percent at the end of December, 2002. This decline in interest rates has greatly increased intrinsic stock values, and we explain why in Chapter 6.

The DCF approach uses both cash flow and interest rate measures as the two primary influences on intrinsic stock value. The direct relationship of a stock's value to corporate cash flow is examined in Chapter 5. The inverse relationship of a stock's value to a change in a corporation's weighted average cost of capital (WACC), especially through changes in interest rates, is described in Chapter 6.

Investor Expectations Regarding Returns of a Stock

What are reasonable market expectations in the way of return on a particular stock? It depends in large part on the risk of the stock and the expected growth of the company's earnings and free cash flows. Remember the first principle of finance: With increasing risk, a rational investor should require increasing expected return.

Let's assume that the risk-free, 10-year Treasury bond yields 7.0 percent, that the equity risk premium is 3 percent, and the stock is of average risk (beta = 1.0) relative to the stock market as a whole. According to the Capital Asset Pricing Model that we described in Principle 10 of Chapter 2, our expected return for this stock is 10.00 percent. (We rigged this example to result in a nice round number.) The CAPM equation that follows shows the relationship between expected return, the risk-free rate, beta, and the equity risk premium.

Expected Return from Stock = Risk-Free Rate
+ Beta*(Equity Risk Premium)

Expected Return from (Beta = 1) Stock = 7.0% + 1.0*(3.0%) = 10%

Beta is a measure of price volatility (risk) of an asset. If the risk of the stock is greater than average (e.g., the stock has more volatility and a beta of 2.0), a rational investor would require an expected return that is greater than that of a lower-beta stock. For example, based on a Treasury bond yield of 7 percent and an equity risk premium of 3 percent, the expected return of a beta = 2 stock is:

Expected Return from (Beta = 2) Stock = 7.0% + 2.0*(3.0%) = 13%

If you buy a $100 (beta = 1) stock on January 1 (which is difficult because the U.S. stock market is closed) that pays no dividend and has the risk characteristics described above, your expectation is that the stock will increase in value by 10 percent to $110 on December 31. Your hope is that it will become the next hot stock and will make you a millionaire.

If you assume the same yield/risk profile, you expect that the stock will increase in price by another 10 percent to $121 by the following December 31st. If the $100 stock has a beta = 2, your expectation is a progression in price to $113 (year 1) to $127.69 (year 2).[3]

As long as the stock performs in accordance with its perceived risk profile, your gain of 10 percent or 13 percent per year would have fulfilled your expectations. If the stock price exceeds your target levels, you're happy! If the stock price increases to less than your target levels, or decreases, you might still be happy, but you have been underpaid for the risk associated with owning that stock.

Stock Price—Too High?—Too Low?—Just Right?

If you pay too much for a stock—it doesn't matter how good the company and its management are—your investment will perform poorly. According to all measures of corporate performance, the company may be a great company, and its operations may be very efficient. Nevertheless, if the stock's price when you purchase it is much higher than the company's business operations can support, you've made a bad investment decision.

As an investor, your major concern is whether a stock's price is equal to, above, or below its true value at the time you buy it. This book and the ValuePro 2002 software show you how to estimate a stock's value and avoid purchasing overpriced stock.

How Are Expectations of Growth Factored into Stock Prices?

Many investors don't understand how expectations of future corporate performance are reflected in the current price of a stock. Suppose DEF Growth Company announces that quarterly revenue and earnings have increased by 10 percent and DEF's stock price immediately declines by 25 percent. Why would this happen? Easy! If stock market analysts and institutional investors are expecting earnings or revenue growth for momentum stocks of 30 percent per year, those expectations are already factored into today's stock market price—especially for growth stocks. Any performance that does not meet or exceed those growth expectations usually results in a sizeable drop in the stock's price.

Growth stocks are companies whose rate of revenue or earnings growth (15 percent and up) greatly exceeds the growth rate of the economy as a whole (3 percent to 5 percent). If earnings growth for the stock meets market expectations, all other things equal, the stock return should be approximately equal to the return of a stock with a similar beta. For instance, according to our grossly hypothetical examples above, we would expect returns of 10 percent for a beta = 1.0 stock, and returns of 13 percent for a beta = 2.0 stock. We would *not* expect a return equal to the 30 percent associated with the earnings or revenue growth rate of the company! Read this paragraph again—it is very important that you understand its implications!

If growth equals expectations, the market reacts quietly to the earnings report. After the stock market closed on July 16, 1998—during the height of the high-tech boom, Microsoft reported a healthy 28-percent gain in its fiscal-fourth-quarter earnings (and Microsoft's fiscal year ends on June 30th), which was in-line with analysts' earnings estimates. In NASDAQ trading, Microsoft shares closed at $117-3/8, unchanged for the day. In after-hours trading that day, shares of Microsoft fell slightly to $116-7/8—an insignificant reaction to a 28-percent growth in earnings.

If growth exceeds expectations, all else being equal, the expected stock return should exceed the above-stated hypothetical 10 percent to 13 percent returns—perhaps by a very large margin. For example, on August 19, 2002, The Lowe's Companies, a home improvement retail chain, reported a 42-percent gain in second quarter earnings. The results surprised analysts who expected a 29-percent gain. That day, the shares of Lowe's rose $4.21 to close at $41 (an 11 percent gain) while the general stock market, as measured by the S&P 500, increased by approximately 2.36 percent.

If revenue or earnings growth turns out to be lower than expected, watch out! The return on that stock will probably be negative and could be disastrous. For example, after the close of business on September 18, 2002, Electronic Data Systems, the world's second-largest computer services company, cut its third and fourth quarter earnings and revenue guidance significantly. According to Thomson First Call, analysts had expected EDS to earn 88 cents per share in the fourth quarter. EDS warned that it expected net income of only 12 to 15 cents a share in the third quarter and 57 cents to 59 cents a share in the fourth quarter, and that fourth quarter revenue would drop between 3 percent and 7 percent. The next day on September 19th, EDS's stock price plummeted $19.26 per share—(53 percent), from $36.46 to $17.20, on a day that the S&P 500 Index declined by 3 percent. The stock price of IBM, EDS's main competitor and the market leader in computer services, fell 7 percent that day due to investor suspicions that market forces that negatively affected EDS would exert a similar effect on IBM.

Managed Earnings, Managed Expectations, and Accounting Scandals
The stock market is obsessed with quarterly earnings estimates—so much so that the finance and investor relations departments of com-

panies commit significant resources to inform Wall Street of the company's annual and quarterly revenue and earnings expectations. Prior to March of 2000, companies could reveal certain material nonpublic information to favored analysts and large shareholders who could then use the information to their advantage.

To overcome the inequity of selective disclosure, the SEC issued Regulation FD. Under this regulation, whenever an issuer discloses material nonpublic information to any other person, the issuer must simultaneously or promptly make public disclosure of that same information. If a company falls short of its quarterly earnings estimates, even by the smallest amount, the drop in stock price could be significant. Consequently, many companies had become adept at handling market expectations.

Prior to Regulation FD, the company could give guidance to certain favored equity analysts, who would then influence Wall Street estimates of the company's earnings and revenues, either up or down. Companies also aggressively managed their earnings so that they would always just meet or slightly exceed expectations, often by a penny per share. Companies established rainy-day reserves for deferred revenue that could be tapped if necessary to meet earnings expectations. Microsoft has been accused of setting up such reserves, and financial companies such as commercial and investment banks and insurance companies have also been known to overfund reserves for future revenues and profits.

One company that frequently met expectations to the penny was WorldCom. For several years, and in an effort to achieve operating earnings estimates, WorldCom finance personnel regularly categorized short-term operating expenses as long-term capital expenditures. WorldCom transferred more than $9 billion in operating expenses, resulting in false accounting statements that supported a stock price that defied gravity. Scott Sullivan and others at WorldCom are awaiting trial and could receive long prison terms for their roles in an accounting scam that has caused considerable pain to millions of investors.

Mr. Sullivan may have some high-ranking corporate company joining him in the big house. Enron has admitted to hiding losses and debts in off-balance-sheet partnerships that were supposedly independent, but actually were not. Global Crossing and Qwest inflated profits by entering into sham transactions with other telecom companies in which they swapped fiber optic cable capacity and booked the swaps as revenue. Xerox paid a $10 million fine to the SEC and has restated downward more than $6.4 billion in revenue over a five-year period. Adelphia is under civil and criminal investigations for hiding more than $3 billion in loans to the Rigas family and for inflating its actual number of customers. Former CEO Dennis Kozlowski and CFO Marc Swartz of Tyco have been indicted and charged with stealing more than $170 million from Tyco and running a criminal enterprise aimed at defrauding investors. Many others companies have taken accounting practices beyond the pale.

Some companies have corporate incentive programs that are poorly designed and may unwittingly encourage corporate management to play loose with the rules. One such company was Computer Associates. In an incredibly stupid and bizarre compensation scheme, CA's three top executives—Charles B. Wang, Sanjay Kumar, and Russell Artzt—were granted 20.25 million shares of Computer Associates to divide if shares of the stock closed above $53.33 for any 60 trading days during a 12-month period. In May of 1998, the goal was achieved, and the shares, which were worth over $1.1 billion at the time, were granted. Sound excessive?

Just two months after the grant, CA announced that its profits and sales would fall short of expectations resulting in its shares being pummeled. Nice timing! The SEC is currently investigating CA to see whether top executives artificially inflated the company's sales and earnings for the sole purpose of receiving the $1.1 billion grant. Now who would do something like that for only $1.1 billion? If ever there were a compensation scheme that encouraged some innovative accounting by top executives, this was it.

Without reverting to accounting chicanery or fraud, it is impossible for the managers of most growth companies to meet the expectations that often are factored into consensus analyst estimates and the pricing of growth stocks. A company can't continually grow at 30 percent to 50 percent per year over a long period of time. Because of unrealistic expectations of greedy investors and the lack of guts of a CFO or CEO to be truthful with stock market analysts, the prices of growth stocks soar to levels that could never be supported by the operations of the company's businesses. Unrealistic expectations for growth from both Wall Street and Main Street were a principal cause of the high-tech bubble and its subsequent collapse.

The bursting of the bubble, the revelations of corporate corruption and misappropriation, and the concern of potential investor outrage at the voting booths spurred Washington to pass bipartisan legislation quickly and almost unanimously. On July 30, 2002, President George W. Bush signed into law the Sarbanes-Oxley Act of 2002. The act strengthens securities and accounting laws and attacks corporate fraud. It creates a board with the responsibility of oversight of the accounting industry and the power to punish accountants for mistakes or wrongdoing. Under the act, a company's CEO and CFO are required to certify the contents of the company's quarterly and annual reports. A CEO or CFO who violates the act faces a prison term.

Managed Earnings: Our Recommendation

We think that the Sarbanes-Oxley Act will be effective in reducing greatly (not eliminating completely) the Enron, WorldCom, Global Crossing types of accounting scams that the market has recently witnessed. If not, our money is coming out of the stock market. No rational investor wants to participate in a market where an accounting scorecard means nothing.

When we value a stock, we use a reasonable and rational technique. We won't make the mistake of paying too much for a JDSU or LU. In our valuations, we employ two different growth rates—one that reflects analyst estimates (but those growth estimates most likely are too high in the long run) and one that reflects growth rates that are consistent with the growth of the economy (3 percent to 5 percent) and see where the valuations play out.

The intelligent investment decision rule in today's market (especially for growth stocks) is: If you believe that a company's performance will exceed expectations, buy the stock; if you believe the company will perform below expectations, sell the stock. If you want to be able to make intelligent investment decisions, it's essential to know how today's stock prices reflect expectations of growth rates, net operating profit margins, net investment levels, and interest rates.

Stock Valuation—Art, Science, or Magic?

The economics underlying the movements and price levels of the stock market are a mystery to most people. At the end of trading each day, stock analysts on CNNfn, CNBC, and other financial news networks attribute stock price movements to any number of factors: government reports on consumer or wholesale prices; changes in interest rates and the bond market; the increasingly bullish or bearish sentiment of investors; statements by Federal Reserve Chairman, Alan Greenspan; or company earnings reports exceeding or falling short of expectations.

Even more puzzling for many market players is what factors determine the absolute price of a stock. Why is the Dow Jones Industrial Average at 8,341.63? Why does McDonald's sell for $16.08 per share? Is stock valuation an art, a science, or just magic?

In this book, we focus on the art and science of stock valuation. We contend that over time, stock prices will gravitate to their underlying intrinsic values. The valuation of common stock is no different from the valuation of any other asset. Asset valuation—be it a financial, real, or human asset—is a generic exercise.

Today's economic value of any asset is simply the total of its cash flows that it expects to generate, discounted back to the present at a rate that reflects both the time value of money and the degree of risk or uncertainty associated with those expected cash flows. Cash flows for common stocks can come from dividends, from the sale or merger of a company, from repurchase of stock by the company (like Microsoft and Intel who have large share repurchase programs), or from the sale of the stock at market prices.

The DCF valuation approach applies to all assets: financial assets such as bonds, mortgages and stock; real assets such as buildings and real estate, art and antiques, and rare coins; and human assets such as a college education and the economic value of a person's life. (Many jurisdictions use DCF valuation techniques to determine the economic value of a life in a wrongful death court case.) For financial assets with fixed payments such as bonds and mortgages, it's relatively simple to apply the DCF approach. Adapting this approach to common stocks (or an individual's life) is considerably more difficult. We address how to overcome these difficulties in the chapters that follow.

Stock Valuation Approaches: Fundamental, Technical, and MPT

Professional stock market participants practice a number of investment approaches and techniques. These philosophies range from the conservative buy-and-hold companies that you know strategy of individual investors, to the aggressive long/short, risk-neutral strategies[4] employed by sophisticated hedge fund managers playing the international markets.

In general terms, the different stock market investment and valuation strategies can be classified as fitting into one of three camps—fundamental analysis, technical analysis, and modern portfolio theory (MPT). The three philosophies have different beliefs about the relationship between the stock prices that we observe in the markets and underlying intrinsic stock values.[5] These different beliefs are summarized in Exhibit 3-4.

An example of fundamental analysis is the valuation procedure that we use in this book—discounted cash flow analysis. According to this

How to Value a Share?

	Technical Analysis	Fundamental Analysis	Portfolio Theory
What Drives Stock Prices?	Psychology Technical Cosmic	Earnings Dividends	Risk & Return
How to Value A Share?	Trends Waves Factors	Forecast Dividends & Earnings	Risk & Return
Relationship Between Value and Prices?	P ✗ V	P will Eventually Equal Value	P = V

EXHIBIT 3-4 Valuation Strategies Chart

approach, the company's current and future operating and financial performance determine the intrinsic value of a company's stock. Fundamental analysts use other approaches to assess intrinsic value as well—primarily target stock price and relative valuation—which we discuss below. To assess a company's prospects, fundamental analysts evaluate overall economic, industry, and company data to estimate a stock's intrinsic value. The assumption underlying fundamental analysis is that a company's stock price over time will gravitate to its intrinsic value.

Technical analysts believe that short-term stock price movements are influenced primarily by changes in market psychology—the supply and demand considerations that we describe in Principle 4. True technicians are not concerned with a company's balance sheet and income statement but instead believe that stock prices reflect the greed versus fear mentality of investors. Underlying technical analysis, there is no necessary relationship between a stock's price and its underlying intrinsic value.

The followers of modern portfolio theory believe that competitive forces in the stock market result in stock prices that always reflect underlying intrinsic values. In MPT terminology, the market is efficient because new information is very quickly incorporated into stock prices and there never are any undervalued or overvalued stocks. We explain some of the theories of MPT in Chapter 2.

Fundamental Analysis

Fundamental analysis starts with the assumption that a stock has a true or intrinsic value to which its price is anchored. Price may diverge from this value in the short run, but over time, price and intrinsic value will converge. The more famous advocates of fundamental analysis include: investors—Benjamin Graham, Warren Buffett, and Peter Lynch; and Wall Street strategists, such as Abby Joseph Cohen of Goldman Sachs, Alan McCann of Merrill Lynch, and John Manley of Salomon Smith Barney. The virtues of fundamental analysis are espoused on the Internet by the Motley Fool (*www.fool.com*/), Stock Valuation with Sense (*www.stocksense.com*/), and VectorVest (*www.vectorvest.com*/).

We estimate that more than 80 percent of Wall Street's analysts primarily use fundamental valuation techniques to base their buy/sell recommendations and to estimate a company's *intrinsic value*. In this analytical style, value is a function of revenue, growth, earnings, dividends, cash flows, profit margins, risk, interest rates, and other factors. Fundamental stock analysts assess a company's stock price versus value using one or more of the following three methods.

Target Stock Price Analysis. This popular technique begins with a forecast of a firm's future earnings per share (EPS). This figure is then multiplied by a projected price/earnings (P/E) ratio to arrive at a target stock price. A typical target stock price analysis would conclude in this manner: "With a 2003 EPS estimate of $1.63/share, and assuming a market P/E ratio of 18, our target stock price for McDonalds is $30 per share. Given the current price of $16.08, we recommend buying the stock."

Relative Value Analysis. Relative value measures are often used in conjunction with the target stock price approach. Relative value analysis employs a measure of value—most commonly the P/E ratio—for a company and similar stocks and industry peers. In addition to the price/earnings ratio, relative value measures include price/book value (*P/BV*), price/sales (*P/S*), or the price/earnings/growth (*PEG*) ratios as yardsticks for comparisons of different companies with varying characteristics.

Because it's simple to compute and understand, the P/E ratio is the relative value measure quoted most frequently by the media. The P/E ratio for the company is compared to P/E ratios of the company's peers in conjunction with other fundamental factors—most notably earnings per share growth, net operating profit margin, and risk—to ascertain whether a stock is overvalued or undervalued. The PEG ratio for the valuation of growth stocks has been a popular metric among investors recently because it is a favorite measure used by The Motley Fool in its publications and Web site.

A relative value analysis may read as follows: "McDonalds current P/E of 15.8 is below the P/Es of other fast food restaurant chains. Given that the company's growth (5 percent for sales and earnings) is in line with industry peers, and its risk profile (as measured by earnings volatility and debt levels) is below that of its competitors, we conclude that McDonalds is undervalued."

Discounted Cash Flow Analysis. We use DCF analysis in this book. While DCF analysis is used to value all types of fixed income investments (bonds, mortgages, etc.), it receives much less attention from the media as a method to value common stocks. An apparent reason for this lack of attention may be the difficulty in explaining the DCF technique in simple terms to stock investors.

In the DCF approach, a stock's value is the sum of the expected cash flows of the company, discounted at an appropriate interest rate. The most basic DCF approach is the *dividend discount model (DDM)*, under which the value of a stock is the present value of the dividends that an investor expects to receive. Using the DDM approach, the analyst estimates future dividend growth and the required rate of return on the stock, and discounts those expected dividends to arrive at a stock's value.

Another DCF approach is the *free cash flow to equity (FCFE)* model, which measures the cash flow left over after payments for working capital, capital expenditures, the interest and principal on debt, and dividends on preferred stock. These cash flows are then discounted at the company's cost of equity to arrive at the stock's value. The final DCF approach is the *free cash flow to the firm (FCFF) approach*, and is the approach that we describe herein at length.

Analysts who use DCF analysis tend to provide a simple value statement, as opposed to detailed assessments to investors, such as: "On a cash flow basis, we estimate that McDonalds fair value is $30 per share. Given the current price of $16.08, we rate MCD as a strong buy."

Many market participants use fundamental analytic techniques as the basis for long-term buy/sell decisions. The basic investment rule associated with fundamental analysis is: If a stock price is well below its intrinsic value, buy the stock; if the stock price is well above its value, sell the stock.

Technical Analysis

Technical analysts chart historic stock price movements, volume of trading activity, and the price/volume aspects of related equity and debt markets to predict or anticipate the stock buying behavior of other market participants. The animal spirits of other market players are more important to technical analysts than to fundamental analysts. Technical analysts believe that stock prices are influenced more by investor psychology and the emotions of the crowd than by changes in the underlying fundamentals of the company. And the actions of the crowd of investors in the stock markets are driven by *fear* on the downside and *greed* on the upside.

The more famous advocates of technical analysis are Ralph Acampora of Prudential Securities, William O'Neil of *Investor's Business Daily*, and Alan Shaw of Salomon Smith Barney. The virtues of technical analysis are featured on the Internet at Stock Charts (*www.stockcharts.com/*), Technical Traders (*www.technicaltraders.com/*), and (*www.bullchart.com/*).

Recall Principle 4—supply and demand drive stock prices in the short run. Technical analysts focus on how market participants will behave in the near term and how stock market pessimism or optimism will affect their behavior. To a technical analyst, when a stock's price trends upward, it is not necessarily because of better operating aspects of the company, but because of increasing demand for the stock and momentum in the company's stock price. Investors who exclusively use technical analysis generally have a shorter-term stock holding orientation and more frequent trading activity than investors who employ only fundamental analysis.

Many market participants use technical analytical techniques as the basis for short-term buy/sell decisions. The basic investment rule associated with technical analysis is: If your indicators signal that a stock's price will rise, buy the stock; if your indicators signal that a stock's price will fall, sell the stock.

Modern Portfolio Theory

Efficient capital markets (discussed in Principle 2 in Chapter 2) is a cornerstone of MPT and is the belief that stock prices *always* reflect intrinsic value, and that any type of fundamental or technical analysis is already embedded in the stock price. Advocates of MPT tend to be finance academicians who have ultra-conservative or libertarian political views. Many teach or studied at the University of Chicago.

To support this claim, they cite academic studies showing, among other things: daily stock price changes are random (the *Random Walk Hypothesis*); stock prices react very quickly to new company disclosures about earnings, dividend changes, and other corporate news; and that investment funds run by professional money managers (mutual and pension funds), on average, tend to underperform a buy and hold the overall stock market strategy as measured by owning an S&P 500 Index Fund.

As a group, these findings suggest that investors cannot use past stock price information or public news releases of firm-specific information to find undervalued stocks, and that even investment fund managers, on average, cannot sleuth the market to detect undervalued stocks. An important exception to these studies is the research performed by Fama and French, and similar research by others, which we discuss in Chapter 2. These studies show that investors can consistently outperform the market by buying undervalued value stocks and selling overvalued growth stocks.

MPT practitioners sometimes express disdain for technical or fundamental analysis. As such, MPT devotees tell investors not to bother to search for undervalued stocks but instead to pick a risk level that they can live with and diversify holdings among a portfolio of stocks. (See Principle 9.)

Stock Value, Stock Price, and Emotions

Many professional investors will tell you that a stock's value is whatever price you can get for it on the open market—nothing more, nothing less. Supply and demand determines the fair price of a stock. It's hard to argue with that declaration, but we'll give it a try.

We believe that a fair price is determined by fundamental analysis resulting in a supportable intrinsic value, not by a chart-reading momentum investor that is operating according to the greater fool theory of valuation. We hate to rely on selling a stock at a ridiculous price based on the assumption that there is always an ample supply of truly foolish buyers for overpriced stock.

Market players are constantly bombarded with information that may influence a stock's price, either positively or negatively. Some info is very stock specific—a report of better or worse than expected earnings, the release of a dynamite new product, the death of the corporation's founder (which in a morbid way usually has a positive effect on stock prices), the settling of a labor strike, or an exciting technological or medical breakthrough.

Does the stock market ever overreact or underreact to new information? Absolutely!

We discuss the EntreMed example in Chapter 2. The company was the subject of a very favorable article regarding its cancer research in a Sunday edition of the *New York Times*. The article contained no new information regarding the company; however, it did give the company front-page exposure to three million readers and potential new investors. The stock price multiplied from its closing price of $12 on Friday to open at $84 on Monday. Is this a rational reaction?

Emotions often play a large role in the stock market. Some market players may translate the information that they receive into overly optimistic or pessimistic influences on a company's expected future cash flows. A stock's price may be bid up for a time to an unrealistically high level, or it may be driven down to an unbelievably low bargain opportunity. Some info may affect an industry as a whole. For example, if Dell Computer Corporation unexpectedly lowers its revenue projections for the year, its stock price most likely will decline, perhaps significantly. That announcement may also negatively affect the stock market price of other computer manufacturers. Logically, investors will conclude that the industry forces that are affecting Dell may also adversely affect IBM and Hewlett-Packard. The announcement may also lower the stock prices of Microsoft, which sells software that's bundled into Dell computers, and Intel, which sells microprocessors to Dell.

Some information may affect the stock market as a whole. For example, political and labor stability, decreasing income taxes, low inflation, and small equity risk premiums (associated with stable interest rates and cost of capital) are major bonuses for the vast majority of stocks. Conversely, labor and political unrest, higher inflation, increased income taxes, and a greater perceived equity risk premium (associated with higher interest rates and cost of capital) are huge downers for stocks in general. Equity risk premiums increased greatly around the 9/11 terrorist attacks and again during the corporate governance scandals of Enron and WorldCom.

With all this info bombarding investors and causing constant reevaluations, market prices seesaw quite a bit. Does a stock's intrinsic value change as frequently as—and in unison with—its price? The evidence is to the contrary. A lot of academic research has been conducted regarding the movement of stock prices and the noise associated with that movement.[6] Because of overly optimistic or pessimistic views in the market, a stock's price may diverge significantly and for a long period of time from a stock's intrinsic value. That happened during the inflating of the Internet/telecom/high-tech bubble. Over time, however, stock value and stock price should converge on a regular basis.

Stock Value, Stock Price, and Analyst Recommendations

Intrinsic value, like beauty, is somewhat in the eye of the beholder and is influenced by the valuation model used and the assumptions made in the analysis. Wall Street (and non-Wall Street, for that matter) analysts incorporate their own spin to the models that they use to calculate a stock's value. An analyst's estimate of intrinsic value will be based upon the current fundamentals (historic revenue growth, net operating profit margins, etc.) associated with the stock, and more importantly, upon analyst's beliefs about the future development of those fundamentals. Some of the assumptions, such as expected growth rates, may be overly optimistic and may result in values that are impossible to justify in relation to the underlying operations of the company.

An analyst who believes that a stock is priced below its intrinsic value would recommend a purchase of the stock. On the flip side—an analyst, fearing retribution from the corporate client, may be more reticent to recommend a sale of a stock that is priced above its intrinsic value. An analyst that gives a stock a sell recommendation has a much more difficult time in getting information from that company in the future. Also, sale recommendations tend to strain relationships between the company and the firm's investment banking department, which may be trying to get a lucrative piece of business from the company, making that analyst persona-non-grata in the investment bank's corporate dining room. Instead of a sell recommendation, an analyst calls an overpriced stock a *fully valued* stock or a *long-term hold* situation. Be cautious when hearing those terms.

Since the bursting of the high-tech bubble, stock analysts and conflicts of interest have been the focus of much public attention. The bullish stock reports and bearish internal emails of Henry Blodget, the former Internet stock analyst of Merrill Lynch, have caused Merrill embarrassment and were a large factor in the $100 million settlement in late 2002 of an action brought by the New York State Attorney General, Elliott Spitzer. Blodget has been banned from the securities industry and assessed a fine of several million dollars. In August 2002, Jack Grubman, the former telecom analyst at Salomon Smith Barney, resigned amidst SEC investigations alleging that he upgraded or maintained unreasonably high recommendations on stocks of telecom companies that employed Salomon Smith Barney as investment banker. He has also been banned from the securities industry and assessed a fine of $15 million. Grubman has been embarrassed by emails in which he portrays Citicorp CEO Sandy Weill in an unfavorable light, and makes all of us aware of how difficult and expensive it would be to place a four-year-old child in a decent preschool in Manhattan.

In fact, concerns about conflicts of interest of research analysts at brokerage firms led to the August 2002 proposal by the SEC of Regulation Analyst Certification (Regulation AC). The regulation:

- prohibits a brokerage firm from tying analyst compensation to specific investment banking transactions;
- prohibits an analyst from offering favorable research to induce firm business;
- restricts personal trading by analysts in securities of companies the analyst follows; and
- requires disclosure of conflicts of interest in research reports and public appearances of the research analyst.

The former stock research analyst James English in his excellent book, *Applied Equity Analysis*, persuasively argues that the stock analyst is an *advocate*, not a neutral observer, and that equity analysis is not prophecy but opinion. According to Dr. English, the analyst's job is to present a position. If the analyst works for and is paid by a firm with investment banking activities, the investor should understand that conflicts will occur and may bias a valuation. The investor never should blindly accept the recommendation of an analyst. It's the investor's own responsibility to ferret out the opinions of other analysts or develop his own view of the stock.

Given the stock inputs that you develop, the DCF approach, and the ValuePro 2002 software, *you* can determine a stock's intrinsic value, on the same basis as models used by Wall Street analysts. The benefit is that you, free of conflicts of interest, control the inputs—the fundamentals—and you can see how those input changes are transformed into changes in a stock's value.

You determine the most likely revenue growth rate or the profit margin that you think the company can achieve, or the discounting rate that the financial markets will demand. We'll describe in great detail how you can reasonably estimate these inputs and show you that you don't have to be a clairvoyant to do so. With the valuation approach and the spreadsheet software, you are now in charge of your stock-picking destiny. You are the master of the stock valuation universe. *You* are now able to empower yourself with information!

When to Buy, When to Sell: Our Recommendation

Most investors that we know (with the exception of some staunch academician friends who actually believe in MPT), use either a combination of fundamental and technical analysis in coming up with investment picks and timing, or they use no analysis at all, relying solely on hot tips from their golfing partners.

How do we view the fundamental versus technical versus MPT valuation debate? We always prefer to buy a stock that is priced below its intrinsic value. However, when the stock's price trend is upward, the trend can carry an overvalued stock even higher. Many investors that primarily use technical analysis have benefited from using this type of momentum trading strategy.

Conversely, if the market is bearish and stocks are tanking, we believe that the worst place to be is in a stock whose price is at a significant premium to its intrinsic value. An overvalued stock is a great short-selling opportunity in a bear market. We believe that technical price trends as well as fundamental value and diversification are all important. If an investment philosophy works for you, use it to your benefit. However, don't turn your back on other investment and valuation techniques, especially the values churned out using the DCF approach.

The MPT side of the story presumes that fundamental and technical analysis will get you nowhere in the investment world, since all this information is already reflected in the stock price. While academics tend to believe this notion, investment professionals do not. The empirical evidence is beginning to turn against the idea that stock prices always reflect intrinsic stock values. The Fama and French article that we have described previously is the most obvious and best study showing that markets may not be efficient or semiefficient. Other academic studies using the F&F approach have similar results.

Since 1990, *The Wall Street Journal* has tested the notion of stock market efficiency in its "Investment Dartboard" column. The *Journal* compares the six-month total return performance of four stocks, one selected by each of four different investment professionals, with the performance of four stocks picked through the random method of tossing darts at the stock listings pages of the *Journal*. In 1999, four different amateur investors that read the *Journal* were invited to participate in each contest. The final contest ended on September 11, 2002. The aggregate performance strongly supports the pros over both the darts and the amateurs. In the 147 contests over the 12-year period, the pros have beaten the darts in 90. On a relative return basis, the pros have earned an average six-month return of 9.6 percent over the period, compared to 5.1 percent for the DJIA, and 2.9 percent for the randomly selected dart stocks,[7] creating a significant difference in returns.

In the 35 contests since 1999 when amateurs were first invited to participate, the professionals have averaged a six-month profit of 4.7 percent, while the picks of the amateurs lost 5.4 percent, the dart stocks lost an average of 2.4 percent, and the Dow Jones Industrial Average fell by an average of 1.7 percent—a resounding victory for Wall Street and the proponents of fundamental analysis.

We believe strongly that there is value to careful stock selection and that an investor should own a diversified portfolio of common stocks. Within that portfolio, the investor should value each stock individually using the DCF technique that we describe. When a stock's price is *overvalued* and it exceeds its intrinsic value by more than *X* percent (the investor picks that percentage, e.g., 15 percent), the investor should sell that stock and replace it with another stock that is *undervalued* by more than *X* percent (e.g., 15 percent).

This approach allows an investor to benefit from the diversification that is advocated by modern portfolio theory, while also making the value play that we so strongly believe in but that has confounded academicians. We also believe that in any analysis leading to a buy/sell stock decision, the investor should heed the fear and avoid the greed factors that regularly bubble through the stock market.

Tax decisions often complicate the timing of purchase and sale of stock, and we do not address this complex issue in the book.

Finally, no matter how good your analysis and how much you feel that a stock is undervalued, the market may not agree with you or may know something that you do not yet know. Our recommendation is that if you buy a stock and the price drops significantly, by 20 percent or more below your purchase price, sell it. Cut your losses and move on. Also, periodically update the valuations of your stocks. If the fundamentals of a stock have changed and the change negatively affects its intrinsic value, sell the stock if and when it gets X percent below its revised intrinsic value level.

Where Do We Go Next?

Valuing common stocks is a mystery to most investors. Recent extreme volatility in the stock market no doubt has added to the mystique. Indeed, many market observers insist that these gyrations support the notion that stock valuation is less art and science and more magic. This book's focus is on the art and science of stock valuation and how you can profitably use it in your investment decisions. In the pages that follow, we explain how you can apply the stock valuation principles used by professional money managers and Wall Street investment bankers to value your favorite stocks.

The crucial concept we attempt to hammer home throughout this book is that the value of a stock—like the value of any other financial instrument—is equal to the discounted value of its expected cash flows, adjusted for risk and timing. For many investors, there are two general sources of confusion in the stock valuation process. First, how do we estimate future cash flows? We clear up this question in Chapter 5. Second, what is the appropriate rate to discount uncertain cash flows? We discuss this concern in Chapter 6. This book teaches you how to address these questions and use your answers to generate investment profits.

Since we believe that it is helpful to know about the company in which you're considering an investment, Chapter 7 shows the what, where, and how of getting information instantaneously. Chapter 8 shows you how to use the DCF approach to value stocks such as Citigroup, Merrill Lynch, and Berkshire Hathaway.

So let's go! If you get stuck on a term that is unfamiliar or a concept that is difficult to grasp, either reread the section or refer to the Glossary. It's now time to learn how to value a stock.

Notes

1. Jeremy J. Siegel, *Stocks for the Long Run*, McGraw-Hill, New York, NY, 1998, pages 13, and 79–80.

2. Siegel, pages 153–154.

3. $100 * 1.10 = $110 * 1.10 = $121; $100 * 1.13 = $113 * 1.13 = $127.69.

4. The collapse of Long Term Capital Management has shown that there are no completely risk-neutral investment strategies.

5. For a description of the fundamental valuation techniques discussed in this section, see Aswath Damodaran, *Investment Valuation*, John Wiley & Sons, Inc., New York, NY (1996), and Tom Copeland, Tim Koller, and Jack Murrin, *Valuation—Measuring and Managing the Value of Companies*, John Wiley & Sons, Inc., New York, NY (1996).

6. Siegel describes tests of the efficient market theory and the movement of stock prices in great detail.

7. Georgette Jasen, "Investment Dartboard," *The Wall Street Journal*, September 12, 2002, c9.

CHAPTER 4

How to Value a Stock

Some Definitions Relating to Cash Flow

Many corporate board members, CEOs, and teachers of finance (including the authors of this book) believe that Ebeneezer Scrooge had it right the first time—before the spirits enlightened him. The number-one priority of a business is to make money for its stockholders, with more profits being preferred to less.

The goal of management should be to make stockholders happy by selling real products and services and earning real profits with real cash; not by inventing bogus revenues, such as when Global Crossing and Qwest swapped fiber optic cable capacity; not by reporting phantom profits, such as Enron generated from scam transactions; not by using aggressive or bogus accounting to boost stock prices artificially and trigger exorbitant stock grants, as the management of Computer Associates has done.

If management succeeds at its task of creating a profitable and well-run business, the firm's stock price should rise and management should be amply rewarded. Managers who perform poorly will become consultants and will exit quietly. And if to the detriment of creditors and shareholders managers try to enrich themselves by bending the rules and breaking the laws, they should wind up wearing orange jumpsuits and swinging sledgehammers.

Operating Income, Operating Expense, and Net Operating Profits

How does a corporation make money? It develops and operates business lines and divisions where it manufactures products or provides services. A company generates *revenue* by selling its products and services to another party. While generating revenue, a company incurs *operating expenses* such as *costs of goods sold* (*CGS*—which includes depreciation charges for the expense of plant and equipment), *sales and general administrative expenses* (*SG&A*), and *research and development costs* (*R&D*).

$$\text{Operating Expenses} = \text{CGS} + \text{SG\&A} + \text{R\&D}$$

Stockholders sincerely hope that corporate revenues are greater than the expenses associated with producing them. The difference between a firm's operating revenue and operating expense is called operating income or *net operating profit* (*NOP*).

$$\text{Net Operating Profit} = \text{Operating Revenues} - \text{Operating Expenses}$$

How is net operating profit measured? NOP is the income generated from continuing operations of the firm and should reflect the future revenue-generating ability and the expense requirements of the operating businesses that comprise the firm's ongoing operations. NOP is the income that a company earns from its ongoing operations without taking into account the payment of income taxes on corporate earnings, the interest payments on the company's debt, or the dividend payments on preferred stock. For manufacturing and technology companies, NOP *excludes* interest income, investment income, extraordinary gains or losses, and income from discontinued operations.

When valuing a stock, investors are very concerned with revenue, operating expenses, and net operating profits. The corporation's *net operating profit margin* (*NOPM*) is an important cash flow measure that helps to quantify a corporation's ongoing operating profitability. The formula for NOPM is:

NOPM = Net Operating Profit/Revenue

As an example, let's look at the revenue, expense, and operating income for the Microsoft Corporation. Microsoft is the dominant player in the software market for personal computers (PCs). Its operating systems, which include MS-DOS (Microsoft disk operating system) and all of the Windows software, power over 85 percent of the PCs currently in use. Microsoft also developed and markets the top-selling software application package in the world—Office Suite, which includes Word (word processing), Excel (spreadsheet), Power Point (graphics), and Outlook (communication) software. Microsoft also is the largest provider of services and software for the Internet with its Explorer serving as the number-one Internet browser. At the end of 2002, Microsoft's market capitalization was the largest of any company in the world.

We have printed the 2002 Consolidated Statement of Income page, Exhibit 4-1, taken from Microsoft's corporate Web site. Initially, we focus on entries for Microsoft's revenues, total operating expenses, and operating income.

Using these entries, we divide Microsoft's yearly operating income by its net revenues (*operating income/ net revenues*) and calculate that Microsoft's NOPM equaled 47.9 percent, 46.3 percent, and 42.0 percent in years 2000, 2001, and 2002 respectively—an average of 45.4 percent during this period. We also see that its net revenues increased from $22,956 million to $25,296 million to $28,365 million representing revenue growth of 10.2 percent in 2001 and 12.1 percent in 2002. Microsoft's growth rates were substantially higher in the 1990s. Still, these are impressive NOPMs and revenue growth rates for such a large company. The fact that growth rates and NOPMs are trending downward over time is consistent with what usually happens to these percentages as a company grows and competition eats into operating profit margins. Unfortunately, shrinking growth rates and NOPMs are bad for stock values. In Chapter 5, we show how to use these ratios for valuation purposes, along with cash flow measures that are taken from the company's balance sheet and cash flow statements.

In millions, except earnings per share			
Year Ended June 30	2000	2001	2002
Revenue	$ 22,956	$ 25,296	$ 28,365
Operating expenses:			
Cost of revenue	3,002	3,455	5,191
Research and development	3,772	4,379	4,307
Sales and marketing	4,126	4,885	5,407
General and administrative	1,050	857	1,550
Total operating expenses	11,950	13,576	16,455
Operating income	11,006	11,720	11,910
Losses on equity investees and other	(57)	(159)	(92)
Investment income/(loss)	3,326	(36)	(305)
Income before income taxes	14,275	11,525	11,513
Provision for income taxes	4,854	3,804	3,684
Income before accounting change	9,421	7,721	7,829
Cumulative effect of accounting change (net of income taxes of $185)	–	(375)	–
Net income	$ 9,421	$ 7,346	$ 7,829
Basic earnings per share:			
Before accounting change	$ 1.81	$ 1.45	$ 1.45
Cumulative effect of accounting change	–	(0.07)	–
	$ 1.81	$ 1.38	$ 1.45
Diluted earnings per share:			
Before accounting change	$ 1.70	$ 1.38	$ 1.41
Cumulative effect of accounting change	–	(0.06)	–
	$ 1.70	$ 1.32	$ 1.41
Weighted average shares outstanding:			
Basic	5,189	5,341	5,406
Diluted	5,536	5,574	5,553

EXHIBIT 4-1   Microsoft 2002 Income Statement

Corporate Free Cash Flow

To produce revenue, not only must a corporation incur operating expenses, it also must invest money in real estate, buildings and equipment, and in working capital to support its business activities. A company's *new investment*, its annual investment in plant, property, and equipment, may be quite substantial and represent a significant cash outflow for the company. For example, during the late 1990s, the McDonald's Corporation invested about 20 percent of its total yearly revenues to expand its number of restaurants and make the improvements and capital expenditures that the fast food business requires. These were big cash outflows. Partially offsetting capital expenditures is the *depreciation* deduction that a company receives as it annually expenses its prior capital expenditures for tax purposes. Depreciation is a noncash expense and is not a cash outflow. The *net investment* that a company makes to support its operations is:

Net Investment = New Investment − Depreciation

Working capital is the company's investment in its accounts receivable plus its inventories (both being cash outflows), minus its accounts payable (a cash inflow).

Working Capital = (Accounts Receivable + Inventories)
− Accounts Payable

The net change in working capital is the yearly change that is required to support the growing revenues and operations of the company.

The corporation must pay income tax, another cash outflow, on its earnings. From Exhibit 4-1, we see that Microsoft had a provision for $3684 million in income taxes in 2002, which when divided by its income before income taxes of $11,513 million, is equal to a tax rate of 32.0 percent.

Capital expenditures, working capital, and income tax payments represent real cash outflows from the corporation—hard-earned dollars flowing out of the firm that are not available to pay the good guys, the shareholders.

How do we blend these cash flow measures together to come up with a stock's value? We use a discounted free cash flow to the firm approach to calculate the intrinsic value of a company's stock. The number that results from adjusting the earnings measure associated with NOP for the actual cash flows of taxes, net investment in long-term assets, and net change in working capital is known as *free cash flow to the firm* (*FCFF*).

FCFF is an important measure to stockholders. This is the cash that is left over after the payment of all hard cash expenses and all operating investment required by the firm. FCFF is the actual cash that is available to pay the company's various claim holders, especially the stockholders. The following equation is used to calculate the annual FCFF:

FCFF = NOP − Taxes − Net Investment
$$\hspace{4cm} - \text{Net Change in Working Capital}$$

The accounting definition of earnings and profits are fine for accounting purposes, but from a stock valuation standpoint, stockholders should be more concerned about the amount of free cash flow to the firm.

How do all of these cash flows and acronyms relate to a stock's value? It boils down to this: on any corporate investment, a corporation creates additional value for stockholders if and only if it earns a rate of return, after all net cash flow adjustments, that exceeds the corporation's weighted average cost of capital. This occurs only when the investment generates additional free cash flow to the firm.

We have stated that the value (not necessarily the price) of an investment is equal to the present value of its expected cash flows, appropriately discounted for risk and timing. So the value of a firm is not determined by historic performance, or even current performance. The firm's value is determined by investors' belief about the company's *future* performance. Future performance is difficult to predict—particularly when you're putting your hard-earned money behind your prediction in the way of a stock purchase. However, there are some tried-and-true methods to estimate growth and other valuation inputs that are used by analysts and savvy investors for valuation purposes. We talk about those later, and we provide some tips on how to make well-informed assumptions—ones that we're willing to put our dollars behind!

The Free Cash Flow to the Firm Approach

This book uses the free cash flow to the firm approach to value the corporation. The FCFF approach has two underlying assumptions: the company will maintain a relatively constant capital structure; and company management will act in the best interests of its owners (a sometimes erroneous assumption, given the recent exploits of John Rigas of Adelphia and Andrew Fastow of Enron) to maximize stockholder value.

The first assumption implies that the company will have stable percentages of debt, preferred stock, and common stock in its market capitalization ratio. This assumption affects the calculation of the company's WACC over time. As the market capitalization of a company increases, the amount of debt, preferred stock, and common stock should increase proportionately. The second assumption implies that the cash inflows the firm receives will be reinvested only in profitable business projects, or else the free cash flow will be paid out to the stockholders. The term "reinvested in profitable business projects" means that those projects will create additional free cash flow for the firm, and therefore will earn a rate of return that is higher than the company's WACC and will add to stockholder value.

What does this assumption mean for a corporation? If Microsoft has a WACC of 10 percent, Microsoft should not invest in projects that have an expected rate of return that is less than 10 percent. Otherwise, it should pay out its free cash flow to shareholders. It's easier to find investments and projects with higher rates of return in growth sectors, such as computers, pharmaceuticals, and information technology, rather than in more mundane economic sectors. That's why most high-growth, high-tech companies, such as Microsoft or Intel, invest their free cash flow in projects or acquisitions. It's much harder to find projects with high rates of return in mature, low-growth industries such as banking, manufacturing, and utilities.

Free Cash Flow—Share Repurchase Programs versus Dividends

If no profitable investment opportunities are available, a company should return its free cash flow to its stockholders. Free cash flow can be distributed to stockholders as dividends, which are taxable payments, or through the corporation's repurchase of shares in the open market. Presently, share repurchase is how many corporations prefer to pay out free cash flow. For instance, Microsoft used free cash flow to repurchase over $6 billion of stock in its fiscal year ending June 30, 2002. That's a huge chunk of change and is more money than most corporations have in the way of annual revenues.

Does the value of a stock depend on its dividend policy? No! Dr. Merton H. Miller and Dr. Franco Modigliani are two Nobel Laureates in economics who have written extensively about corporate capital structure and dividend policy. In their 1961 article, "Dividend Policy,

Growth and the Valuation of Shares," in the *Journal of Business*, they proved that the dividend policy of the firm should not affect the current value of a stock. However, dividend policy greatly affects the expected future value of a stock.

Here's an example that illustrates the relationship between dividend policy and stock price. Assume that XYZ Dividend Company has an invested capital base of $1 billion, is financed solely by equity, and has 100 million shares outstanding. It operates in a competitive industry in which the cost of equity capital is 10 percent, and the marginal after-tax return on new investment is also 10 percent. Assume that XYZ earns $100 million per year after taxes and net investment, and pays all of its earnings to shareholders in the form of dividends. Based on its cost of capital, XYZ's operations support market equity of: [$100 million/(.10)] = $1 billion, or $10 per share based on 100 million shares outstanding. XYZ for the foreseeable future expects to generate $100 million per year after taxes and pay all of its earnings out to shareholders as dividends. If its required yield remains at 10 percent, it will have a $1 billion—$10 per share—constant stock market value. Table 4-1 shows how XYZ's stock will perform over time.

The stockholders of XYZ Dividend Company receive $100 million per year in dividends, equal to $1 per share in stock outstanding—a 10 percent return on the company's market equity of $1 billion. The stock price remains stable at $10 per share because the shareholders are receiving their required 10 percent in the form of the $1 per share dividend. Our hypothetical performance of XYZ Dividend Company is similar to the actual performance of an electric utility in the stock market.

A company that is identical to XYZ Dividend Company—let's call

TABLE 4-1 XYZ Dividend Company-Stock Price

	100% Dividend Payment					
Year	Market Equity	Earnings	Required Return	Dividend	Net Invest	Stock Price
1	$1 billion	$100 million	10%	$100 million	0	$10
2	$1 billion	$100 million	10%	$100 million	0	$10
3	$1 billion	$100 million	10%	$100 million	0	$10

it UVW Growth Company—operates in the same industry and has the same initial $100 million per year earnings after taxes. UVW is financed 100 percent by equity, has 100 million shares outstanding, and faces the same marginal after-tax return on new investment of 10 percent. Instead of paying dividends to its shareholders, UVW invests all of its earnings back into its business and receives a return on its new investments of 10 percent per year. So the earnings of UVW increase from $100 million in year one, to $110 million in year two, to $121 million in year three. Based on a 10-percent cost of equity capital, the market equity that UVW Company can support increases from $1 billion (equal to $10/share) in year one, to [$110 million/(.10)] = $1.1 billion (equal to $11 per share) in year two, to [$121/(.10)] = $1.21 billion (equal to $12.10 per share) in year three. Shareholders of UVW receive their 10 percent rate of return through an increase in UVW's share price. See Table 4-2.

Shareholders of UVW Growth Company receive no current dividend payment, but they expect to receive an increase in stock price as UVW reinvests its earnings in investment projects that earn 10 percent per year.

Shares of both *XYZ and UVW are each worth $10 per share today—* the year-one price. Their current stock prices do not depend on their respective dividend policies. What does change is the future path of the price of stocks XYZ and UVW: a flat $10 per share for XYZ because it pays its 10-percent earnings to shareholders as dividends, and an expected 10-percent-per-year increase in price of the shares of UVW because its earnings are reinvested at an after-tax return of 10 percent per year.

TABLE 4-2 UVW Growth Company-Stock Price

| | | | 0% Dividend Payment | | | |
Year	Market Equity	Earnings	Required Return	Dividend	Net Invest	Stock Price
1	$1 billion	$100 million	10%	0	$100 million	10.00
2	$1.1 billion	$110 million	10%	0	$110 million	11.00
3	$1.21 billion	$121 million	10%	0	$121 million	12.10

This explanation of the Modigliani and Miller dividend invariance hypothesis shows that the current stock price is independent of the company's dividend policy.

Now, we have another tough question to discuss. If management believes that its shares are grossly overpriced, should a company repurchase its stock? Absolutely not! Buying a company's overpriced shares in the open market hurts the remaining shareholders and transfers wealth from the company to the selling shareholders. If a company does not have business opportunities in which to invest its free cash flows, and it does not want to initiate or increase dividends, it is a better alternative to invest excess funds temporarily in safe investments—even if the investment pays a rate of return that is less than the company's cost of capital. Companies such as Microsoft, Intel, and Cisco have been faced with this dilemma and have invested free cash flow in high-quality, short-term securities.

Who determines if a company's stock is overpriced? It's rare that you hear a CEO or CFO complain that his company's stock is overvalued. When you hear this comment, it should send a strong sell signal to you as an investor. On September 23, 1999 at a conference for business writers in Seattle, Microsoft's President Steve Ballmer stated, "There's such an overvaluation of tech stocks it's absurd. And I'd put our company's stock in that category." At the time, Microsoft was trading at $96 per share, and based on its 5.2 billion shares outstanding, had market equity of $500 billion. Mr. Ballmer's comments triggered a decline of 108.33 points in the NASDAQ Composite Index to 2749.83, down 3.79 percent for the day. The NASDAQ Index climbed to a high of about 5200 in March of 2000. Microsoft's stock ended 2002 at $51.70 per share. Mr. Ballmer was right on. If only we would have listened, we could have avoided so much pain.

It is unusual to hear a CEO reveal his belief that his company's stock is overvalued. Mr. Ballmer knew that Microsoft's operations, with revenue of $22 billion in 2000 and operating income of $11 billion, could not be expected to support market equity of over $500 billion—an amount 45 times Microsoft's operating earnings and 22.7 times its sales. We doubt that Jeff Skilling of Enron or Bernie Ebbers of World-Com would ever have given investors the same honest advice about their companys' stocks, regardless of the heights to which they had climbed.

Let's assume that corporate management does not believe that the stock of the company is overvalued. More likely, most management believes that its company's stock is too cheap. Under share repurchase programs, companies buy their own stock in the open market and reduce the number of shares outstanding. Share repurchases benefit the remaining stockholders by reducing the supply of the outstanding stock and increasing the stock's price.

Some investors prefer to buy stock of a company that pays out free cash flows through a share repurchase program. These investors expect to see a stock's price grow steadily over time, like our hypothetical UVW Growth Company, rather than to receive quarterly dividend payments. Investors in higher tax brackets find it painful to pay taxes on dividends that they receive. Also, if investors don't currently need the dividends for spending purposes, they are forced to decide where they want to reinvest those dividends and incur additional transaction costs in doing so. They can decide when to sell their shares, and then pay taxes at lower long-term capital gains tax rates. Share repurchase programs allow investors to minimize their tax payments while still allowing the corporation to maintain the philosophy of paying out excess free cash flow.

Other investors buy stock in a company—a utility like Consolidated Edison, for example, or our hypothetical XYZ Dividend Company—for the dividend stream that it pays, along with the possibility of dividend growth. The differing dividend/stock repurchase philosophies create what is termed a *clientele effect*. Retirees and other investors who are interested in predictable current returns usually purchase stock in companies that pay out their free cash flow through dividends. By contrast, investors who are interested more in capital gains and the growth of a stock's price gravitate to low- or no-dividend-paying companies that pay out their free cash flow through stock repurchase programs.

Free Cash Flow—the Corporation's Investment Decision

The investment rule underlying the free cash flow approach is simple: Invest in a project or business strategy if and only if the project generates additional free cash flow to the firm. This investment will result in an increase in shareholder value. A company should undertake projects that increase FCFF. If the project decreases the discounted free cash flow to the firm, the result is a decrease in shareholder value.

Rather than invest in a project that reduces shareholder value, the company should pay the money to investors through share repurchases or dividend payments.

The FCFF Approach—Where Does It Work?

The stocks that the FCFF valuation approach handles well represent 95 percent of all common stock traded on U.S. and international stock markets. However, in valuing highly levered companies (such as real estate investment trusts (REITs) and financial institutions), companies with no current free cash flow (such as EntreMed), and portfolio companies (such as Berkshire Hathaway or Internet Capital Group), the FCFF approach needs some minor adjustments.

Typically, the balance sheets of commercial banks and investment banks have a book value, not market value, of approximately 90 percent debt and 10 percent equity. We discuss market versus book values in Chapter 6. Also, financial institutions require very little investment in property, plant, and equipment. The bulk of their investments are in financial obligations that have characteristics that more closely resemble working capital investments. The balance sheets of financial companies are more important to their valuations than the balance sheets of industrial companies. Of particular interest is the excess of marketable current assets over current liabilities. We visit this topic in greater depth when we value Citigroup and Merrill Lynch in Chapter 8.

Adjustments must be made for companies that currently have little or no free cash flow or companies that are suffering net operating losses. These adjustments involve changing NOPMs over time and estimating the probability of and potential revenues from high-risk products, whose cash flows depend upon regulatory approval or future scientific breakthroughs. The value of the shares of some companies, which have no current cash flows and whose future is highly dependent on speculative products, may be better handled using an option pricing approach, which is beyond the scope of this book.

Most of this fine-tuning can be handled using the FCFF approach, and we discuss how we do it in the chapters that follow.

Why DCF and Not EPS?

Wall Street often focuses on a corporation's quarterly earnings-per-share number. Investment services, such as First Call and Zacks, and research analysts from stock brokerage firms estimate quarterly earnings. And pity (or better yet, short) the stock of a company that does not achieve or exceed those estimates.

There is no doubt that, all other things being equal, we prefer that a company in which we own stock has more earnings than less. However, all other things are not equal. Often, EPS comes up short in measuring returns. Why? With EPS calculations, no consideration is given to dividends or to the time value of money. (Remember Principle 7.) EPS ignores the risk associated with a stock. (Recall Principle 1.) No consideration is given as to when (*timing*) an investor expects to receive the cash flows. In fact, no discounting process at all is associated with EPS measure. (Remember Principle 10.). EPS implicitly and explicitly ignores the risks and timing of returns that are dealt with in a discounted cash flow analysis. EPS also fails to incorporate expectations of future corporate performance.

Analysts prefer to work with discounted cash flows rather than earnings-related ratios for two additional reasons. First, earnings may be calculated in a number of ways, ranging from using various types of inventory control accounting, to the use of different methods for depreciation, to numerous ways to recognize revenue. Management may manipulate these methods to increase reported earnings. Second, EPS does not address the investments in fixed assets and working capital that are necessary to support the growth of the firm. If EPS growth requires too much additional investment, then earnings *growth* actually may result in a decrease in free cash flow and a decrease in the company's stock value.

Prior to the enactment of the Sarbanes-Oxley Act of 2002, many corporations managed their EPS and earnings growth through accounting gimmicks to achieve or exceed the expectations of Wall Street. Gimmicks du jour go in and out of favor as aggressive, but legal, methods to boost an income statement. Telecom companies swapped fiber optic cable capacity and immediately booked income. This was aggressive, but probably not illegal. Andrew Fastow, mimicing the Wizard of Oz, operated behind dark curtains and used smoke and mirrors to push certain Enron activities to off-balance-sheet entities to hide losses and debts. Some of Enron's transactions may have been legal, but many were scams. And WorldCom brought a new level of audacity to corporate accounting by booking over $9 billion in ordinary expenses as capital expenditures. We hope that the SEC, the

Justice Department, and the various state Attorneys General truly clamp down on scam accounting and sham transactions and prosecute perpetrators to the fullest extent permitted by law. Without reliable accounting numbers, stock valuation is a worthless exercise.

The Discounted FCFF Valuation Approach

The Four-Step Process

The discounted FCFF valuation approach uses a four-step process to value the stock of a company. In this section we value the common stock of Microsoft, at a point in time prior to its announcement on January 16, 2003 of a two-for-one stock split to take effect on January 28th. If you follow along with us closely, you'll quickly learn the basics about valuing a stock.

Step 1: Forecast Expected Cash Flow. The first order of business is to forecast the expected cash flows for the company. We use the most likely assumptions regarding the company's growth rate, net operating profit margin, income tax rate, fixed investment requirement, and incremental working capital requirement. It's easier than it sounds. In Chapter 5 we describe these cash flow inputs and how to estimate them reasonably. The expected cash flows are separated into two time periods. First, the excess return period in which the corporation generates cash flows from operation; and second, the residual value period—the time period after the excess return period, in which the corporation is not able to create additional free cash flow.

Step 2: Estimate the WACC. Next, we estimate the company's WACC. Its weighted average cost of capital is the discounting rate that we use in the valuation process. We show how to estimate a company's WACC in Chapter 6.

Step 3: Calculate the Enterprise Value of the Corporation. We then use the company's WACC to discount the expected cash flows during the excess return period to get the aggregate of the corporation's cash flow from operations. We calculate the company's residual value, which usually represents 60 percent to 90 percent of the corporation's total value, by dividing the company's net operating profit after taxes (*NOPAT*) at the end of the excess return period, by its WACC. We then discount that future value back to today, also at a discount rate equal to the company's WACC. We add the cash flow from operations, the residual value, and the short-term assets to get today's value of the corporation as a whole—the corporate or enterprise value. We describe this procedure in greater depth later in this section.

Corporate Value = Cash Flow Operations + Residual Value
+ Short-term Assets

The ValuePro 2002 Software shows this calculation at the top of the General Pro Forma Page. Again, this simple spreadsheet program does the work automatically.

Step 4: Calculate Intrinsic Stock Value.   We subtract the value of the company's short-term liabilities and senior liabilities—debt and preferred stock—from the enterprise value to get value to common equity, as shown in the following.

Value to Common Equity = Corporate Value
− (Debt + Preferred) − Short-term Liabilities

We then divide value to common equity by the number of shares outstanding to get the per share intrinsic value of common stock.

Where do we get all this information for a valuation? The inputs necessary to accomplish Step 1—forecast expected cash flow—are the focus of Chapter 5. The inputs and information needed to accomplish Step 2—estimate the WACC—are the subjects of Chapter 6. But before we jump ahead, let's now spend a little time discussing the theory of competitive advantage that underlies the calculation of cash flow from operations described in Step 3 above.

Excess Return Period and Competitive Advantage

Because of a competitive advantage enjoyed by the firm, the company is able to earn returns on new investments that are greater than its cost of capital during the *excess return period*. Examples of companies that experienced a significant period of big-time competitive advantage are IBM in the 1950s and 1960s, Apple Computer in the 1980s, and Microsoft, Intel, and Cisco in the 1990s.

Success invariably attracts competitors with their own lower-cost versions of the product or service, and whose aggressive practices cut into market share and revenue growth rates. The pricing and marketing activities of competitors also drive down net operating profit margins. A lower NOPM reduces return on new investment to levels that approach the corporation's WACC. When a company loses its competitive advantage and the return from its new investments just equals its WACC, the corporation is investing in business strategies in which the aggregate net present value is 0. Worse yet, companies can generate negative returns and destroy shareholder value—witness IBM in the 1980s, Apple in the 1990s, and the telecom companies in the 2000s.

Increasing size attracts additional competition. As industries develop and market sectors grow, companies serving those sectors can have relatively small revenue—$10 to $100 million—and not make the radar screens of competitors or attract their interest. However, when a company hits the $100 million revenue threshold, potential competitors start to notice and begin to enter the sector space, cutting into growth and profit margins. So small-cap firms that initially may have very little competition in a specialty market sector can make some hay and generate abnormal profits from operations.

The length of time over which a company can earn abnormal profits depends on the particular products being produced, the industry in which the company operates, and the barriers for competitors to enter the business. Markets that have a high barrier to entry, such as products with patent protection, strong brand names, or unique marketing channels, might have an excess return period that is quite long—10 to 15 years or longer. More typically, the excess return period for most companies will be 5 to 7 years or shorter. All else equal, a shorter excess return period results in a lower stock value.

What happens after the excess return period? Does the company dry up, shrivel, or go bankrupt? *No!* For valuation purposes, the company loses its competitive advantage over its competitors. The loss of competitive advantage means that the company's stock value may still grow, but only at the market's required rate of return for the stock—not at an abnormally high growth rate level. For example, if the common stock price of RST Company (which does not pay dividends) is $10, and its required rate of return is 12 percent, its stockholders expect it to grow to ($10 * 1.12) = $11.20 after year one; ($11.20 * 1.12) = $12.54 after year two; ($12.54 * 1.12) = $14.03 after year three; ad infinitum. Once the excess return period ceases and the company has no more profitable new investments, the company should pay all of its free cash flow to shareholders through dividends or share repurchases.

When return on investment equals a company's WACC, investors are just compensated for the risk that they are taking in owning the company's stock and no additional value is created from new business investments. The stock price is still growing in value, but its growth does not exceed its risk-adjusted market expectation (or match investors' hopes). At that point in time, the after-tax earnings of the company can be treated and valued as what is known as a cash flow perpetuity—equal to the company's net operating profit after tax divided by its WACC ($NOPAT/WACC$). This number is discounted to the present also at the company's WACC.

This discounted value is called the company's *residual value*—a very important number, and generally represents 60 percent to 90 percent of the total value of the company. The residual value is very sensitive to projections of the company's NOPAT and its WACC, as described in the section that follows.

Excess Return Period: Our Recommendation

What is our preferred excess return period? This is a judgment call. We use the 1-5-7-10 Rule—and suggest that you do likewise.

We group companies into one of four general categories and excess return periods. We then value them using a 10-year excess return period to calculate what we consider to be their maximum value, and a more conservative 1-year, 5-year, or 7-year return period to calculate a reasonable or minimum value. Here are the criteria we use to determine the lower, more conservative excess return period:

1. *Boring companies* that operate in a highly competitive, low-margin industry in which they have nothing particular going for them—a 1-year excess return period;

2. *Decent companies* that have a recognizable name and decent reputation and perhaps a regulatory benefit (e.g., a utility like Consolidated Edison), but don't control pricing or growth in their industry—a 5-year excess return period;

3. *Good companies* with good brand names, large economies of scale, good marketing channels, and consumer identification (e.g., McDonald's)—a 7-year excess return period; and

4. *Great companies* with great growth potential, tremendous marketing power, brand names, and in-place benefits (e.g., Intel, Microsoft, Coca Cola and Disney)—a 10-year excess return period.

We do not believe in going out more than 10 years with an excess return period. Some fundamental stock valuation models, like the dividend discount model, incorporate earnings and dividend growth in excess of the company's WACC, out to an infinite time period. Cash flows in these models are discounted until the hereafter. We think that 10 years is a reasonable amount of time to incorporate the product cycles of today's markets.

Does a corporation really lose its competitive advantage and the benefit of its excess return period? For well-managed corporations, the answer is probably no. Most well-run companies will continue to innovate, reduce operating costs, increase efficiency, create new business strategies, and maintain their competitive advantage for a long time. Some will go bankrupt. Some will be acquired or merge. But the concept of an excess return period or forecast period is one that should result in a more conservative, less aggressive stock valuation. When we invest, we would rather err on the side of conservatism than overpay for a stock.

The Three Valuation Categories

In calculating corporate or enterprise value, the FCFF approach and the spreadsheet software divides corporate assets and liabilities and discounts cash flows into three categories and time periods:

Cash Flow from Operations. First, during the excess return period, we calculate free cash flow to the firm. This is the difference between operating cash inflows and cash outflows. The free cash flows are then discounted. The discount factors are a function of the firm's WACC and the timing of the expected cash flows.

Corporate Residual Value. Second, we find the corporation's residual value. This is the value calculated by taking the company's NOPAT at the end of the excess return period, dividing it by the company's WACC, and discounting it (also at the WACC) to today's value. At the end of the excess return period, we assume that the corporation is just receiving a return on investment equal to its WACC. Therefore, the net present value (*NPV*) of additional investment by the corporation is zero, and no additional value is created for stockholders.[1]

Short-term Assets. Third, we add the firm's short-term assets to the mix. We include only real current assets that could be sold or liquidated at close to face value, such as investment securities, inventories, accounts receivable, and other current corporate financial investments. We do not include intangible assets, such as goodwill, which would be difficult to sell or value, or long-term assets such as property plant and equipment, which are essential to generating the company's cash flow from operations. Here, the current balance sheet of the firm comes into play. For example, according to its balance sheet on June 30, 2002, Microsoft had $38.6 billion in cash and excess marketable securities on its books. These assets have no business operating risk and should not be discounted in the valuation procedure.

Corporate value is the sum of the discounted cash flow from operations, plus discounted corporate residual value, plus short-term assets.

Corporate Value = Cash Flow Operations
                      + Residual Value + Short-Term Assets

Once total corporate value is calculated, we subtract the amount of short-term liabilities and the market value of debt and preferred stock, and then divide that amount by the shares of stock outstanding to get the per share intrinsic stock value.

Intrinsic Value = (Corporate Value − Debt − Preferred
                      − Short-term Liabilities)/Shares Outstanding

Mathematically, this is as difficult as the DCF approach gets. No calculus, no differential equations—just addition, subtraction, multiplication, and division. And through the magic of a microprocessor, the computations occur instantaneously.

Microsoft—A Simple DCF Example

So how complex is it to value stocks like a pro? Not very! To illustrate the valuation process, we now take you through a simplified valuation of Microsoft. The four steps are: forecast expected cash flow; estimate the required rate of return (the WACC); discount the expected cash flow by the WACC; and calculate per share intrinsic value.

Step 1: Forecast Microsoft's Expected Cash Flow

Expected cash flow to shareholders includes cash dividends, if any, and the expected increase (or decrease) of the stock's price during the investor's holding period of the stock. As we show in Chapter 3, it's easy for the bank to estimate the expected cash flow from Mary's mortgage because she agrees to pay the bank exactly $734 per month. Accurate estimations of cash flow for common stock are more challenging. Here we describe ways to help you overcome the complications associated with cash flow estimation.

The DCF valuation analysis that we use estimates expected free cash flow to the firm. Free cash flows are cash amounts that are available to be paid to stockholders. Earnings per share is an accounting measure and an accountant's way of measuring corporate performance. Discounted free cash flows are an investor's way of measuring potential returns to shareholders. DCF is more wallet oriented, hence more meaningful to you—unless you happen to be an accountant.

The discounted free cash flow approach uses corporate performance measures that focus solely on real cash dollars flowing into and out of the company. Corporate activities that produce additional net cash inflows to the company, such as increased revenue growth or increased net operating profit margins, have a positive effect on stock value. These are good activities.

Corporate activities that produce net cash outflows from the company, such as higher income tax rates, higher capital investment or working capital requirements, or lower net operating profit margins due to increasing labor costs or other costs of production, have a negative effect on stock value. These payments may be necessary from the corporation's perspective but they are not particularly good activities for the stock's value.

Microsoft has been a darling of Wall Street for many years. Since its initial public offering in March of 1986, Microsoft produced an average annual return of almost 50 percent per year to investors until 2000. (See Exhibit 4-2.) With the bursting of the high-tech bubble, Microsoft's return dropped into negative figures.

We discuss how to estimate corporate cash flows in Chapter 5, where we focus on five cash flow measures. We refer to these cash flow

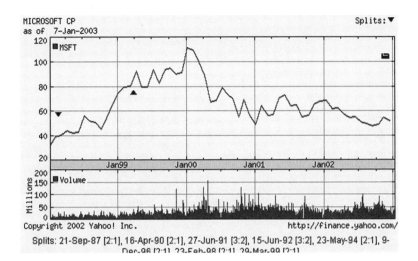

EXHIBIT 4-2 Microsoft Five-year Stock Price Chart

measures as *The Five Chinese Brothers* (taken from the Chinese folk tale of the same name). The cash flow measures and the initial estimates for Microsoft are: the revenue growth rate—11 percent, the net operating profit margin—42 percent, the net fixed capital investment rate (equal to the investment rate minus the depreciation rate—see below), the incremental working capital investment rate—9.8 percent, and the company's income tax rate—32 percent. Briefly, these may be described as:

The Five Chinese Brothers:

Revenue Growth Rate	Annual Growth in Revenue
Net Operating Profit Margin	Operating Income/Revenue
Tax Rate	Taxes/Pretax Income
Working Capital Investment	Change in Working Capital/Revenue
Fixed Capital Investment	Net Capital Investment/Revenue

To compute net capital investment, we have provided the depreciation rate—3.8 percent, depreciation divided by revenue, and the investment rate—2.7 percent, capital expenditures divided by revenue.

We examined the historic ratios for Microsoft and used them in calculating the sample inputs listed above. We used analyst consensus estimates for Microsoft's projected growth rates. We show our sample

ValuePro 2002
General Input Screen
Intrinsic Stock Value $38.86
General Inputs

Company Ticker.....	MSFT		
Excess Return Period (years)	10	Depreciation Rate (% of Rev.)	3.80
Revenues ($mil)	28365	Investment Rate (% of Rev.)	2.70
Growth Rate (%)	11.00	Working Capital (% of Rev.)	9.82
Net Operating Profit Margin (%)	42.00	Short-Term Assets ($mil)	47827
Tax Rate (%)	32.00	Short-Term Liabilities($mil)	11640
Stock Price($)	45.15	Equity Risk Premium (%)	3.00
Shares Outstanding (mil)	5415	Company Beta	1.00
10-year Treasury Yield (%)	7.00	Value of Debt Out. ($mil)	0
Bond Spread to Treasury (%)	0.00	Value of Pref. Stock Out. ($mil)	0
Preferred Stock Yield (%)	0.00	Company WACC (%)	10.00

EXHIBIT 4-3   Microsoft General Input Screen

inputs in Exhibit 4-3, the general input screen of the ValuePro 2002 software program. Our valuation spreadsheets will become more meaningful to the reader as we progress through the book.

Net operating profit (NOP) for Microsoft during the excess return period is projected to grow more than 2.5 times, from $13,224 million in 2003 to $33,827 million in the year 2012. To convert from net operating profit to free cash flow to the firm, we must: (1) add depreciation (a noncash expense), and (2) subtract income taxes, incremental working capital and fixed capital investment. (Also see Exhibit 4-4.) Free cash flow (FCFF) projections for Microsoft (in millions of dollars) are:

Year	2003		2004		2005		2006	...		2012
FCFF	$9,032	+	$10,026	+	$11,128	+	$12,363	+ ...	+	$23,104

Step 2: Estimate Microsoft's Discount Rate—The WACC

What is the appropriate rate to use to discount Microsoft's uncertain (but expected) cash flow? There are several discounted cash flow methods used in the capital market. The method used in this book calculates *the after-tax weighted average cost of capital* (WACC) of the company and uses that WACC to discount the company's after-tax free cash flow. Again, we show you how to estimate a company's WACC long-

ValuePro 2002
General Pro Forma Screen
10-year Excess Return Period
MSFT

Disc. Excess Return Period FCFF	$85,552
Discounted Residual Value	$88,684
Short-Term Assets	$47,827.0
Total Corporate Value	$222,062

Total Corporate Value	$222,062
Less Debt	$0
Less Preferred Stock	$0
Less Short-Term Liabilities	($11,640)
Total Value to Common Equity	$210,422
Intrinsic Stock Value	$38.86

(2)	(3)	(4)	(5)	(6)	(7)	(8)	(9)	(10)	(11)	(12)	(13)
12 Months Ending	Revenues	NOP	Adj. Taxes	NOPAT	Invest.	Deprec.	Change in Invest.	Change in Working Capital	FCFF	Discount Factor	Discounted FCFF
01/10/2003	28,365										
01/10/2004	31,485	13,224	4,232	8,992	850	1,196	-346	306	9,032	0.9091	8,211
01/10/2005	34,949	14,678	4,697	9,981	944	1,328	-384	340	10,026	0.8264	8,286
01/10/2006	38,793	16,293	5,214	11,079	1,047	1,474	-427	378	11,128	0.7513	8,361
01/10/2007	43,060	18,085	5,787	12,298	1,163	1,636	-474	419	12,353	0.6830	8,437
01/10/2008	47,797	20,075	6,424	13,651	1,291	1,816	-526	465	13,711	0.6209	8,514
01/10/2009	53,054	22,283	7,130	15,152	1,432	2,016	-584	516	15,220	0.5645	8,591
01/10/2010	58,890	24,734	7,915	16,819	1,590	2,238	-648	573	16,894	0.5132	8,669
01/10/2011	65,368	27,455	8,785	18,669	1,765	2,484	-719	636	18,752	0.4665	8,748
01/10/2012	72,559	30,475	9,752	20,723	1,959	2,757	-798	706	20,815	0.4241	8,828
01/10/2013	80,540	33,827	10,825	23,002	2,175	3,061	-886	784	23,104	0.3855	8,908
	80,540	33,827	10,825	23,002	3,061	3,061	0	0	230,023	0.3855	88,684

EXHIBIT 4-4   Microsoft General Pro Forma Screen

hand, and if you use the ValuePro 2002 software, it automatically does all the work based on the inputs that you feed it.

How do you calculate a WACC? Finance theory (as discussed in Principle 10 describing the Capital Asset Pricing Model) tells us that a company's WACC discounting rate is a function of three general categories of risk/return adjustments required by the market:

- As a *base rate of return* for any investment, the market's current long-term risk-free rate of interest (which incorporates expectations of inflation). We use the current 10-year (the maturity coincides with the maximum length of our excess return period) U.S. Treasury bond yield.

- For the expected return associated with the company's debt and preferred stock, a spread above the risk-free rate that reflects the company's *risk of default.*

- For the expected return associated with the company's common stock, the market's assessment of the current equity risk premium and the *systematic risk (beta)* associated with the company's stock.

To arrive at the company's WACC, the cost of capital inputs described above must be adjusted for two factors: the tax deductibility of interest payments; and the percentage of debt, preferred stock, and common stock employed by the company in financing its operations.

While this calculation may seem complex, it is actually quite simple with a calculator or software such as ValuePro 2002.

The discount rate that is used in the valuation process, and the movement of interest rates in general, can have an enormous effect on the market value of the stock.[2] The discount rate that is used to value a stock reflects the three risk factors described previously. Investments with similar risks should have similar discount rates.

Factors that reduced the discount rate, such as a decrease in interest rates due to expectations of lower inflation, or a decrease in the equity risk premium due to the fall of communism and an increase in free trade among nations, greatly increased stock market valuations in the 1990s. An important reason for the percentage increases in general stock market valuations, in excess of the growth rate of corporate earnings during the 1990s, was the significant reduction of interest rates and their related lowering of corporate WACCs. A lower WACC increases a stock's value.

Conversely, factors that increase the discount rate, such as higher inflation, bogus corporate accounting, and restrictive government policies, will have a significant negative effect on stock market prices. Likewise, factors that increase the equity risk premium, such as terrorist attacks, production and distribution bottlenecks, and currency and trade crises, also will increase WACCs and negatively affect stock prices. A higher WACC reduces a stock's value. (We discuss all the WACCy stuff in detail in Chapter 6.)

The WACC is easier to compute for Microsoft than for most firms since the company is financed completely by common stock. Microsoft has no debt or preferred stock outstanding. In this simple example, the WACC for Microsoft was entirely a function of its cost of common stock. The capitalization and the WACC for Microsoft looked like this:

Capital Source	Capital Amount	Discounting Rate
Debt	0	0
Preferred Stock	0	0
Common Stock	$244,487 million	10%
WACC		10%

At one point in time in 1999, Microsoft had a market capitalization of over $600 billion. Microsoft's stock price has been reduced by more than one-half. Market capitalization is defined as the market value of debt, preferred stock, and common stock outstanding. Since Microsoft had no debt or preferred stock outstanding, its market capitalization was equal to the number of common shares outstanding times the stock price per share. Microsoft's market cap (on August 12, 2002) was as follows:

Common Shares Outstanding * Stock Price = Market Capitalization

5415 million   * $45.15   = $244.5 billion

The cost of common stock for Microsoft is a function of the level of interest rates (the 10-year U.S. Treasury), the risk of Microsoft relative to the overall stock market (its beta), and the equity risk premium. While we will not go into particulars for Microsoft in this example, we used a WACC of 10 percent.

Step 3: Calculate Microsoft's Total Corporate Value

Step 3 discounts the expected cash flow by the required rate of return. In the DCF approach, the required rate of return is the firm's WACC. Recall the mortgage example from Chapter 3. The concept is the same.

Step 3 involves two stages: (1) calculating the discounted value of the expected cash flows over the 10-year excess return period, and (2) calculating the value of Microsoft beyond this 10-year period—its residual value. Exhibit 4-5 gives the discounted expected cash flows for 2003–2012 for Microsoft. The sum of the discounted cash flows over the 10-year excess return period is $85,552 million.

Exhibit 4-4 shows the total corporate value calculation. We start with the sum of the discounted free cash flows ($85,552 million) and add the present value of the expected cash flows beyond the end of the excess return period (year 2012). Residual value equals net operating profit after tax (NOPAT) divided by the WACC. The residual value for Microsoft is [$23,002 million/(.10)] = $230,023 million. Since this is the value at a point in time 10 years from today, we discount it at the 10-year discount factor of 0.3855 to get its present value of $88,684 million.

To calculate the enterprise value of the corporation, we sum the discounted free cash flow over the 10-year excess return period ($85,552 million), the discounted residual value ($88,684 million), and

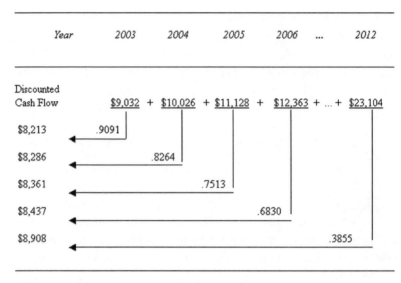

EXHIBIT 4-5   Microsoft Discounted Free Cash Flow

the short-term assets ($47,827 million) associated with the firm's balance sheet, and come up with a value of $222,062 million for Microsoft.

Step 4: Calculate Microsoft's Intrinsic Stock Value

The final step involves computing the total value to common equity by subtracting the market value of the firm's liabilities and dividing that amount by shares outstanding. Microsoft has no debt or preferred stock outstanding, and its total short-term liabilities are $11,640 million. Exhibit 4-4 shows the total value to common equity calculation. The estimated market value of Microsoft's common stock is $210,422 million. Dividing this figure by the number of shares outstanding (5415 billion shares) on August 12, 2002 gives an estimated stock value per share of $38.86.

Notice that the $38.86 intrinsic value was about 16 percent less than the closing price on August 12th of $45.15. We would have sold Microsoft if we owned it, or at least refrained from purchasing it until the price declined to a lower level. And we hadn't adjusted the intrinsic stock value for the dilution associated with stock options—an adjustment that would have resulted in a further decrease in the value of Microsoft. We discuss the subject of stock options in Chapter 6.

Valuation—Growth versus Value, Large Cap versus Small Cap

Often we read about mutual funds and investment managers specializing in *value* stocks or *growth* stocks or *large cap* stocks or *small cap* stocks. How should the classification of a stock into one of these categories affect its value?

Growth stocks are stocks that are expected to have high revenue or earnings growth rates, usually 15 percent and above, over the foreseeable future. Growth stocks are characterized by high price to earnings (P/E) ratios and low book value to market value of equity (BE/ME) ratios. Growth stocks usually are the hot stocks in the current fad or go-go sectors of the stock market. Most recently, the growth sectors were high-tech industries like telecommunications, computers, pharmaceuticals, and information technology.

Value stocks are stocks that are expected to have low revenue or earnings growth rates, and are stocks of companies in mature businesses such as utilities, banks and brokerage, manufacturing, and the automobile industries. Low P/E and high BE/ME ratios characterize these stocks. Value stocks are associated with companies in sectors of the stock market that are out of favor with investors, or in boring industries that don't have a compelling story that attracts the attention of TV business reporters.

Large cap stocks are stocks that have market capitalization of equity in excess of $5 billion. Mid cap stocks have market equity of $1 to $5 billion and small cap stocks have market capitalizations that generally are less than $1 billion.

Depending upon the cycle of the moon and recent successes or failures in fund management, different investing approaches either come into or go out of favor. Investors concentrating in large caps performed well during the 1997–1999 stock market climb—with gains in the S&P 500 of 31 percent, 26.7 percent, and 19.5 percent, before reversing course to −10.1 percent in 2000, −13 percent in 2001, and −23.4 percent in 2002. According to Siegel, small cap stock returns exploded during the period between 1975 and 1983, when the compound annual return of small cap stocks averaged 35.3 percent.[3] Recently, small caps have not done nearly as well. Different investment styles, such as value versus growth, hot sector mutual funds, and large cap versus small cap approaches come into and go out of vogue on Wall Street on a regular basis.

Recall the discussion from Chapter 2 regarding efficient markets and the study performed by Fama and French. Although F&F never used *growth* or *value* to classify stocks, they found that stocks with high BE/ME ratios, what most investors would term value stocks, consistently and significantly outperformed stocks with low BE/ME ratios—growth stocks.

It is our belief that, whether a stock is large cap or small, growth or value, the valuation procedure is exactly the same. Investors should care only about expected future cash flows and the risks associated with those expected cash flows. The market price of any growth or value stock, large or small cap, can be greatly under or over its intrinsic value. Relative to value stocks, growth stocks will have higher, and often unrealistic, expected growth rates. Relative to large cap, small cap stocks may have higher betas and WACCs. But the valuation procedure for each category should be identical.

Our valuation approach gives you the information that you need to determine which stocks are overvalued and which stocks are cheap, which stocks should rise, and which are poised to plummet. And we welcome you to try it.

Valuation—The Next Step

Now that we've numbed you with discussions of free cash flows, DCF versus EPS, and all those pesky acronyms—NOP, FCFF, NOPAT, and WACC, it's time to wake up. We're about to apply the theory and show you how to do something really useful in the way of cash flow analysis! In the next chapter, we show you how to calculate FCFF, and we explain which variables are most important to the calculation. And we continue to help you lay the groundwork for your financial independence and your ability to make your own decisions regarding investing in stocks.

Notes

1. In calculating the Residual Value of the corporation, it is assumed that there is no net new investment, i.e., investment =

depreciation, and there is no additional working capital required. As an example, at the end of an Excess Return Period of 10 years, if the company's NOPAT = $1million and its WACC = 10 percent, the company's future residual value = $1million/(.10) = $10 million, which amount would be discounted to the present at the discount factor equal to 1.0 divided by (1.0 plus the company's WACC), that sum taken to the tenth power = $1.0/(1.0 + .1)^{10} = (.3855)$. Residual Value = $10 million * .3855 = $3,855,000.

2. Malkiel explains how the stock market drop of 508 points (22.6 percent) on October 19, 1987 could have been caused solely by an increase in both interest rates and the equity risk premium (pp. 203–206).

3. Siegel, page 95.

CHAPTER 5

Forecasting Expected Cash Flow

The Five Chinese Brothers

Remember the folk tale "The Five Chinese Brothers?" Although identical in appearance, each brother had a unique trait or ability. One couldn't be burned. One could hold his breath indefinitely. One had a neck made of iron. You get the idea. By using all five of their individual talents, the five Chinese brothers managed to escape from every form of torture that the jealous villagers could dream up. And so the five Chinese brothers lived happily ever after.

Similarly, in our DCF approach, five cash flow measures will lead to happy endings in your stock portfolio. The five cash flow measures on which we focus are: growth rate, net operating profit margin, company income tax rate, net investment, and incremental working capital investment. These cash flow measures are the most important inputs in determining the free cash flow to the firm. Free cash flow to the firm represents the difference between a corporation's cash inflow and cash outflow.

Free Cash Flow to the Firm = Cash Inflow − Cash Outflow

Naturally, many operating decisions of a company affect these cash flow measures in one way or another. Decisions relating to salaries, hiring, executive bonuses, and new suppliers affect net operating profit margins. Decisions regarding research and development expenditures, new products, and advertising campaigns affect growth rates, periods of competitive advantage, net operating profit margins, and net investment. And management choices relating to these variables occur each and every day within a large company.

This chapter shows how these five cash flow measures affect the value of the corporation, and this is where the rubber really begins to meet the road. The cash flow estimation process is sometimes as tedious as toenail clipping, but it's the most important part of valuation. In the process of estimating cash flow, you learn a great deal about the company that you are valuing. Here, we study Cisco (CSCO: *www.cisco.com/*) and discuss the inputs that we use to estimate Cisco's expected cash flow.

Growth Rates and the Excess Return Period

When we talk about growth in the context of valuation, we're most concerned about the corporation's growth of earnings or profits. Growth in earnings is the result of either:

- Growth in revenues generating more cash flowing into the firm;
- Reduction in expenses and an increase in NOPMs resulting in less money flowing out of the firm; or
- A combination of increasing revenue and decreasing expenses.

All else equal, corporate managers and Wall Street analysts prefer growth in revenues to be the cause of an increase in earnings.

We keep the valuation process as simple as possible, at least for a first cut at valuing a stock. If we assume that the valuation inputs are held constant over time (meaning that the net operating profit margin, net investment rates, and income tax rate don't change over the excess return period), then the growth in cash flow to the firm is the same whether we apply the assumed growth rate directly to revenues, or if we change both revenue growth and NOPMs to come up with the proper growth rate in earnings. It's far simpler to use a constant revenue growth rate to replicate growth in earnings, rather than changing a combination of inputs. In the more detailed custom valuations that we perform in Chapter 8, we get fancy and change inputs over time so that growth may be captured by a combination of increasing revenues and decreasing NOPMs. For now, let's keep things simple and assume that when we discuss growth, we're applying the growth rate to the revenue of the firm.

The current revenue of the corporation and the expected growth (positive or negative) of revenue during the excess return period are extremely important inputs for valuing a company. These variables act as the first step in forecasting the expected cash inflow to the corporation. The term *revenue growth rate* is self-explanatory. How it is estimated is a bit trickier.

Where do you get growth rates? Do you have to be a swami or a fortuneteller to come up with a good prediction? That could be helpful, but thankfully, it is not necessary. Some Web sites such as Yahoo Finance, First Call, and Zacks have five-year expected profit or revenue growth projections. Many Wall Street brokerage firms also forecast these numbers. Finally, the corporation's recent history and trend of growth can act as a good initial indicator of potential growth.

Growth Rates: Value versus Growth Stocks and Reversion to the Mean

Just as science tells us that the universe can't expand forever, mathematics tells us that a corporation cannot forever grow at a rate appreciably higher than the growth rate of the economy in which it operates. It is impossible for a company to grow its operations every year at an unreasonably high rate of growth. Some companies, like Cisco and Tyco, maintained high growth rates during the 1990s by buying growth—acquiring smaller companies at high prices and merging them into the parent company. While this did buy hyper-growth, it came at a significant cost—the newly issued shares by the company to finance the purchase of the target, and the subsequent dilution of the company's shares outstanding.

Characterized by high price-to-earnings and low book-value-to-market-value ratios, growth stocks don't remain growth stocks forever. Eventually, new technologies replace the old, patent protection expires, and competitors enter the fray and cut into market share and reduce profit margins to a reasonable percentage. The promise that once seemed so bright for the company and its industry gives way to business as usual. In short, growth stocks soon become normal stocks and may even become value stocks. Therefore, it's a mistake to use a growth rate that is too high for too long a period of time when you're valuing a stock. It may be a very costly mistake. Eventually, the growth rates for all companies begin to approach the growth rate for the economy in which they operate.

Analysts' Growth Rates

Wall Street analysts are generally an optimistic group, and their estimates of growth rates bear this out. A 1999 study[1] undertaken by the Board of Governors of the Federal Reserve examined analyst expectations of the 1-year growth rate of earnings per share of the S&P 500 during the 18-year period from 1979 to 1996. The study found that the analysts' consensus expectations exceeded the actual growth rate in 16 of the 18 years of the period surveyed, and by an average amount of 9 percent. This is a significant difference in expectations over reality, and shows a definite upward bias of analysts' growth estimates.

If analysts' one-year estimates are that far off base, what about their longer-term estimates; and why are we concerned about analyst estimates? Good questions. Expectations of future economic performance are embedded in stock prices. If we don't properly account for those expectations, we won't be able to estimate which stocks are currently undervalued and overvalued. In fact, Alfred Rappaport and Michael J. Maubossin, in their book, *Expectations Investing,*[2] use observed stock prices to determine the market's consensus expectations of growth in earnings.

Growth Rates: Our Recommendation

When valuing a stock, we look at scenarios that are based on at least two different growth rates. Our first valuation uses a growth rate based on consensus analyst estimates, which we realize are optimistic and often result in a high intrinsic value. Our second valuation uses a more conservative growth rate that is usually based on the expected growth rate for the economy in which the company operates (3 percent to 5 percent for U.S. stocks), resulting usually in a lower valuation. All other things equal, these two values act as a bracket for intrinsic value. A third growth rate that we often check is the expected growth rate for the industry or sector in which the company operates.

If the observed stock price is higher than our highest valuation, we avoid or sell the stock. If the stock price is between our highest and lowest valuations and we believe that there's a reasonable chance that the earnings of the company will equal or exceed analyst estimates, we consider a purchase of the stock. If the stock price is lower than our lowest valuation, we consider this stock to be a good buying opportunity, and it warrants additional analysis.

Cisco's Revenue Growth Rate

Cisco Systems, Inc. is the company that we value over the next two chapters. Cisco provides a broad line of products for transporting data, voice, and video either around the world on the Internet or within private intranet networks. Cisco manufactures routers, servers, switching technology, network security, and optical networking and management software. Cisco markets its products through its direct sales force, as well as through other distribution systems. Its competitors include: Alcatel, Lucent, Nortel Networks, Siemens AG, Ciena, and Ericsson. Cisco generated $18,915 in revenues (net sales) in 2002, of which 83 percent was from the sale of products and 17 percent was from the sale of services.

In the 1990s the stock price of Cisco, one of the bellwether high-tech stocks of the Internet era, rocketed into the stratosphere. In 2000 at its highest point, the market equity of Cisco was the greatest of any company in the world and approached $600 billion. Since that high mark, its market equity has fallen 83 percent, and is now at $97.8 billion. At this level, Cisco's stock is selling at a price/earnings ratio of 53, and a price/sales ratio of over 5, still rich by historical standards. On August 6, 2002, Cisco announced that it has increased its share repurchase program by $5 billion, authorizing a total repurchase of $8 billion in stock. A graph of Cisco's stock price is shown in Exhibit 5-1.

We downloaded Cisco's 2002 Annual Report from its corporate Web site and have reproduced its 2002 Income Statement as Exhibit 5-2.

To get a perspective on Cisco's growth and performance over the years, we have used other information sources to include five years of

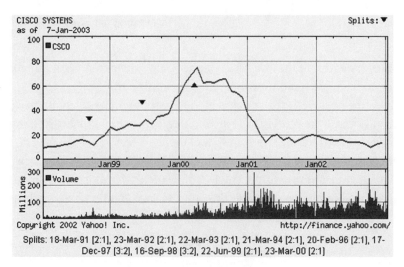

Splits: 18-Mar-91 [2:1], 23-Mar-92 [2:1], 22-Mar-93 [2:1], 21-Mar-94 [2:1], 20-Feb-96 [2:1], 17-Dec-97 [3:2], 16-Sep-98 [3:2], 22-Jun-99 [2:1], 23-Mar-00 [2:1]

EXHIBIT 5-1   Cisco's Five-Year Stock Price Chart

Consolidated Statements of Operations
(In millions, except per-share amounts)

Years Ended	July 27, 2002	July 28, 2001	July 29, 2000
NET SALES:			
Product	$15,669	$19,559	$17,002
Service	3,246	2,734	1,926
Total net sales	18,915	22,293	18,928
COST OF SALES:			
Product	5,914	10,198	5,970
Service	988	1,023	776
Total cost of sales	6,902	11,221	6,746
GROSS MARGIN	12,013	11,072	12,182
OPERATING EXPENSES:			
Research and development	3,448	3,922	2,704
Sales and marketing	4,264	5,296	3,946
General and administrative	618	778	633
Restructuring costs and other special charges	–	1,170	–
Amortization of goodwill	–	690	154
Amortization of purchased intangible assets	699	365	137
In-process research and development	65	855	1,373
Total operating expenses	9,094	13,076	8,947
OPERATING INCOME (LOSS)	2,919	(2,004)	3,235
Interest and other income (loss), net	(209)	1,130	1,108
INCOME (LOSS) BEFORE PROVISION FOR INCOME TAXES	2,710	(874)	4,343
Provision for income taxes	817	140	1,675
NET INCOME (LOSS)	$ 1,893	$ (1,014)	$ 2,668
Net income (loss) per share—basic	$ 0.26	$ (0.14)	$ 0.39
Net income (loss) per share—diluted	$ 0.25	$ (0.14)	$ 0.36
Shares used in per-share calculation—basic	7,301	7,196	6,917
Shares used in per-share calculation—diluted	7,447	7,196	7,438

EXHIBIT 5-2   Cisco Systems 2002 Income Statement

revenue data (an annual report typically has only three years of revenue data) in Table 5-1 below. Consider Cisco's revenue growth, from $6452 million in 1997 to $18,915 million in 2002—almost a three-fold increase over the five-year period.

It's simple to calculate the yearly growth rate in revenue—divide one year's revenue by the previous year's revenue and subtract 1.0. For example, Cisco's one-year growth rate in 2001 is calculated by dividing 2001 revenue of $22,293 million by its 2000 revenue of $18,928 million and subtracting 1.0. In math terms, we get:

($22,293/$18,928) − 1.0 = 1.178 − 1.0 = .178 = a 17.8% growth rate.

Even if growth rates turn negative as it did for Cisco in 2002, the same equation holds. Cisco's one-year growth rate in 2002 is:

($18,915/$22,293) − 1.0 = .8485 − 1.0 = (15.15)%

The five-year average revenue growth rate for Cisco was 26.62 percent, while its compound annual growth rate ($CAGR$)[3] was 24.0 percent. Remember Principle 5 in Chapter 2. It is far more accurate and conservative to rely on compound annual growth rates rather than simple average growth rates, which overestimate the actual performance of a stock.

TABLE 5-1 Cisco Systems

Five-year Revenue History (in millions of dollars)			
Year	**Revenue**	**$ Increase**	**% Increase**
2002	$18,915	−3,378	−15.15%
2001	22,293	3,365	17.78%
2000	18,928	6,755	55.49%
1999	12,173	3,685	43.41%
1998	8,488	2,036	31.56%
1997	6,452	—	—
5-year average growth rate			26.62%
5-year compound average growth rate			24.00%

How did Cisco's profits perform during this period? Cisco's net operating profit margin decreased from 24.9 percent in 2000, to 4.8 percent in 2001, and then increased to 19.5 percent in 2002. Its net operating profit decreased from $4719 million in 2000 to $1076 million in 2001, before rebounding in 2002 to $3683 million. We talk about net operating profit margins and net operating profits in the following section.

Shrinking growth rates along with decreasing NOPMs and lower profits are not good signs for what had been a growth stock. It appears that competitors are successfully attacking the Internet hardware domain where Cisco was once the dominant provider and that demand for Cisco's products has waned. Also, as a firm increases in size it becomes more and more difficult to keep growing at an extraordinarily high growth rate. The growth rate eventually has to converge to or go below the economy's growth rate. So even Cisco is obeying the laws of the universe.

It's also easier for a CEO to talk about revenue and earnings growth than it is to develop the products and strategies to actually accomplish that growth. As an investor you need to look past the public relations spiel, be realistic in growth estimates, and be aware of how reasonable growth prospects affect stock value.

What about Cisco's growth rates? As we have discussed earlier in this section, most investors talk about and look at a company's growth in earnings or profits, as opposed to its revenue. Growth in earnings will come from one of two sources: growth in revenue—known as *top-line growth* (because revenue is the initial entry on an income statement); or growth in operating income as a result of higher net operating profit margin—known as *bottom-line growth* (because operating income is the result of a lot of addition and subtraction on an income statement). Bottom-line growth may be caused by higher revenue, or more likely in today's downsizing environment, by a reduction in costs.

Exactly where the growth in earnings comes from—revenue growth versus increasing NOPMs—although important to some people, does not significantly change the valuation outcome in the DCF analysis. When discussing growth rates, we apply the growth to revenue because revenue is subject to less manipulation than earnings.

When valuing a stock, we use the most recent publicly available information about the company. This means that we examine the company's most current quarterly report and earnings release. Many companies post these reports on their corporate Web sites. The SEC site is also a great central repository of quarterly and annual corporate information. The most recent quarterly report gives a good indication of the revenue and earnings prospects of the company. Analysts cover these quarterly report filings and earnings releases. A negative surprise almost always results in a steep drop in a stock's price. A positive surprise often results in a jump in the stock's price.

Why are there such significant reactions to relatively small surprises in earnings? Recall that a stock's value is based in large part upon expected future cash flows. If growth rates drop or NOPMs decline, when analysts and investors plug these lower numbers into a discounted cash flow pricing model, the resulting change in intrinsic value can be significant.

To keep this example simple, we focus now on Cisco's Annual Report and save using quarterly data and earnings surprises until the valuations in Chapter 8. What are Wall Street analysts saying about Cisco's expected future growth rates? On August 14, 2002, we checked out analyst estimates for Cisco by going to the Yahoo Finance Web site (*http://finance.yahoo.com/*). Yahoo Finance uses research data provided by Thomson Financial Network/First Call, which polled the 40 analysts that follow Cisco and found that 13 analysts rate Cisco a strong buy, 17 rate Cisco a buy, and 10 rank Cisco as a hold. The consensus estimate for a long-term (five-year) growth in earnings is 20 percent per year. We also checked Zack's (*www.zacks.com/*) Web site for detailed analyst estimates on Cisco and found a consensus 5-year growth estimate of 20.05 percent. To us, a 20-percent growth estimate smacks of optimism, but we use it to develop the high-side estimate of Cisco's intrinsic stock value.

Let's assume that we like Cisco's Internet strategy and believe that greater revenue growth will follow as it peddles its routers, servers and software around the globe. For simplicity, and to be consistent with analyst estimates, we use a constant revenue growth rate of 20 percent, an aggressive assumption in light of Cisco's past three years of revenue growth—from 55 percent to 17 percent to −15 percent—not a positive trend. We also introduce some more conservative assumptions by playing a *what-if* 5-percent growth scenario, consistent with the high end of the growth of the U.S. economy.

Excess Return Period: Our Recommendation

Even if the company is a great company worthy of a 10-year excess return period, we often also check how the company's intrinsic stock value should react if the demand for the company's product contracts and its excess return period is reduced. When we're valuing a company using the ValuePro 2002 software, we can easily see how reducing a company's excess return period from 10 to 7 to 5 years affects intrinsic value. In certain situations, reducing the excess return period results in an increase in stock value. This occurs when a company currently is earning less than its WACC on its new investment. Playing what-if games with the company's excess return period allows you to see how its cash flows truly affect stock value.

Cisco's Excess Return Period

Recall the 1-5-7-10 Rule from Chapter 4. We think Cisco is a great company—worthy of a 10-year excess return period. Why?

The length of the excess return period should correspond to the time period over which the investor expects the corporation's business strategy to be successful. This means that the strategy will generate free cash flow—it will earn a rate of return on new investment in excess of the company's WACC. Business strategies based on patent protection, superior marketing channels, or valuable brand names should have a relatively longer-term excess return period.

Cisco has terrific products, great brand name recognition, and efficient marketing channels. However, competitors seem to be making inroads into the markets that Cisco has dominated for years. Intense competition in the Internet hardware markets has resulted in shrinking profit margins and lower sales growth. Still, we think Cisco is well positioned in its industry, and we use a 10-year excess return period as we go through the rest of the cash flow analysis.

Valuation Inputs Relating to Revenue Growth and Excess Return Period

As of August 14, 2002, our inputs relating to revenue, revenue growth rate, and excess return period on our general input screen (see Exhibit 5-5, later in this chapter) are:

TABLE 5-2   Cisco Systems

	Projected Revenue Schedule (in millions of dollars)		
Year	Revenue	$ Increase	% Increase
2002	$18,915		
2003	$22,698	$3,783	20.00%
2004	$27,238	$4,540	20.00%
2005	$32,685	$5,448	20.00%
2006	$39,222	$6,537	20.00%
2007	$47,067	$7,844	20.00%
2008	$56,480	$9,413	20.00%
2009	$67,776	$11,296	20.00%
2010	$81,331	$13,555	20.00%
2011	$97,597	$16,266	20.00%
2012	$117,117	$19,519	20.00%

Revenues ($mil)	$ 18,915
Revenue Growth Rate (%)	20.0 percent
Excess Return Period (years)	10

Given the above inputs, we come up with the following (long-hand) 10-year excess return period projected revenue schedule for Cisco, as shown in Table 5-2. We also show Cisco's general pro forma screen, as generated by the ValuePro 2002 software, at the end of this chapter. (See Exhibit 5-6.)

The FCFF approach allows for individual yearly inputs of different revenue growth rates over the excess return period. For example, valuation analyses can be based on growth rates increasing or decreasing over time, and they can accommodate numerous multistage growth assumptions. We examine multistage growth approaches in Chapter 8.

Net Operating Profit Margin and NOP

In this section, the acronyms begin to flow heavily. They're only letters, and they're all described in our List of Acronyms. The *net operating profit margin (NOPM)* is equal to the corporation's *net operating profit (NOP)* divided by *operating revenue*—revenue from continuing operations. To arrive at this ratio, we take operating revenue and subtract the *costs of goods sold (CGS), selling, general and administrative expenses (SGA),* and *research and development costs (R&D)* and divide the resulting number by operating revenue:

$$\text{NOPM} = \frac{\text{Operating Revenue} - (\text{CGS} + \text{SGA} + \text{R\&D})}{\text{Operating Revenue}} = \frac{\text{Net Operating Profit}}{\text{Operating Revenue}}$$

SGA, CGS, and R&D data also comes from the corporation's income statement. The net operating profit margin of a company is a crucial determinant of its intrinsic stock value.

If the NOPM is negative, or it is insufficient to cover the net investment required to support the company's growth, there is a significant likelihood that the intrinsic value of the company will be zero—not a good number if you are a shareholder. Obviously, the company can't continue to operate forever in a manner that destroys shareholder wealth. Be aware that the DCF method of valuation yields may yield a zero intrinsic value if the firm doesn't generate positive cash flows. We describe how to change growth rates and profit margins over time, so that the DCF method can properly value turnaround situations.

Also, different companies may use different names and labels for revenue and expense figures in their annual reports. For instance, on the cash inflow side Cisco reports "net sales," McDonald's uses "total revenues," Microsoft has "revenue," and Intel uses "net revenue." More confusing differences in labeling occur on the expense side. Cisco reports that restructuring and special charges are part of operating expenses. We disagree and have not included them in our calculations of NOP and NOPM. Be careful when you examine annual reports and be sure to group entries consistently!

There is no authoritative financial accounting entity that dictates the format of financial statements that a company must use. Companies in different industries prepare their financial statements in various ways. For example, high-tech and industrial companies report NOPMs in the manner that we described above. Interest income, dividend income, and interest expense are not included in the calculation of net operating profits or of NOPMs. For financial companies, interest income, dividend income and interest expense are included in the calculation of net operating profit and NOPMs. *Practitioners Publishing Guide*, in its four-volume set—*Guide to Preparing Financial Statements*, gives samples of the different financial statement presentations that are used for 50 industries.[4] When you review financial statements, do not expect all companies to have identical formats or templates.

NOPMs: Our Recommendation

Due to competitive pressures, changing technology, or the general economy, the NOPM of a company can fluctuate greatly from year to year. If the company has shown a pattern of increasing or decreasing NOPMs, we generally use the most recent NOPM for our initial valuation. If the company has erratic NOPMs, such as Cisco has shown in Table 5-3 that follows, we use the average of the company's NOPM over the last three years.

If a company has had negative or very low NOPMs that create an intrinsic value of zero, we would look more closely at the stock. We may play a what-if game and assume that the board of directors of the company, at some point, will do the right thing and replace manage-

TABLE 5-3   Cisco Systems

Year	Revenue	CGS	SG&A	R&D	NOP	NOPM
			Three-Year NOPM History (in millions of dollars)			
2002	18,915	6,902	4,882	3,448	3,683	19.47%
2001	22,293	11,221	6,074	3,922	1,076	4.83%
2000	18,928	6,746	4,579	2,704	4,719	24.93%
Three-Year Average						16.41%

ment. Or that management will institute changes that will shift the performance of the company to an NOPM that is representative of the average NOPM of the industry in which the company operates. We can find the average NOPM by looking at the NOPMs of a subset of other companies in the industry. If those corporate changes occur and we think that NOPMs will increase, we can plug our higher expected NOPM into the valuation process and assess what the company's stock value could be in the future. Then we can decide whether a purchase of the stock may be a good speculative investment, based on a reasonable risk-versus-reward ratio.

Cisco's NOPM

Let's look again at Cisco's 2002 income statement (Exhibit 5-2) to calculate its NOP and its NOPM over the last three years. (See Table 5-3.)

As an example, let's calculate Cisco's NOPM for 2002:

$$\text{NOPM} = \frac{\$18,915 - (\$6,902 + \$4,882 + \$3,448)}{\$18,915} =$$

$$\frac{\$3,683}{\$18,915} = .1947 = 19.47\%$$

Cisco's NOPM has been erratic, fluctuating from 24.93 percent in 2000 to 4.83 percent in 2001 to 19.47 percent in 2002. Now that we know how Cisco has performed in the past, we must estimate its expected performance. For now, we assume that Cisco continues to operate at the 3-year average of 16.41 percent for its NOPM for the foreseeable future.

Valuation Input Relating to NOPM

The input relating to NOPM for the ValuePro 2002 software on the general input screen is:

Net Operating Profit Margin (%)   16.41%

Based on analysts' expected long-term growth rate of 20 percent per year, and an estimated NOPM of 16.41 percent per year, we get the projected NOPM and NOP shown in Table 5-4. NOP is also shown in the general pro forma screen. (See Exhibit 5-6 later in this chapter.)

The FCFF approach allows for different yearly inputs of net operating profit margins over the excess return period and can accommodate

TABLE 5-4   Cisco Systems

	Projected NOPM and NOP (in millions of dollars)		
Year	Revenue	%NOPM	NOP
2002	$18,915		
2003	$22,698	16.41%	$3,725
2004	$27,238	16.41%	$4,470
2005	$32,685	16.41%	$5,364
2006	$39,222	16.41%	$6,436
2007	$47,067	16.41%	$7,724
2008	$56,480	16.41%	$9,268
2009	$67,776	16.41%	$11,122
2010	$81,331	16.41%	$13,346
2011	$97,597	16.41%	$16,016
2012	$117,117	16.41%	$19,219

numerous assumptions in the valuation process. This allows NOP (operating income) to vary as the product of revenues (with varying growth rate capabilities) times NOPMs (with varying percentage capabilities).

The FCFF approach allows an infinite number of NOPM/revenue growth rate input combinations to create more multistage growth valuation options than we ever want to think about.

Income Tax Rate and Adjusted Taxes

We all are painfully aware that the geopolitical units where we reside have great resourcefulness in expropriating a large portion of our income in the form of taxation. Likewise, corporations have to pay the various jurisdictions where they do business—federal, state, local, and international governments—their respective pounds of flesh. In our calculation of corporate free cash flow, we make appropriate adjustments for taxes to see what is left over for the good guys—the stockholders.

The free cash flow to the firm approach takes net operating profit, estimates an adjusted tax payment based on the corporation's income tax rate, and subtracts adjusted taxes to calculate NOPAT. We call them adjusted tax payments because the actual tax payments to the various governmental taxing entities are arrived at through complex calculations following arcane tax laws, with the associated $600 per hour New York tax lawyer's fee tacked on. These calculations include deferred components and complicated tax code treatments that a regular person can't even begin to understand.

Sometimes, due to taking advantage of tax laws, a company's tax rate is significantly below the maximum marginal corporate tax rate—which in the United States is 35 percent. At other times, due to previous deferrals, the company's tax rate may be significantly above the maximum marginal tax rate. If the company remains profitable, in the long run the tax rate should approach or average close to the maximum marginal tax rate.

The tax deductions for interest expense associated with debt and the tax shield that debt provides are not included in the cash flow section of the FCFF approach. They are introduced into the FCFF valuation process by adjusting the weighted average cost of capital. These adjustments, which are described in Chapter 6, reduce the cost of the debt component of the WACC to convert it to an after-tax WACC.

The FCFF approach to calculate NOPAT is to multiply NOP by $(1 -$ Tax Rate).

$$\text{NOPAT} = \text{NOP} - \text{TAXES} = \text{NOP} * (1 - \text{Tax Rate})$$

Tax Rates: Our Recommendation

If you believe that the company will become or continue to be profitable, will deplete their accelerated deductions, and will eventually pay taxes at the maximum marginal corporate tax rate, you may want to look at a what-if scenario that uses the maximum corporate tax rate, currently 35 percent, in the valuation calculation. That's a simple exercise if you are using DCF software such as ValuePro 2002.

Cisco's Tax Rate

We find Cisco's tax rate from its income statement by dividing its income before provision for income taxes by its provision for income taxes. The 2002 income statement for Cisco (see Exhibit 5-2) shows income before provision of income taxes of $2710, ($874), and $4343 million for 2002, 2001, and 2000 respectively, and a provision for income taxes of $817, $140, and $1675 million. Since Cisco had a loss in 2001, the rate calculation for that year is not meaningful. The tax rate for 2000 was ($1675/$4343) = 38.57 percent, and for 2002 it was ($817/ $2710) = 30.15 percent. The average tax rate for these two years is 34.36 percent.

Valution Input Relating to Tax Rate

The input relating to the tax rate for the ValuePro 2002 software on the general input screen is:

Tax Rate (percent)   34.36 percent

The FCFF approach allows for individual yearly inputs of tax rates over the excess return period and can accommodate numerous tax rate assumptions in the valuation process. We use this number for our 10-year calculation of NOPAT, shown in Table 5-5.

Net Investment

Net investment is the dollar amount needed to fuel the growth of the firm, and includes new investment in property, plant, and equipment, minus the depreciation expense associated with previous investments. The information for this calculation comes from the company's cash flow statement. In math terms, net investment is:

Net Investment = New Investment − Depreciation Expense

Net investment depends to a great extent on management decisions that are specific to and frequently guarded by a company. Often, management does not want competitors to be aware of projects that the company is undertaking, and information about planned investment may be difficult to obtain. Investment in property, plant, and equipment is necessary to maintain both service and sales, and to grow revenues and profits. Sometimes an industry may go on an investment binge, and companies mistakenly overbuild their facilities and infrastructure. Examples of overbuilding in the l990s and early 2000s are

TABLE 5-5   Cisco Systems

	Projected Taxes and NOPAT (in millions of dollars)			
Year	NOP	Tax Rate	Taxes	NOPAT
2002				
2003	$3,725	34.36%	$1,280	$2,445
2004	$4,470	34.36%	$1,536	$2,934
2005	$5,364	34.36%	$1,843	$3,521
2006	$6,436	34.36%	$2,212	$4,225
2007	$7,724	34.36%	$2,654	$5,070
2008	$9,268	34.36%	$3,185	$6,084
2009	$11,122	34.36%	$3,822	$7,300
2010	$13,346	34.36%	$4,586	$8,761
2011	$16,016	34.36%	$5,503	$10,513
2012	$19,219	34.36%	$6,604	$12,615

the telecom companies and fiber optic cable providers. During that period, the new investment-to-revenue-ratios for those companies were so high that there was no possibility for a telecom company to generate positive free cash flow.

Net Investment: Our Recommendation

We've found that the easiest way to estimate net investment as a valuation input is to do the following:

1. During the excess return period, which assumes revenue growth, project that new investment and depreciation expense continue at the historic average percentages of revenue.

2. After the excess return period, which assumes that the return from new investment equals the company's WACC, set new investment equal to depreciation so that the company adequately maintains property, plant, and equipment.

The estimation procedure described here assures that to maintain its revenue growth, a company's new investment will keep pace on a percentage basis with total revenue. When revenue growth stops, new investment just keeps pace with depreciation expense, and net investment equals zero. That is:

$$0 = \text{New Investment} - \text{Depreciation Expense}$$

Some analysts believe that it's more accurate to project net investment and new investment in terms of a percentage of incremental revenue growth. We find that adjustment confusing and we prefer to use the percentage of revenue approach. Also, when new investment ratios get exceedingly high and out of control, such as in the telecom industry's binge investment years, for valuation purposes we assume that new investment will return to more sustainable prior levels.

Cisco's Net Investment

Let's now look at Cisco's investment ratios and depreciation ratios to get comfortable with this calculation. In addition to growth of its current operations, Cisco has a history of buying growth through the purchase of companies. The 2002 statement of cash flow (see Exhibit 5-3) shows that Cisco acquisition of property and equipment was $2641 million in 2002, $2271 million in 2001, and $1086 million in 2000.

As shown in Table 5-6, over the last three years Cisco has invested approximately 10 percent of revenue in the purchase of property, plant, and equipment and has expensed most of it—8.31 percent—in the way of depreciation. If we assume that over the next 10 years it continues to cost Cisco similar investment and depreciation amounts to increase sales, then the schedule of net investment for Cisco is shown in Table 5-7.

Valuation Inputs Relating to Net Investment

The inputs relating to new investment and depreciation expense, used to calculate net investment on the general input screen for the Value-Pro 2002, software are:

New investment rate (percent of revenue)	9.96 percent
Depreciation rate (percent of revenue)	8.31 percent

Consolidated Statements of Cash Flows
(In millions)

Years Ended	July 27, 2002	July 28, 2001	July 29, 2000
Cash flows from operating activities:			
Net income (loss)	$ 1,893	$ (1,014)	$ 2,668
Adjustments to reconcile net income (loss) to net cash provided by operating activities:			
Depreciation and amortization	1,957	2,236	863
Provision for doubtful accounts	91	268	40
Provision for inventory	149	2,775	339
Deferred income taxes	(573)	(924)	(782)
Tax benefits from employee stock option plans	61	1,397	2,495
Adjustment to conform fiscal year ends of pooled acquisitions	–	–	(18)
In-process research and development	53	739	1,279
Net (gains) losses on investments and provision for losses	1,127	43	(92)
Restructuring costs and other special charges	–	501	–
Change in operating assets and liabilities:			
Accounts receivable	270	569	(1,043)
Inventories	673	(1,644)	(887)
Prepaid expenses and other current assets	(28)	(25)	(249)
Accounts payable	(174)	(105)	286
Income taxes payable	389	(434)	(365)
Accrued compensation	307	(256)	576
Deferred revenue	678	1,629	662
Other accrued liabilities	(222)	251	369
Restructuring liabilities	(64)	386	–
Net cash provided by operating activities	6,587	6,392	6,141
Cash flows from investing activities:			
Purchases of short-term investments	(5,473)	(4,594)	(2,473)
Proceeds from sales and maturities of short-term investments	5,868	4,370	2,481
Purchases of investments	(15,760)	(18,306)	(14,778)
Proceeds from sales and maturities of investments	15,317	15,579	13,240
Purchases of restricted investments	(291)	(941)	(458)
Proceeds from sales and maturities of restricted investments	1,471	1,082	206
Acquisition of property and equipment	(2,641)	(2,271)	(1,086)
Purchases of technology licenses	–	(4)	(444)
Acquisition of businesses, net of cash and cash equivalents	16	(13)	24
Change in lease receivables, net	380	457	(535)
Purchases of investments in privately held companies	(58)	(1,161)	(130)
Lease deposits	320	(320)	–
Purchase of minority interest of Cisco Systems, K.K. (Japan)	(115)	(365)	–
Other	159	(516)	(424)
Net cash used in investing activities	(807)	(7,003)	(4,377)
Cash flows from financing activities:			
Issuance of common stock	655	1,262	1,564
Repurchase of common stock	(1,854)	–	–
Other	30	(12)	(7)
Net cash (used in) provided by financing activities	(1,169)	1,250	1,557
Net increase in cash and cash equivalents	4,611	639	3,321
Cash and cash equivalents, beginning of fiscal year	4,873	4,234	913
Cash and cash equivalents, end of fiscal year	$ 9,484	$ 4,873	$ 4,234

EXHIBIT 5-3 Cisco Systems 2002 Statement of Cash Flow

The FCFF approach allows for individual yearly inputs of new investment and depreciation expense ratios over the excess return period, and it can accommodate numerous capital investment and depreciation assumptions in the valuation process.

TABLE 5-6   Cisco Systems

	Investment and Depreciation History (in millions of dollars)					
Year	Revenue	Investment	% Investment	Depreciation	% Depreciation	Net Investment
2002	$18,915	$2,641	13.96%	$1,957	10.35%	$684
2001	$22,293	$2,271	10.19%	$2,236	10.03%	$35
2000	$18,928	$1,086	5.74%	$863	4.56%	$223
3-year average			9.96%		8.31%	

Incremental Working Capital

Working capital is needed to support the sales effort of a company. In the calculation of incremental working capital, we want to find short-term assets and liabilities, the levels of which depend directly on the

TABLE 5-7   Cisco Systems

	Projected Net Investment Schedule (in millions of dollars)			
Year	Revenue	Investment	Depreciation	Net Investment
2002	$18,915			
2003	$22,698	$2,261	$1,887	$375
2004	$27,238	$2,714	$2,264	$450
2005	$32,685	$3,256	$2,717	$539
2006	$39,222	$3,907	$3,260	$647
2007	$47,067	$4,689	$3,912	$777
2008	$56,480	$5,627	$4,695	$932
2009	$67,776	$6,752	$5,633	$1,119
2010	$81,331	$8,102	$6,760	$1,342
2011	$97,597	$9,723	$8,112	$1,611
2012	$117,117	$11,668	$9,735	$1,933

amount of revenue. The current assets and current liability categories that most directly relate to sales are: *accounts receivable*—monies owed to the company from customers; *inventories*—monies used by the company to finance its products prior to their sale; and *accounts payable*—monies owed by the company to other entities. We define working capital as accounts receivable plus inventory minus accounts payable:

Working Capital = [(Accounts Receivable + Inventory)
$$- \text{Accounts Payable}]$$

Often a company's change in net working capital, either positive or negative, is approximately proportional to its change in revenue. Some firms, like Intel whose incremental working capital averaged 14.8 percent of revenue, have a very large amount of cash tied up in working capital. Other firms, such as some electric utilities that have an easy-pay plan in which customers deposit monies in the summer based upon a level monthly-pay plan for their peak electricity use in the winter, have a cash inflow due to a surplus of working capital.

Incremental Working Capital: Our Recommendation
The components to calculate incremental working capital are listed on the balance sheet of the company. Most often, the company's intrinsic stock value is least sensitive to this cash flow input. Many analysts use the trend in balance sheet data, such as a significant increase in inventories or accounts receivable, as an early warning sign that may indicate problems at a company. Such balance sheet sleuthing is beyond the scope of this book.

We use a simple averaging process to calculate the ratio that we use for incremental working capital, and we suggest that you do likewise. This ratio, either positive or negative, is multiplied by the increase or decrease in revenue—not the absolute level of revenue. For example, if the company's working capital ratio is 10 percent, and its estimated increase in revenue is $100 million, its incremental working capital requirement is $100 million * (10 percent) = $10 million. Likewise, if the company's growth rate is zero, its incremental working capital requirement is zero.

Consolidated Balance Sheets
(In millions, except par value)

	July 27, 2002	July 28, 2001
ASSETS		
Current assets:		
Cash and cash equivalents	$ 9,484	$ 4,873
Short-term investments	3,172	2,034
Accounts receivable, net of allowance for doubtful accounts of $335 at July 27, 2002 and $288 at July 28, 2001	1,105	1,466
Inventories, net	880	1,684
Deferred tax assets	2,030	1,809
Lease receivables, net	239	405
Prepaid expenses and other current assets	523	564
Total current assets	17,433	12,835
Investments	8,800	10,346
Restricted investments	–	1,264
Property and equipment, net	4,102	2,591
Goodwill	3,565	3,189
Purchased intangible assets, net	797	1,470
Lease receivables, net	39	253
Other assets	3,059	3,290
TOTAL ASSETS	**$37,795**	**$35,238**
LIABILITIES AND SHAREHOLDERS' EQUITY		
Current liabilities:		
Accounts payable	$ 470	$ 644
Income taxes payable	579	241
Accrued compensation	1,365	1,058
Deferred revenue	3,143	2,470
Other accrued liabilities	2,496	2,553
Restructuring liabilities	322	386
Total current liabilities	8,375	7,352
Deferred revenue	749	744
Total liabilities	9,124	8,096
Commitments and contingencies (Note 8)		
Minority interest	15	22
Shareholders' equity:		
Preferred stock, no par value: 5 shares authorized; none issued and outstanding	–	–
Common stock and additional paid-in capital, $0.001 par value: 20,000 shares authorized; 7,303 and 7,324 shares issued and outstanding at July 27, 2002 and July 28, 2001, respectively	20,950	20,051
Retained earnings	7,733	7,344
Accumulated other comprehensive loss	(27)	(275)
Total shareholders' equity	28,656	27,120
TOTAL LIABILITIES AND SHAREHOLDERS' EQUITY	**$37,795**	**$35,238**

EXHIBIT 5-4   Cisco Systems 2002 Balance Sheet

Cisco's Incremental Working Capital

Let's take a look at Cisco's working capital (taken from Cisco's balance sheet, see Exhibit 5-4) over the past two years to see the effect that an increase in revenue will produce.

Table 5-8 shows that Cisco has a significant amount of cash tied up in net working capital—an average of 9.63 percent of revenue.

TABLE 5-8   Cisco Systems

	Two-Year Working Capital History (in millions of dollars)					
Year	Revenue	Acct. Rec.	Inventory	Acct. Pay.	Working Cap	%Work. Cap.
2002	$18,915	$1,105	$880	$470	$1,515	8.01%
2001	$22,293	$1,466	$1,684	$644	$2,506	11.24%
2-year average						9.63%

For our estimate of incremental working capital, we make projections that show working capital expanding at a rate of 9.63 percent times the yearly increase in revenue, as shown in Table 5-9.

Valuation Input Relating to Incremental Working Capital

The input relating to incremental working capital for the ValuePro 2002 software on the general input screen is:

Working Capital (% of change in revenue)   9.63%

TABLE 5-9   Cisco Systems

	Projected Working Capital (in millions of dollars)		
Year	Revenue	Increase Rev.	Inc. Work. Cap
2002	$18,915		
2003	$22,698	$3,783	$364
2004	$27,238	$4,540	$437
2005	$32,685	$5,448	$525
2006	$39,222	$6,537	$630
2007	$47,067	$7,844	$755
2008	$56,480	$9,413	$907
2009	$67,776	$11,296	$1,088
2010	$81,331	$13,555	$1,305
2011	$97,597	$16,266	$1,566
2012	$117,117	$19,519	$1,880

The FCFF approach allows for individual yearly inputs of incremental working capital ratios over the excess return period, and it can accommodate numerous working capital investment assumptions in the valuation process.

Free Cash Flow to the Firm

Estimating Free Cash Flow During Excess Return Period

That was painful, but we're home free! We now have all of the estimates that we need for the calculation of free cash flow to the firm. We take the net operating profit after tax and subtract net investment and incremental working capital to get free cash flow to the firm. Remember our FCFF equation from Chapter 4:

FCFF = NOP − Taxes − Net Investment
$$− \text{Net Change in Working Capital}$$

Earlier in this chapter we saw that *NOPAT = NOP − Taxes*. And it doesn't take a mathematician to see that:

FCFF = NOPAT − Net Investment − Net Change in Working Capital

Table 5-10 uses this equation and now makes those calculations of Cisco's FCFF.

Estimating Residual Value

The residual value of a company measures the free cash flow generated by the company after the excess return period. In this example, residual value is a measure of Cisco's future profits and cash flows from year 11 to infinity. The residual value also is a large component—usually 60 percent to 90 percent—of the value of a company.

Recall our discussion regarding the time frame after the excess return period—we assume that the rate of return on investment equals the company's WACC, that new investment equals depreciation, and that the company's incremental working capital requirement is zero. The valuation of the longer-term cash flows is a simple capitalization of the firm's net operating profit after tax (NOPAT). To calculate residual value, we divide NOPAT at the end of the excess return period by the company's WACC (NOPAT/WACC), and then bring the resulting number back to the present at the relevant present value factor.

TABLE 5-10 Cisco System

	Projected Free Cash Flow to the Firm (in millions of dollars)				
Year	Revenue	NOPAT	Net Invest.	Inc Work. Cap.	FCFF
2002	$18,915				
2003	$22,698	$2,445	$375	$364	$1,706
2004	$27,238	$2,934	$450	$437	$2,047
2005	$32,685	$3,521	$539	$525	$2,457
2006	$39,222	$4,225	$647	$630	$2,948
2007	$47,067	$5,070	$777	$755	$3,538
2008	$56,480	$6,084	$932	$907	$4,245
2009	$67,776	$7,300	$1,119	$1,088	$5,094
2010	$81,331	$8,761	$1,342	$1,305	$6,113
2011	$97,597	$10,513	$1,611	$1,566	$7,335
2012	$117,117	$12,615	$1,933	$1,880	$8,803

Let's use our Cisco valuation as an example. As shown in Table 5-10 above, NOPAT for Cisco in year 10 (2012) is $12,615 million. If we assume that Cisco has a WACC of 10.04 percent and a discount factor in year 10 of (.3841), Cisco's residual value is: [(NOPAT)/(WACC)] * discount factor = [($12,615 million)/(.1004)] * (.3841) = $48,268 million. We show you where these WACC and discount factors come from in Chapter 6. Cisco's $48.3 billion residual value represents approximately 60 percent of Cisco's total value to common equity, as shown on the top of Exhibit 5-6.

Valuation Exercise: Estimating Free Cash Flow for Cisco

Suffering through the pain and agony of creating all of these schedules longhand is reminiscent of the third grade at Saint Michael's Elementary School in Levittown, PA in 1958. Sister Mary Ignatius would be impressed by the ease with which a spreadsheet solves the divine

ValuePro 2002
General Input Screen
Intrinsic Stock Value $10.87
General Inputs

Company Ticker.....	CSCO		
Excess Return Period (years)	10	Depreciation Rate (% of Rev.)	8.31
Revenues ($mil)	18915	Investment Rate (% of Rev.)	9.96
Growth Rate (%)	20.00	Working Capital (% of Rev.)	9.63
Net Operating Profit Margin (%)	16.41	Short-Term Assets ($mil)	17433
Tax Rate (%)	34.36	Short-Term Liabilities($mil)	8375
Stock Price($)	14.45	Equity Risk Premium (%)	3.00
Shares Outstanding (mil)	7447	Company Beta	1.93
10-year Treasury Yield (%)	4.25	Value of Debt Out. ($mil)	0
Bond Spread to Treasury (%)	0.00	Value of Pref. Stock Out. ($mil)	0
Preferred Stock Yield (%)	0.00	Company WACC (%)	10.04

EXHIBIT 5-5 Cisco General Input Screen

mystery of stock valuation with a few clicks of the miraculous mouse! Exhibit 5-5 shows the general input screen from the ValuePro 2002 integrated valuation software program. In this valuation, we use the analyst estimated growth rate of 20 percent per year, and all of the inputs that we have listed previously.

Given the inputs, ValuePro 2002 produces the general pro forma cash flow schedule for the excess return period that you specify—10 years in Exhibit 5-6.

Revenue, compounded at its estimated 20-percent rate growth, is shown in column 3. NOP, found by multiplying revenue by the NOPM of 16.41 percent, is shown in column 4. Adjusted taxes, equal to NOP times the tax rate of 34.36 percent, is shown in column 5. NOPAT, equal to NOP minus adjusted taxes (column 4 minus column 5) is shown in column 6.

New investment, equal to revenue times the 9.96-percent estimated investment rate, is shown in column 7. Depreciation, equal to revenue times the 8.31 percent estimated depreciation rate, is shown in column 8. And net investment, equal to new investment minus depreciation (column 7 minus column 8) is shown in column 9. The change in working capital, equal to the change in yearly revenue times the incremental working capital rate of 9.63 percent, is shown in column 10.

ValuePro 2002
General Pro Forma Screen
10-year Excess Return Period
CSCO

Disc. Excess Return Period FCFF			$23,613		Total Corporate Value			$89,314				
Discounted Residual Value			$48,268		Less Debt			$0				
Short-Term Assets			$17,433.0		Less Preferred Stock			$0				
Total Corporate Value			$89,314		Less Short-Term Liabilities			($8,375)				
					Total Value to Common Equity			$80,939				
					Intrinsic Stock Value			$10.87				

(2)	(3)	(4)	(5)	(6)	(7)	(8)	(9)	(10)	(11)	(12)	(13)
12 Months Ending	Revenues	NOP	Adj. Taxes	NOPAT	Invest.	Deprec.	Change in Invest.	Change in Working Capital	FCFF	Discount Factor	Discounted FCFF
01/11/2003	18,915										
01/11/2004	22,698	3,725	1,280	2,445	2,261	1,886	375	364	1,706	0.9088	1,550
01/11/2005	27,238	4,470	1,536	2,934	2,713	2,263	449	437	2,047	0.8258	1,691
01/11/2006	32,685	5,364	1,843	3,521	3,255	2,716	539	525	2,457	0.7505	1,844
01/11/2007	39,222	6,436	2,212	4,225	3,907	3,259	647	630	2,948	0.6820	2,011
01/11/2008	47,067	7,724	2,654	5,070	4,688	3,911	777	755	3,538	0.6198	2,193
01/11/2009	56,480	9,268	3,185	6,084	5,625	4,693	932	907	4,245	0.5632	2,391
01/11/2010	67,776	11,122	3,822	7,300	6,750	5,632	1,118	1,088	5,094	0.5119	2,608
01/11/2011	81,331	13,346	4,586	8,761	8,101	6,759	1,342	1,305	6,113	0.4652	2,844
01/11/2012	97,597	16,016	5,503	10,513	9,721	8,110	1,610	1,566	7,336	0.4227	3,101
01/11/2013	117,117	19,219	6,604	12,615	11,665	9,732	1,932	1,880	8,803	0.3841	3,382
	117,117	19,219	6,604	12,615	9,732	9,732	0	0	125,650	0.3841	48,268

EXHIBIT 5-6 Cisco General Pro Forma Screen

Column 11 shows the *free cash flow to the firm*—equal to column 6 minus (column 9 plus column 10). Columns 12 and 13 are used to discount and total those FCFF numbers. You'll note that FCFF is calculated for the 10-year excess return period. At the end of the 10-year period, ValuePro 2002 calculates the residual value by dividing Cisco's NOPAT, estimated to be equal to $12,615 million, by the Cisco's WACC (which as we'll see later, turns out to be equal to 10.04 percent) to get a $125,650 million future residual value in 2013. You'll see how and where we get the inputs to calculate Cisco's WACC in Chapters 6 and 7.

We then discount the company's yearly free cash flow and the residual value at the discount factors, shown in column 12, associated with the WACC. Column 13 shows the product of FCFF (column 11) times the discount factors (column 12). The sum of these discounted numbers, along with short-term assets, is the enterprise value of $89,314 million, shown above column 5 in Exhibit 5-6. From the enterprise or corporate value, we subtract the value of debt and preferred stock (but Cisco has neither debt or preferred stock outstanding) and short-term liabilities to get total value to common equity of $80,939 million, as shown in Exhibit 5-6. We divide value to common equity by the amount of shares outstanding (using diluted shares outstanding here—more about that in Chapter 6) to calculate the per-share intrinsic stock value of $10.87, which is exactly what we want to know.

Based on historic data and analyst expected growth rate of 20 percent, the $10.87 intrinsic value for Cisco's stock is significantly less than

ValuePro 2002
General Input Screen
Intrinsic Stock Value $4.64
General Inputs

Company Ticker.....	CSCO		
Excess Return Period (years)	10	Depreciation Rate (% of Rev.)	8.31
Revenues ($mil)	18915	Investment Rate (% of Rev.)	9.96
Growth Rate (%)	5.00	Working Capital (% of Rev.)	9.63
Net Operating Profit Margin (%)	16.41	Short-Term Assets ($mil)	17433
Tax Rate (%)	34.36	Short-Term Liabilities($mil)	8375
Stock Price($)	14.45	Equity Risk Premium (%)	3.00
Shares Outstanding (mil)	7447	Company Beta	1.93
10-year Treasury Yield (%)	4.25	Value of Debt Out. ($mil)	0
Bond Spread to Treasury (%)	0.00	Value of Pref. Stock Out. ($mil)	0
Preferred Stock Yield (%)	0.00	Company WACC (%)	10.04

EXHIBIT 5-7 Cisco General Input Screen—5-percent Growth

its closing price of $14.45 on August 14, 2002. On the basis of these assumptions, a *sell* recommendation was in order on that date. Could it be that the market knows something that we do not, or that market players are using valuation assumptions that are more advantageous to Cisco's stock value than we are? Let's test the lower 5-percent growth rate assumption for Cisco and see how that affects its value. That valuation is shown in Exhibit 5-7.

Changing that assumption certainly did not help Cisco's intrinsic stock value—it dropped 57 percent to $4.64 based on a 5-percent long-term growth rate.

In Chapter 6, we discuss how to estimate a company's weighted average cost of capital and use that number in the valuation process. And in that chapter you'll learn about a company's WACC and market capitalization.

The cash flow estimation process may be tedious but it is not difficult. It's important for you to know that if you properly follow the free cash flow to the firm approach, you'll gain the talent of at least one of the five Chinese brothers—*you won't get burned.*

Notes

1. See Steven Sharpe, "Stock Prices, Expected Returns and Inflation," unpublished paper, Federal Reserve Board, Washington, D.C., 1999.

2. Rappaport, Alfred, and Michael J. Mauboussin, *Expectations Investing*, Harvard Business School Press, Boston, MA, 2001.

3. The CAGR for revenue growth is calculated by dividing the most recent revenue number (*A*) (e.g., $18,915 for 2002) by an earlier revenue number (*B*) (e.g., $6,452 for 1997); taking the resulting ratio to the 1/T power, where T is the number of years in the compounding period; and subtracting 1.0 to bring it into percentage terms. In math talk the previous sentence looks like this: $[(A/B)^{\wedge}1/T - 1.0]$. The calculation of the CAGR for the five-year period (1997–2002) for Cisco is: $[(18,915/6,452)^{\wedge}(1/5) - 1.0] = 1.2400 - 1.0 = 24.0\%$.

4. Many thanks to C. J. Wagner of Seligman Freidman for his assistance in clarifying details relating to financial accounting statements.

CHAPTER 6

Estimating the Cost of Capital

Don't Count Until You Discount

"Don't count until you discount." Writing this chapter brings to mind that oft-repeated phrase of Professor Russ Ezzell, who taught Finance 410 at The Pennsylvania State University. The discounting of expected cash flow is based upon two fundamental concepts underlying finance theory. The first concept is that of *positive interest rates* and may be characterized by the saying, "A dollar invested today is worth more than a dollar promised tomorrow." The second is that of *risk aversion*, discussed in Principle 3 of Chapter 2, and can be captured by the phrase, "A safe dollar is worth more than a risky one."

The FCFF approach and the ValuePro 2002 software follow Dr. Ezzell's advice and develop a set of expected cash flows for a corporation, and then discount those cash flows to account for their timing and risks. In Chapter 5, we have examined the expected free cash flow of the corporation. In this chapter, we address the estimation of the company's discount rate.

In accordance with generally accepted finance theory, a company's after-tax weighted average cost of capital is the rate that's used to discount the company's after-tax free cash flow. A company's WACC is the weighted average of the company's current cost of debt and equity calculated by using current debt, preferred stock and common stock market values. In this chapter, we show you how to calculate a company's WACC.

The WACC as a Portfolio Return

To understand a company's weighted average cost of capital, it is helpful to think of a company's WACC in relation to the weighted average return on your own investment portfolio. You may have $10,000 in a U.S. Treasury bond that has an interest rate of 6 percent. You may own $10,000 of a preferred stock with a dividend of 8 percent. And you also may own $80,000 market value of common stocks with an average expected return of 10 percent. The expected weighted average return of your $100,000 (in total) investment portfolio equals:

$$\text{Expected Portfolio Return} = $$
$$\frac{(\$10,000 \times .06) + (\$10,000 \times .08) + (\$80,000 \times .10)}{\$100,000} =$$

$$\frac{\$9,400}{\$100,000} = 9.4\%$$

A company's WACC is similar to your investment portfolio's weighted average return. It's simply the weighted average cost of the various obligations—debt, preferred stock, and common stock—that are issued by the firm to finance its operations and investments.

The company's WACC is an important number, both to the stock market for valuation purposes and to the company's management for capital budgeting purposes. When analyzing a potential investment opportunity, projects that have an expected return greater than the company's WACC create free cash flow and generate additional positive net present value for stockholders. These corporate investments should result in an increase in stock prices.

Conversely, projects that have expected returns that are lower than the company's WACC reduce free cash flow and decrease the value of the company. Management should just say no! Negative NPV projects decrease stock value. In fact, investing in negative NPV projects has caused the early exit of many a chief executive in recent years.

How to Measure the Cost of Capital

In WACC calculations, the capital claims of the company are classified as debt, preferred stock, and common equity. The company may have outstanding many different issues of preferred stock and debt with varying dividends or coupons. Other than the effect on market value of outstanding debt and preferred stock, the historic interest rates on a corporation's debt and the dividend rates on its preferred stock issues are unimportant numbers. The past capital structure of the corporation is not as important as the expected future capital structure of the corporation and expected market yield levels of its debt and equity.

The percentage weights (discussed in the next section) used in the FCFF approach to calculate the WACC are the percentages that the company plans to use in its capital structure. Generally, we use the current capital structure of the company to estimate what its capital structure will look like in the future. The discount rates should be current rates demanded today (as a proxy for expected rates) by the market for securities with similar risk and cash flow characteristics.

Because of the tax benefits associated with the deduction of interest payments by the corporation, debt is treated in a special manner in the FCFF approach. The after-tax cost of debt is used in the calculation of the corporation's WACC. The ValuePro 2002 software is designed such that, when given the current yield on the company's debt and the company's tax rate, the after-tax adjustment to the WACC is calculated automatically.

Interest Rates, the Company's WACC, and Stock Values

Let's take a closer look at the relationship among interest rates, a company's WACC, and its stock value. Assume that changes in interest rates and in a company's WACC don't affect the amount of the firm's free cash flows or earnings. However, changes in interest rates and WACC greatly affect the present value of those same cash flows and earnings. Lower interest rates will result in a lower weighted average cost of capital. A lower cost of capital will raise the present value of a company's earnings, cash flow, and its stock value. Conversely, higher interest rates and WACCs result in a lower present value of FCFF and a lower stock value.

How much do changes in interest rates affect a stock's value? To get a better handle on this question, it's helpful to understand the mathematics of compounding and discounting—Principle 7 of Chapter 2. Suppose that an investor owns a $10,000 U.S. Treasury bond that pays all of its interest at maturity in 10 years (called a "zero-coupon" or "stripped bond"). Assume that the yield or discount rate associated with that bond is 6 percent. Remember our discussion of discount factors? The discount factor for the bond, 1.0 divided by 1.06 raised to the tenth power, is equal to $(1/(1.06)^{10}) = 0.5584$. The present value of this U.S. Treasury bond is: $(\$10,000 * .5584) = \$5584$.

If interest rates decrease by 1 percent and the new discount rate associated with the bond is 5 percent, its discount factor is: $(1/(1.05)^{10}) = 0.6139$. The present value of the bond is now: $(\$10,000 * .6139) = \$6139$, an increase of $555, or 10 percent, over the value of the same bond discounted at 6 percent.

And if interest rates were to drop by an additional 1 percent so that the discount rate associated with the bond is 4 percent, its discount factor is: $(1/(1.04)^{10}) = 0.6756$. Its present value would equal $6756—an increase of $617, or 10 percent over the value of the same bond discounted at 5 percent.

Now, let's explore the parallel analysis for stock valuation. Stocks, particularly growth stocks, have most of their values associated with expected growth in cash flow and earnings far in the future. By definition, common stock has no stated maturity or principal value, and growth stocks specifically are way out there in terms of average life of cash flow.

If for the moment we ignore the 1-5-7-10 Rule, which effectively shortens the average life of cash flows for valuation purposes, stock values are extremely sensitive to changes in interest rates. From our interest rate analysis above, a 1-percent change in interest rates can result in a 10-percent or more change in stock values.

Stock price/interest rate sensitivity is a two-edged sword. Stock values, particularly those of growth stocks that pay little or no dividends, benefit greatly when interest rates are falling. We saw this clearly during the late 1990s. Conversely, rising interest rates will act to drive down stock values as quickly as falling interest rates propelled stock values skyward in the 1990s. This is the effect that the discounting rate has on stock values!

WACC and Market Capitalization

Let's look at the WACC and market capitalization for a company that has debt, preferred stock, and common stock outstanding. As our test case, we take a freeze-frame look at the capital structure of Consolidated Edison of New York (ED: *www.ConEdison.com/*), an electric utility provider that has plenty of debt and preferred stock, along with common stock. After studying ConEd's balance sheet, we return to our valuation of Cisco, which has a boring capital structure consisting solely of common stock.

Let's examine ConEd's capital structure as of December 31, 2001, and find the amounts of debt, preferred stock, and common stock outstanding. We look at its balance sheet (Exhibit 6-1) and income statement (Exhibit 6-2) to get the necessary information.

From the balance sheet, we find that ConEd has $5501 million of outstanding long-term debt. If we want a detailed description of a company's capital structure, we can access online its regulatory filings at the SEC. We examine Note B of ConEd's 10K for 2001 filed with the SEC through its EDGAR service. We see that ConEd has 25 different taxable debentures aggregating $4.105 billion with maturities from 2002 to 2041 and interest rates ranging from 6.375 percent to 8.125 percent. ConEd also is the obligor in $1.191 billion of tax-exempt debt that was issued on ConEd's behalf by the New York State Energy Research and Development Authority. The 13 tax-exempt issues have maturities from 2014 to 2036 and interest rates ranging from 1.81 percent to 7.5 percent. ConEd also has at least four series of preferred stock outstanding with an aggregate face value of $269.6 million. Is ConEd's capital structure confusing enough?

The income statement indicates that ConEd has 212.1 million average shares outstanding—*basic,* and 212.9 million average shares outstanding—*diluted.* We generally use the diluted shares outstanding when we look at capital structure and value a stock. This larger number better takes into account the effects of stock options and of convertible debt and preferred stock. ConEd's balance sheet shows that the *book value* of the common stock outstanding is $5666 million. On August 26, 2002, the stock of ConEd closed at a price of $42.53 per share. The market equity of ConEd's stock is:

212.9 million shares outstanding * $42.53 = $9,054 million

Condensed Consolidated Balance Sheet Consolidated Edison, Inc.

At December 31 (Thousands of Dollars)	2001	2000
Assets		
Net plant	$ 12,248,375	$ 11,935,170
Cash and temporary cash investments	271,356	94,828
Accounts receivable – customer, less allowance for uncollectible accounts	613,733	910,344
Fuel, gas in storage, and materials and supplies, at average cost	220,699	242,929
Other current assets	324,307	395,245
Total current assets	1,430,095	1,643,346
Total investments	216,979	526,089
Goodwill and intangible assets	529,330	488,702
Other noncurrent assets and deferred charges	2,571,332	2,173,938
Total deferred charges	3,100,662	2,662,640
Total	$ 16,996,111	$ 16,767,245
Capitalization and Liabilities		
Total common shareholders' equity	$ 5,666,268	$ 5,472,389
Preferred stock	249,613	249,613
Long-term debt	5,501,217	5,415,409
Total capitalization	11,417,098	11,137,411
Minority interests	9,522	8,416
Long-term debt due within one year	310,950	309,590
Notes payable	343,722	255,042
Accounts payable	665,342	1,020,402
Other current liabilities	890,551	730,999
Total current liabilities	2,210,565	2,316,033
Total noncurrent liabilities and deferred credits	3,358,926	3,305,385
Total	$ 16,996,111	$ 16,767,245

EXHIBIT 6-1   ConEd Balance Sheet

Market Value versus Book Value

Financial theory states that the market capitalization of a company is equal to the total market value, not book value, of the outstanding debt, preferred stock and common stock of the company.

Market Capitalization = Market Value
(Common Stock + Preferred Stock + Debt)

The FCFF approach uses the various market values to calculate a company's market capitalization, along with debt and equity weightings. To illustrate this point, consider the book value $5666 million ver-

Condensed Consolidated Income Statement Consolidated Edison, Inc.

Year Ended December 31 (Thousands of Dollars)	2001	2000	1999
Operating revenues			
Electric	$ 6,887,863	$ 6,938,128	$ 5,792,673
Gas	1,465,957	1,261,970	1,000,083
Steam	503,736	452,135	340,026
Non-utility	776,406	779,158	358,541
Total operating revenues	9,633,962	9,431,391	7,491,323
Operating expenses			
Purchased power and fuel	4,024,372	3,995,491	2,254,073
Gas purchased for resale	859,961	789,080	485,155
Other operations and maintenance	1,492,241	1,604,644	1,626,602
Depreciation and amortization	526,235	586,407	526,182
Income tax and other taxes	1,603,680	1,439,633	1,579,512
Total operating expenses	8,506,489	8,415,255	6,471,524
Operating income	1,127,473	1,016,136	1,019,799
Other income (deductions)	(758)	(12,263)	31,972
Income before interest charges	1,126,715	1,003,873	1,051,771
Interest charges	430,880	407,445	337,563
Net income	695,835	596,428	714,208
Preferred stock dividends requirements	13,593	13,593	13,593
Net income for common stock	$ 682,242	$ 582,835	$ 700,615
Earnings per common share – Basic	$ 3.22	$ 2.75	$ 3.14
Earnings per common share – Diluted	$ 3.21	$ 2.74	$ 3.13
Dividends per common share	$ 2.20	$ 2.18	$ 2.14
Average number of shares outstanding (millions) – Basic	212.1	212.2	223.4
Average number of shares outstanding (millions) – Diluted	212.9	212.4	223.9

EXHIBIT 6-2 ConEd Income Statement

sus market value $9054 million of ConEd's common stock. ConEd's book value versus market value ratio ($5666/$9054) is 62.6 percent.

The *book value of debt and preferred stock* is an accounting measure that relates to how much money was raised by the company when each security initially was issued. The *book value of common stock* is also an accounting measure that relates to the amount of money raised when the stock was issued, plus the amount of aggregate earnings that have been retained over the life of the company.

The *market value of debt and preferred and common stock* is the price at which the specific obligation would trade in today's market, times the amount outstanding. Because of the frequent trading of stocks and the fact that stock prices are readily observable, it's easy to determine the market value of common stock. Since debt and preferred stock trade less frequently and often only in the dealer-to-dealer market, market prices of these securities are not easily observable and are harder to determine.

If we're expecting a 10-percent return on a share of ConEd, and its market value is $42.53 per share, our expectation is that we will earn 10 percent per year on our $42.53 market value, or $4.25 per year between dividends and stock price appreciation. We'd be disappointed if we received 10 percent on the lower $26.61 book value of the share, or $2.66 per year. Hence, professionals use market values when they look at market capitalization of common stock.

Market versus Book Value: Our Recommendation

In real life, as opposed to the ivory tower of academia in which some of us reside, the current quotes of market value for debt and preferred stock are often difficult to obtain. Absent credit concerns and default risk, the market values of preferred stock and debt for the most part do not stray significantly from their respective book values. In an effort to conserve time and to simplify a valuation, most market professionals use the company's reported book values for debt and preferred stock when they examine the capitalization of the corporation.

Market professionals always use the market value of common stock when they examine the capitalization of the corporation. As we will see in valuation examples, the market value of common stock sometimes bears little relationship to its book value. Stock prices are readily available. In keeping with this market practice, we use book values for debt and preferred stock and market values for common stock in all of our valuation examples.

Market Versus Book Value for ConEd

We use the book values of ConEd's debt and preferred stock outstanding and both the book value and market value of common stock to develop ConEd's market capitalization schedule, as shown in Table 6-1 below.

Market versus Book Value for Cisco

Cisco, like most tech companies that have a high degree of business and operating risk, has no debt or preferred stock outstanding. According to Cisco's balance sheet (Exhibit 5-4), as of July 27, 2002, the book value of Cisco's common stock was $28,656 million and, ac-

TABLE 6-1   Consolidated Edison, Inc. Market Capitalization

| | 12/31/2001 (millions of dollars) | | | |
| | Book Value | | Market Value | |
	Total	%	Total	%
Debt	$5,501.2	48.6%	$5,501.2	37.1%
Preferred stock	$249.6	2.2%	$249.6	1.7%
Common stock	$5,566.2	49.2%	$9,054.6	61.2%
Total capitalization	$11,317.0	100.0%	$14,805.4	100.0%

cording to its income statement (Exhibit 5-2), it has 7301 shares outstanding in its per-share calculation-basic, and 7447 shares outstanding in its per-share calculation-diluted. We use the higher diluted number to determine Cisco's market equity. Cisco's closing stock price on August 14, 2002, the date we valued Cisco, was $14.45, resulting in total market equity for Cisco's stock of $107,609 million (see Table 6-2 below). The book equity to market equity (BE/ME) ratio for Cisco, a high-tech company that prior to 2002 had very high growth rates, is: ($28,656/$107,609) = 26.6 percent, significantly lower than the 62.6-percent ratio for ConEd, which no one would mistake for a growth stock.

TABLE 6-2   Cisco Systems Market Capitalization

| | 7/27/2002 (millions of dollars) | | | |
| | Book Value | | Market Value | |
	Total	%	Total	%
Debt	$0.0	0.0%	$0.0	0.0%
Preferred stock	$0.0	0.0%	$0.0	0.0%
Common stock	$26,656.0	100.0%	$107,609.2	100.0%
Total capitalization	$26,656.0	100.0%	$107,609.2	100.0%

Estimating ConEd's WACC

Before estimating all of the component costs that make up a WACC, let's try a simple example for ConEd. Let's assume the following: The pretax cost of debt for ConEd is 5.25 percent, which represents a 1.0-percent *spread to Treasuries*; ConEd's after-tax cost of debt (assuming a tax rate of 35 percent) is: [5.25% * (1 − .35)] = 3.41%; its cost of preferred stock is 6.56 percent; and the cost of common equity is 5.67 percent. ConEd's WACC on August 26, 2002, based on these assumptions, a market value weighting of common stock, and book value weightings of debt and preferred stock (see Table 6-1), was:

ConEd's WACC =37.1%(3.41%) + 1.7%(6.56%)

+ 61.2%(5.67%) = 4.84%

Below, we show our inputs for the ValuePro 2002 software relating to the cost of capital and market capitalization. We explain how and where these numbers come from in the pages that follow.

Valuation Inputs Relating to Cost of Capital and Market Capitalization—ConEd

Our initial inputs for the ValuePro 2002 software relating to ConEd's cost of capital and market capitalization are:

Stock Price ($)	$42.53
Shares Outstanding (mil)	212.9 million
10-Year Treasury Yield (%)	4.25%
Bond Spread to Treasury (%)	1.0%
Preferred Stock Yield (%)	6.56%
Equity Risk Premium (%)	3.0%
Company Beta	0.4725
Value of Debt Outstanding ($mil)	$5,501.2 million
Value of Preferred Stock Outstanding ($mil)	$249.6 million

As we can see from the last entry in the right-hand column of the Exhibit 6-3, the WACC for ConEd in this example is 4.84 percent. The FCFF approach allows for individual yearly inputs of the WACC over

ValuePro 2002
General Input Screen
Intrinsic Stock Value $41.06
General Inputs

Company Ticker.....	ConEd		
Excess Return Period (years)	10	Depreciation Rate (% of Rev.)	5.46
Revenues ($mil)	9633.9	Investment Rate (% of Rev.)	11.46
Growth Rate (%)	4.00	Working Capital (% of Rev.)	1.76
Net Operating Profit Margin (%)	11.70	Short-Term Assets ($mil)	1353.5
Tax Rate (%)	35.00	Short-Term Liabilities($mil)	2226.8
Stock Price($)	42.53	Equity Risk Premium (%)	3.00
Shares Outstanding (mil)	212.9	Company Beta	0.47
10-year Treasury Yield (%)	4.25	Value of Debt Out. ($mil)	5501.2
Bond Spread to Treasury (%)	1.00	Value of Pref. Stock Out. ($mil)	249.6
Preferred Stock Yield (%)	6.56	Company WACC (%)	4.84

EXHIBIT 6-3 ConEd General Input Page

the excess return period. We'll look at this type of changing WACC adjustment in a valuation in Chapter 8. A changing WACC allows us to incorporate the effect of different leverage, capital structures, and discounting rates in the valuation process.

The Cost of Common Equity and Shares Outstanding

The *cost of common equity* is the annual rate of return that an investor expects to earn when investing in shares of a company. That return is composed of the dividends paid on the shares plus any increase (or minus any decrease) in the market value of the shares. For example, if an investor expects a 10-percent return from ConEd's stock and buys a share at $42.53, her expectation is to receive $4.25 through a combination of dividends (currently $2.22 per share during 2002) and the appreciation of the stock price (presumed to be $2.03 to give her the 10-percent expected return totaling $4.25) during the year.

The Risk-Free Rate and Expected Returns

Let's take a look at the rate of return, in general, an investor should expect from a stock. We use the CAPM pricing model that we discuss in Principle 10 of Chapter 2. The return expected of any *risky* common stock should be composed of three components:

1. A return commensurate with a risk-free security (R_f) of a comparable term or maturity and that incorporates expectations of inflation;

2. A return that incorporates the market risk associated with common stocks as a whole (R_m); and

3. A return that incorporates the business and financial risks of the company, known as the company's *beta*.

The first measure of return (R_f) relates to the rate of return currently available on a risk-free security. A rational investor who values a risky security, such as common stock, would expect it to earn a return greater than that of a risk-free security. If the yield on a 10-year Treasury Bond is 5 percent, an investor should expect a return greater than 5 percent for a common stock.

Expected Return Relating to Common Stock

The second measure of return (R_m) relates to the return and the risks associated with stocks in general. A risk premium (the *equity risk premium*) is associated with the stock market as a whole, and that risk premium should be priced into any equity investment. For example, if you expect to earn 8 percent on average from a diversified stock portfolio, and the risk-free rate is 5 percent, the equity risk premium (R_{erp}) = 8% − 5% = 3.0%.

Equity Risk Premium (R_{erp}) = Expected Return on Market (R_m)
$$- \text{Risk Free Rate } (R_f)$$

There is much debate about how to measure or estimate the equity risk premium. R_{erp} is an *expectation* of the excess return associated with the investment in a diversified portfolio of common stocks versus the expected return of a risk-free security. It is the additional return that an investor expects to receive above the yield of a risk-free security to compensate for the price volatility associated with the stock market.

Dr. Aswath Damodaran[1] of New York University finds that the difference in compound annual rates of return between the stock market and Treasury Bonds has *decreased significantly* in recent years. He notes that the stock market to T-Bond risk premium, on a compound annual return basis, has decreased from 5.5 percent for the period 1926–1990, to 3.25 percent for the period 1962–1990, to 0.19 percent for the period 1981–1990. In his text, despite the decrease in observed R_{erp}, he uses the longer-term 75-year average, 5.5 percent equity risk premium in his cost of capital calculations and in his valuation examples.

Investors also have noticed this decrease in the historic equity risk premium, and it appears to us that their expectations of this risk premium have lessened. During the late 1990s the risk premium certainly dropped, perhaps even into negative numbers, with the promise of a *New Economic Paradigm*. (What a joke!) Wall Street analysts, business journalists, and telecosm gurus promoted the notion that the new era of the Internet and high-tech companies would create unlimited growth. Investors were encouraged to bid up the price of many stocks to unreasonably high market equity levels that never could have been supported by the operating profits generated by those companies.

We believe that a reasonable equity risk premium for the stock market of late-2002 is approximately 3 percent,[2] which is what we use in our valuations. Since the terrorist attacks of 9/11 and the corporate governance and accounting scandals of Enron, WorldCom, Tyco, Adelphia, and others, volatility has increased in both the equity and debt markets through December 2002. Concerns remain that the price of risk may be increasing. The Federal Reserve has been generous in maintaining liquidity in the financial markets. However, the stock market must continue to deflate from the overvaluation of the high-tech bubble. Coupled with ongoing fears of turban capped terrorists plotting mass destruction in caves, and Brooks Brothers-clad CEOs and CFOs plotting the next accounting scam to cash in stock options, the outlook is not a promising mix for stock prices. However, in the past when things look bleakest, it often is a good time to buy stocks.

Expected Return Relating to an Individual Stock

The third measure of return versus risk—*beta* is related to a specific stock. What is the risk of the market sector of the firm's principal business (its operating or business risk)? How risky is the financial structure or leverage of the firm (its financial risk)? Beta measures the risk of the company relative to the risk of the stock market in general. Greater risk (operating or business), as measured by a larger variabil-

ity of returns, increases a company's beta. Likewise, with greater leverage (higher debt/value ratio) and increasing financial risk, the company's stock should also have a larger beta. With a larger beta, an investor should expect a greater return.

The beta of a firm of average risk in the stock market is 1.0. The
beta of a firm with below-average operating risk, such as a firm operating in a regulated industry, is less than 1.0. For example, according
to Value Line, the beta of Consolidated Edison is 0.4725. The betas of
firms with above-average operating risk, such as Microsoft or Cisco,
which operate in quickly changing industries such as software and
computers, are greater than 1.00. Microsoft's beta, according to Yahoo
Finance through its Market Guide alliance, is 1.72. According to Yahoo
Finance, Cisco's beta is 1.93. Clearly, megabytes are more volatile than
megawatts.

Expected Return and the Capital Asset Pricing Model

As you recall from Chapter 2, the financial model that uses beta as its
sole measure of risk (a single-factor model) is the Capital Asset Pricing Model (*CAPM*). Many market analysts use CAPM to value a stock.
The relationship between risk and return that is determined by the
model and is incorporated into our FCFF analysis and ValuePro 2002
software is:

$$\text{Expected Return of a Stock } (R_s) = [R_f + (\text{beta} * R_{erp})]$$

In English, this equation translates to: "The expected return on a stock
is equal to the risk-free rate, plus the specific stock's beta, times the
equity risk premium (e.g., 3.0 percent)." For ConEd and Cisco, in numbers it looks like this:

Expected Return on ConEd Stock = [4.25% + (0.4725 * 3%)] = 5.67%

Expected Return on Cisco Stock = [4.25% + (1.93 * 3%)] = 10.04%

The CAPM equations result in a linear relationship between the expected return on a stock and its specific risk measure, beta. A graph of
this risk/return relationship with a risk-free rate of 4 percent, a stock
market risk premium of 3 percent, and the expected return for a stock
with a beta of 1.4 is shown in Exhibit 6-4:

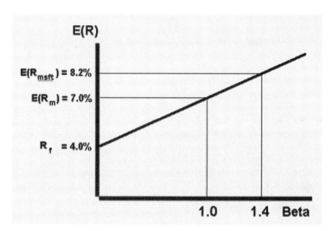

EXHIBIT 6-4 CAPM Graph

There's a lot of academic theory behind the Capital Asset Pricing Model, the equity risk premium, and the calculation of beta. We describe some of the theory in Chapter 2.

Cost of Common Equity: Our Recommendation

The cost of capital inputs that are the most difficult to estimate are the company's beta and the equity risk premium. Neither number can be directly observed in the market. When first valuing a company, we usually find the company's beta on the company's profile link on the Web site, Yahoo Finance. If we are seriously considering an investment in the company, we'll check several sources that publish betas, such as AOL Personal Finance whose data is provided by S&P ComStock, and MSN Investor to get a couple of different estimates of beta. Then, we typically use the average of the betas, or the highest beta value in order to have a more conservative estimate of intrinsic value.

Our estimate of the equity risk premium has been a steady 3 percent for the past several years, with one exception. Due to the enormous uncertainty and fear that gripped the stock market in the weeks immediately after 9/11, we upped our risk premium to 5 percent. That change had a uniformly negative effect on stock value and drove down intrinsic values for stocks by 15 percent to 35 percent. After the United States began its retaliation and the war in Afghanistan looked as if it was going to be successful, we reduced our equity risk premium to 3 percent.

The Amount of Stock Outstanding—the Problem with Options

The final input associated with the cost of common equity is the *amount of stock outstanding.* Since this number is the divisor in the calculation of intrinsic stock value, the amount of stock outstanding is a very important input. Many corporations, especially high-tech companies like Microsoft, Cisco, and Intel, make stock options a large part of the compensation package for many employees. Eventually, when and if those options become vested and are *in-the-money*—meaning the market price of the stock is greater than the exercise price on the options, they present a serious dilution problem for stockholders and negatively affect stock value.

A major question being debated in the financial markets relates to the dilution effect of stock options and how it affects the calculation of the amount of shares outstanding. Currently, there is much discussion in the financial press, the accounting industry, and in Washington about options and compensation issues for corporate executives. Some corporate officials have resorted to questionable accounting practices for a period of time to boost earnings and stock prices to cash in on options. The EVA (economic value added) mantra of "maximizing the value of stock for current shareholders" has been bastardized into "temporarily pump up the price of shares so that management can cash in on its options and screw the shareholders." The granting of $1.1 billion in shares to the top management of Computer Associates that we describe in Chapter 3 is a good example of a terrible incentive program.

So, what should this number be? Should the input for *shares outstanding* be the actual number of shares outstanding, the number that takes into account any in-the-money options that have been granted, or an amount that takes into account all options that have been granted?

Due to vesting considerations and a lack of marketability of stock options, typical option pricing models such as the Black-Scholes model do not work well when used to value employee stock options (*ESOs*). Most ESOs are awarded on the basis that the options will *vest* (which means to become eligible to be exercised) over a period of time. A typical option award will specify that one-third of the options will vest at the end of year one, one-third will vest at the end of year two, and the remainder will vest at the end of year three. Employees who have been awarded options may quit or be terminated and many of the options that have been awarded may never be exercised. An option award is specific to an individual and can't be sold or assigned, meaning it is totally illiquid. The vesting consideration and lack of liquidity of ESOs render them much less valuable than most pricing models would predict.

Shares Outstanding: Our Recommendation

What we use, generally at least for our first cut at valuation, is the most recent amount of shares-outstanding number that pops up in our AOL Finance screen, as reported by S&P Comstock, or from the stock profile screen on Yahoo Finance. To our knowledge, these Web sites report the actual number of shares outstanding based on the most recent quarterly report filed by the company with the SEC. If a stock looks promising based upon our initial valuation, we examine it more closely using the *diluted* amount of shares outstanding as reported in the corporation's quarterly and annual report. This helps us to get a better handle on our concern regarding the firm's dilution problem. Using diluted shares outstanding produces a more conservative valuation, which is desirable when we consider an investment.

Shares Outstanding—ConEd

For ConEd we use the diluted number of shares outstanding of 212.9 million shares as our input for shares outstanding. The amount of diluted and basic shares outstanding is found on ConEd's income statement, Exhibit 6-2.

Shares Outstanding—Cisco

The amount of shares outstanding for a high-tech growth company such as Cisco is more problematic than for a stodgy utility, such as ConEd. During the past two decades, Cisco has propelled its growth and earnings through the purchase of companies in semirelated market sectors. Cisco has financed this buying spree through the issuance of new stock and through the generous granting of stock options. The growth of shares outstanding, on both a basic and diluted basis, has slowed considerably in the past three years, in large part due to the slump in Cisco's stock price. Still, the future diluting effect associated with options should be a concern for investors. We use the diluted number of shares outstanding of 7447 million, that's <u>7.477 BILLION</u> shares, as shown in Exhibit 5-2.

In summary, the inputs for valuing a stock relating to the cost of common equity are the current rate of return on the 10-year risk-free Treasury Bond—4.25 percent as of August 14, 2002; the company's beta (estimates of which are available from a number of sources—see Chapter 7), the current estimate of the equity risk premium, R_{erp}—using 3 percent as of August 14, 2002; and the amount of common stock outstanding—using diluted shares outstanding.

The After-Tax Cost of Debt and Debt Outstanding

The after-tax cost of debt securities represents the cost to the firm of borrowing funds at *current yields* in the debt markets after taking into account the tax deductibility of interest-to-finance investments for the operation of the company.

It's important to use today's yields or interest rates in calculating the company's WACC, because they represent our best expectation of relative opportunity costs for providers of new capital to the company. By contrast, historic or sunk costs are associated with the coupon rates and original offering yields on outstanding debt and preferred stock issues of the company. These historic rates should not affect the corporation's investment decisions or the calculation of the corporation's WACC.

Because a company's debt securities are risky investments (although not as risky as its common stock), the after-tax cost of debt primarily is a function of three variables: the current yields associated with comparable-maturity risk-free debt, the default risk associated with the specific company's debt, and the company's income tax rate.

The Spread to Treasuries—A Measure of Default Risk

All taxable debt that is issued or traded in the United States capital markets is priced at what is called a *spread to Treasuries*. The spread to Treasuries implies that all corporate debt will have a higher yield (effective interest cost) than yields associated with comparable-maturity U.S. Treasury Bonds. This spread will change over time depending on economic conditions and the relative default risk associated with the specific debt security. The interest rate, or yield, of all debt is vitally dependent on the risk-free rate associated with U.S. Treasury debt. The 10-year risk-free rate is our starting point for the WACC calculation.

The spread to Treasuries is the measure of default risk on a specific company's debt, and it is an input into the FCFF approach and the ValuePro 2002 software. For a large company with little operating risk and low financial leverage (low percentage of debt in the company's market capitalization), the spread to Treasuries might be quite small (0.75 percent to 1.0 percent). For companies with considerable operating risk or high leverage, the spread to Treasuries might be quite large (5.0 percent to 9.0 percent).

The best way to determine default risk is to see how a particular company's debt trades in the market and compare it on a spread basis to comparable-maturity Treasury yields. A small number of debt issues are traded on the New York Stock Exchange. Quotes for listed, publicly traded debt are often available on free Web sites, like Yahoo, in their finance sector. In a pinch, you could always resort to a good financial newspaper, like the *Wall Street Journal* or *Investor's Business Daily* for debt quotes. Many companies will not have outstanding debt that is listed or traded on an exchange. Their debt securities will trade in the dealer-to-dealer market, and trade data and market quotes may not be available to the general public.

Another way to measure default risk and to estimate spreads is to use the default rating systems that are published by the three major credit rating agencies—Standard & Poor's Corporation, Moody's Investor Services, and Fitch & Company. These rating services publish ratings for many corporate debt issuers. The highest credit ratings, which are earned by companies with very low default risk, are AAA/Aaa, and the ratings decline from there.

A viable way of estimating the yield on debt of a company that does not have actively traded bonds is to examine the cost of outstanding traded debt from a default ratings standpoint for a similar company. Then use that yield as a proxy for the cost of debt of the company that you are valuing.

The After-Tax Cost of Debt

The final adjustment to be made to the cost of debt is to take into account the effect of income taxes. Since interest payments (and interest accruals) are tax deductible for the company, an adjustment to the WACC is made to reflect this corporate tax saving. The higher the corporate income tax rate, the greater is the tax savings from issuing debt, and the lower is the after-tax cost of debt. The deductibility of interest payments reduces the cost of debt financing for the corporation. The equation that represents this deductibility is:

After-Tax Cost of Debt = Pretax Cost of Debt * (1 − Corporate Tax Rate)

For example, if the risk-free rate is 4.25 percent, and ConEd's debt trades at a 1.0 percent spread to Treasuries, and its tax rate is 35 percent, the pretax cost of debt = (4.25 percent + 1.0 percent) = 5.25 percent, and the after-tax cost of ConEd's debt is:

ConEd's After-Tax Cost of Debt = [5.25% * (1 − .35)] = 3.41%

After-Tax Cost of Debt and Debt Outstanding: Our Recommendation

It is often difficult to find market value quotes for the outstanding debt of the corporation to determine market capitalization calculations. Absent significant credit risk, we've found that the market value of debt does not diverge too greatly from the book value of debt. So using the book value of debt does not significantly affect the valuation process, and that's what we use in our valuation examples.

In summary, the inputs to the ValuePro Program relating to the cost of debt are: an estimate of the current yield associated with long-term debt of the corporation, as represented as a spread to Treasuries; the company's tax rate; and the amount of debt outstanding. For simplicity, use book value of debt if market value isn't available.

After-Tax Cost of Debt and Debt Outstanding—ConEd

ConEd operates in a regulated industry and has a fairly low degree of business risk, but does have a significant amount of debt outstanding. According to its balance sheet (Exhibit 6-1), ConEd has $5501.2 book value of debt outstanding, the number we will use in the ValuePro 2002 software. We also estimate a spread to Treasuries of 1 percent, and will use the maximum marginal corporate tax rate of 35 percent.

The Cost of Preferred Stock and Amount Outstanding

Preferred stock is a hybrid financial instrument that usually represents a small portion of a company's capital structure. Preferred stock is an ownership claim on the assets of the corporation that is senior to common stock (hence the adjective *preferred*) but is junior to that of debt.

The dividends that corporations pay on preferred stock and common stock, unlike the interest payments on debt, are not tax-deductible payments. However, if a corporation owns stock in another corporation, it is allowed a tax deduction (the *dividends received deduction*, or *DRD*) on the dividends it receives. Because of the tax advantages, it is advantageous for a corporation to own stock in another corporation. Also, the tax act passed in May of 2003 temporarily reduced to 15% the tax rate on dividends on certain common and preferred stocks.

Over the past 20 years, investment bankers and corporate issuers have gotten mighty fancy in the use and structure of preferred stock. Many options and complex dividend structures may be embedded in a preferred stock issue. Examples are convertibility into common shares or into debt, optional redemption by the corporation after a certain date, and dividend-setting mechanisms designed to keep the market value and par value equal. These esoteric features can make it hard to value preferred stock properly.

Some companies have perpetual preferred stock outstanding that is traded on an exchange. If a preferred stock is not listed on an exchange, it may be difficult to get a quoted market rate level for the preferred stock of a company. Preferred stock usually makes up a very small percentage of the capital structure of most companies. We have found that the current market yield of preferred stock with no fancy convertibility or dividend-setting mechanisms is somewhere between the pretax cost of debt and the cost of common equity.

Cost of Preferred Stock and Stock Outstanding: Our Recommendation

When we approach a valuation and can find no good quote for preferred stock or a quote for a preferred stock issue of a comparable company, we ballpark the yield on preferred by splitting the difference between the pretax cost of debt and the cost of common equity.

Likewise, it sometimes may be difficult to find market value quotes for the outstanding preferred stock of the corporation to determine market capitalization amounts. We've found that, if there is not a large amount of preferred stock outstanding, using the book value of preferred stock, as opposed to market value, does not bias significantly the valuation. We use book values for amounts outstanding of preferred stock in our valuation examples.

The valuation inputs relating to preferred stock are today's yield level associated with the preferred stock of the company, and the amount of preferred stock outstanding. For simplicity, use book value for preferred stock if the market value isn't available.

Cost of Preferred Stock and Stock Outstanding—ConEd

ConEd has an issue of preferred stock that is listed on the NYSE, pays a quarterly dividend of $1.25 ($5 per year), and was trading on August 27, 2002 at a price of $76.20 per share for a yield of 6.56 percent. From ConEd's balance sheet (Exhibit 6-1), we find that it has $249.6 million face value of total preferred stock outstanding.

WACC Calculation—ConEd

The inputs for ConEd (discussed above) result in an after-tax weighted average cost of capital for ConEd of 4.84 percent. We show the calculation of the WACC in the weighted average cost of capital screen in Exhibit 6-5.

ValuePro 2002
Weighted Average Cost of Capital Screen
ConEd

Cost of Common Equity					
10-Year Treasury Bond Yield	4.25				
Company Specific Beta	0.47				
Equity Risk Premium	3.00				
Cost of Common Equity	5.67				

Market Capitalization and After-Tax Weighted Average Cost of Capital					
	Current Yield	After Tax Yield	Market Value	% Capitalization	Weighted After-Tax Yield
Long-Term Debt	5.25	3.41	$5,501	37.2%	1.27
Preferred Stock	6.56	6.56	$250	1.7%	0.11
Common Stock	5.67	5.67	$9,055	61.2%	3.47
			$14,805	100.0%	4.84

EXHIBIT 6-5   WACC Screen ConEd

WACC Calculation—Cisco

Recall that Cisco does not have debt or preferred stock outstanding, which makes the calculation of Cisco's WACC relatively easy. Cisco's WACC is its cost of equity, which we calculate under the cost of equity section above, to be 10.04 percent. Cisco is a high-tech firm in a quickly changing industry where obsolescence is a major concern. Cisco's WACC is considerably higher than the WACC for ConEd, a regulated company in the stodgy utility industry. As can be seen by these two examples, the discounting mechanism is the way that the capital asset pricing model introduces risk differences into valuing a stock.

Valuation Inputs Relating to Cost of Capital and Market Capitalization—Cisco

Our initial inputs for the ValuePro 2002 software relating to Cisco's cost of capital and market capitalization are:

Stock Price ($)	$14.45
Shares Outstanding (mil)	7447 million
10-Year Treasury Yield (%)	4.25%
Bond Spread to Treasury (%)	0%
Preferred Stock Yield (%)	0%
Equity Risk Premium (%)	3.0%
Company Beta	1.93
Value of Debt Outstanding ($mil)	0
Value of Preferred Stock Outstanding ($mil)	0

Balance Sheet Items in the Valuation Process: Our Recommendation

The majority of the intrinsic stock value for most companies comes from discounting the expected future operating profits. Therefore, the bulk of the company's value depends on future revenue and earnings—metrics that are captured primarily by the income and cash flow statements of the corporation. Nevertheless, the corporation's balance sheet is important and has its role in the valuation equation, particularly for financial companies, such as Citigroup and Merrill Lynch, and portfolio companies (companies whose value is derived from a portfolio of operating companies), such as ICGE and Berkshire Hathaway (Warren—sorry to mention ICGE and your company in the same dependent clause).

A balance sheet captures a picture of the financial health of a company on one particular day in time. The top portion of the balance sheet lists the company's assets—what the company owns. *Current assets* are assets that are expected to be realized in cash or sold or consumed within one year. Examples of current assets are cash, short-term investments, inventories, accounts receivable, and prepaid expenses. *Long-term assets* are assets that will not be completely consumed during a year. Examples are long-term investments, PP&E, intangible assets such as goodwill and patents, and deferred charges.

The bottom portion of the balance sheet lists the company's liabilities—what the company owes, and the shareholders' equity. *Current liabilities* are obligations of the company that are expected to be paid by the firm within the year. Examples of current liabilities include accounts payable, current maturity of long-term debt, accrued expenses, and the current portion of deferred income taxes. *Long-term liabilities* are obligations of the firm that are not required to be paid by the firm within the current year. Examples of long-term liabilities are long-term debt, lease agreements, warranty obligations, and other funding commitments. *Equity* is ownership, the shareholders' residual interest in the firm—what's left over after subtracting liabilities from assets. Shareholders' equity consists of common and preferred stock, paid in capital in excess of par; treasury stock; and retained earnings.

What role should the balance sheet play in valuation? Let's assume that two similar companies, ABC and XYZ, have identical capital structures, costs of capital, and operating cash flows, and that the expected future cash flows generated by both firms are identical. We assume also that the long-term assets of the corporation, such as PP&E, goodwill, and intangibles, will be consumed through depreciation and amortization charges as the firms operate and generate business over the years. Finally, let's assume that the balance sheets of both firms are identical with one exception—the amount of current assets of ABC exceeds those of XYZ by a million dollars.

Should the corporate or enterprise value of ABC = XYZ? No! The enterprise value of ABC should exceed XYZ by $1 million. This conclusion is based upon the principle of *arbitrage* and the *law of one price*, an advanced practice in finance that professionals use to take advantage of trading opportunities in the market. How do we incorporate this aspect into a valuation?

In valuing a company, we assume that the long-term assets of the firm are illiquid or are completely devoted to generating future profits and cash flow for the firm. Therefore, long-term assets enter the valuation equation through NOPMs, and investment and depreciation ratios. Long-term liabilities of the company enter the valuation equation when they are subtracted from total corporate value, as shown at the top of Cisco's general pro forma screen. (See Exhibit 6-8.) The most reasonable way to bring the balance sheet more substantially into play is through the difference of short-term assets versus short-term liabilities. So we add short-term assets to the corporate value side of the equation and subtract short-term liabilities from total corporate value. We use this procedure in the valuations that follow.

Short-Term Assets—Cisco

According to Cisco's balance sheet of July 27, 2002 (Exhibit 5-4), it has total current assets of $17.433 billion with $9494 in cash and cash equivalents, $3.2 billion in short-term investments, $1.1 billion in accounts receivable, $880 million in inventories, $2 billion in deferred tax assets, and $700 million in miscellaneous current assets. This is a very strong short-term asset base.

Short-Term Liabilities—Cisco

Cisco's current liabilities total $8.375 billion, so Cisco's current asset/current liability ratio is greater than 2.0—a good level of liquidity. Cisco's largest category of short-term liabilities is deferred revenue of $3.1 billion, followed by accrued compensation of $1.3 billion, $579 million in income taxes payable, $470 million in accounts payable, and $2.8 billion in other accrued liabilities.

Valuation Inputs Relating to Short-Term Assets and Liabilities—Cisco

Our initial inputs for the ValuePro 2002 software relating to Cisco's short-term assets and liabilities are:

Short-Term Assets ($mil)	$17,433
Short-Term Liabilities ($mil)	$8,375

ValuePro 2002
General Input Screen
Intrinsic Stock Value $10.87
General Inputs

Company Ticker.....	CSCO		
Excess Return Period (years)	10	Depreciation Rate (% of Rev.)	8.31
Revenues ($mil)	18915	Investment Rate (% of Rev.)	9.96
Growth Rate (%)	20.00	Working Capital (% of Rev.)	9.63
Net Operating Profit Margin (%)	16.41	Short-Term Assets ($mil)	17433
Tax Rate (%)	34.36	Short-Term Liabilities($mil)	8375
Stock Price($)	14.45	Equity Risk Premium (%)	3.00
Shares Outstanding (mil)	7447	Company Beta	1.93
10-year Treasury Yield (%)	4.25	Value of Debt Out. ($mil)	0
Bond Spread to Treasury (%)	0.00	Value of Pref. Stock Out. ($mil)	0
Preferred Stock Yield (%)	0.00	Company WACC (%)	10.04

EXHIBIT 6-6   Cisco's General Input Screen

Valuation Exercise: Cisco

We enter the inputs that we discuss above for Cisco into the ValuePro 2002 software, which creates Cisco's general input screen (Exhibit 6-6), Cisco's weighted average cost of capital screen (Exhibit 6-7), and Cisco's general pro forma screen (Exhibit 6-8). Cisco's WACC is 10.04 percent, equal to its cost of equity.

Each of Cisco's expected free cash flows, shown in column 11 of Exhibit 6-8, is discounted at the WACC of 10.04 percent. The discount factors, shown in column 12 of Exhibit 6-8, range from $[1/(1.1004)] =$

ValuePro 2002
Weighted Average Cost of Capital Screen
CSCO

Cost of Common Equity

10-Year Treasury Bond Yield	4.25
Company Specific Beta	1.93
Equity Risk Premium	3.00
Cost of Common Equity	10.04

Market Capitalization and After-Tax Weighted Average Cost of Capital

	Current Yield	After Tax Yield	Market Value	% Capitalization	Weighted After-Tax Yield
Long-Term Debt	4.25	2.79	$0	0.0%	0.00
Preferred Stock	0.00	0.00	$0	0.0%	0.00
Common Stock	10.04	10.04	$107,609	100.0%	10.04
			$107,609	100.0%	10.04

EXHIBIT 6-7   Cisco's WACC Screen

ValuePro 2002
General Pro Forma Screen
10-year Excess Return Period
CSCO

Disc. Excess Return Period FCFF	$23,613				Total Corporate Value			$89,314			
Discounted Residual Value	$48,268				Less Debt			$0			
Short-Term Assets	$17,433.0				Less Preferred Stock			$0			
Total Corporate Value	$89,314				Less Short-Term Liabilities			($8,375)			
					Total Value to Common Equity			$80,939			
					Intrinsic Stock Value			$10.87			

(2)	(3)	(4)	(5)	(6)	(7)	(8)	(9)	(10)	(11)	(12)	(13)
12 Months Ending	Revenues	NOP	Adj. Taxes	NOPAT	Invest.	Deprec.	Change in Invest.	Change in Working Capital	FCFF	Discount Factor	Discounted FCFF
01/11/2003	18,915										
01/11/2004	22,698	3,725	1,280	2,445	2,261	1,886	375	364	1,706	0.9088	1,550
01/11/2005	27,238	4,470	1,536	2,934	2,713	2,263	449	437	2,047	0.8258	1,691
01/11/2006	32,685	5,364	1,843	3,521	3,255	2,716	539	525	2,457	0.7505	1,844
01/11/2007	39,222	6,436	2,212	4,225	3,907	3,259	647	630	2,948	0.6820	2,011
01/11/2008	47,067	7,724	2,654	5,070	4,688	3,911	777	755	3,538	0.6198	2,193
01/11/2009	56,480	9,268	3,185	6,084	5,625	4,693	932	907	4,245	0.5632	2,391
01/11/2010	67,776	11,122	3,822	7,300	6,750	5,632	1,118	1,088	5,094	0.5119	2,608
01/11/2011	81,331	13,346	4,586	8,761	8,101	6,759	1,342	1,305	6,113	0.4652	2,844
01/11/2012	97,597	16,016	5,503	10,513	9,721	8,110	1,610	1,566	7,336	0.4227	3,101
01/11/2013	117,117	19,219	6,604	12,615	11,865	9,732	1,932	1,880	8,803	0.3841	3,382
	117,117	19,219	6,604	12,615	9,732	9,732	0	0	125,650	0.3841	48,268

EXHIBIT 6-8 Cisco's General Pro Forma Screen

.9088 for year 1, to $[1/(1.1004)^{10}] = .3841$ for year 10. The residual value is equal to $48,268 million and is shown at the bottom of column 13 in Exhibit 6-8.

Recall the calculation of corporate value from Chapter 4:

Corporate Value = Cash Flow Operations
+ Residual Value + Short-Term Assets

This calculation, shown at the top of Exhibit 6-8, has a total corporate or enterprise value of $89,314 million. Also recall from Chapter 4 the calculation of common stock value:

Value to Common Equity = Corporate Value − Debt
− Preferred − Short-Term Liabilities

This calculation also is shown at the top of Exhibit 6-8, and shows a value to common equity of $80,939 million, along with per share *intrinsic stock value of $10.87.*

After the Cost of Capital—The Next Step

In this chapter we have explored the estimation of the rate that's used to discount the estimated free cash flow to the firm. We have looked at the calculation of the weighted average cost of capital, and discussed how to estimate the costs of common equity, debt, and preferred stock.

We have examined the WACC calculation for a company with a complex capital structure, ConEd, in Exhibit 6-5. We have also shown how the WACC for a company with only common stock outstanding, Cisco, is handled by a simple CAPM equation that computes the cost of common equity. We have also seen that using market value for common stock, and book values for debt and preferred stock, is a generally accepted practitioner's way of calculating the WACC of a corporation.

In Chapter 7, we explain where and how an investor can quickly find the information needed to use the DCF approach and make informed, intelligent valuations. Armed with this information, our savvy investor will be ready to conquer the investment world!

Notes

1. A. Damodaran, pp. 48–49.

2. An economic report by Bill Dudley of Goldman Sachs, "The Equity Risk Premium and the Brave New Business Cycle," *U.S. Economics Analyst*, February 21, 1997, gives a good rationale for an " . . . equity risk premium that is consistent with fair value for equities versus bonds is nearly 3 percent," page 6.

CHAPTER 7

Finding Information for Valuations

Save a Tree—Use the Internet

Now that you understand the DCF approach, you may want to test your skill at valuation and see how to make money in the real world. How and where do you find the inputs necessary to take a reasonable stab at valuing a stock?

Prior to the Internet, it was cumbersome to find investment information relating to a company. It involved locating the company's headquarters, contacting the company's investor relations department, and requesting printed annual and quarterly reports. The reports took days or weeks to arrive via the mail. The annual reports give the inputs relating to the company's balance sheet, income statement, and cash flow statement. You could also access information at the local library (assuming that it has a good investment and finance department) and look up back issues of *Value Line* and *Standard & Poor's Stock Guide*—through either hard copy or on microfilm or microfiche. You then could photocopy the relevant pages at $.10 to $.25 per page.

This was a good exercise to do while waiting for annual and quarterly reports to be delivered to your mailbox.

Information that you need to value a stock that is not included in annual reports is: the company's beta, its default risk, the risk-free rate, and the company's expected growth rate. This information comes from other sources. Some info may be gleaned from a good financial newspaper such as *The Wall Street Journal, Barron's, Investor's Business Daily,* or *The New York Times.* But this information-gathering process requires time—and lots of it. That is pre-Internet.

In the post-Internet era, free Web sites give you immediate access to all of the information sources you need to make an informed valuation. We assume that you have access to the Internet, and that all that you now need to know is where to look.

The Internet and Investment Information

The Internet is investor-friendly, with a significant number of Web sites devoted to financial information. Virtually every company with publicly traded stock has its own Web site, which it uses to market products, hire employees, and post annual and quarterly reports, earnings releases, and other financial information.

The format of the financial reports associated with many of these Web sites permits downloading of the entire corporate report. It also may allow selective printing of sections of the report such as the income statement, the balance sheet, and the cash flow schedules. These corporate Web sites should be your primary source of information for most of the corporation-related inputs for valuations.

The Internet is a rapidly evolving information medium. New Web sites spring up daily and old Web sites fold. Some Web sites undergo a facelift or a change of focus, and some free Web sites become subscription based. Any listing and written description of Internet sites is quickly outdated.

Corporate Web Sites

How do you find corporate Web sites on the Internet? You can get on the Internet through America Online or the Microsoft Network, or by using the Netscape browser or the Microsoft Internet Explorer in concert with a local or regional Internet access provider. Each browser, through its *find* function, is capable of searching the Internet for the uniform resource locator (*URL*) address of the Web site of Cisco Systems, or the Microsoft Corporation, or almost any company.

Once you're connected to the Internet, there are a number of Web sites that function as *search engines*. If your browser can't find a corporation's Web site, type in the URL for one of the following search engines. It will take you through its own search procedure to find the Web address that you are looking for:

Google	(*www.google.com/*)
Yahoo	(*www.yahoo.com/*)
Excite	(*www.excite.com/*)
Lycos	(*www.lycos.com/*)
Altavista	(*www.altavista.com/*)
Microsoft Network	(*www.msn.com/*)
America Online	(*www.aol.com/*)

The next best source for corporate information is the Web site of the Securities and Exchange Commission (*www.sec.gov/*). We show the home page of the SEC Web site as Exhibit 7-1. The SEC maintains an information service named EDGAR, for Electronic Data Gathering, Analysis, and Retrieval system. This service collects submissions by companies that are required to file reports—financial and otherwise—with the SEC.

The purpose of EDGAR is to increase the efficiency and fairness of the securities markets by allowing free and immediate access to corporate-related information by investors, corporations, and other economic parties. EDGAR filings are posted to the SEC's Web site no later than 24 hours after their filing. The SEC Web site is well designed and easy to use. However, the SEC-mandated financial reports (10Ks, 10Qs, 8Ks, etc.) are fairly lengthy and have a lot of legal gobbledygook in them.

A great source for direct links to corporate Web sites is Yahoo Finance (*finance.yahoo.com/?u*). In the Yahoo Finance/Profiles link, there is a business summary for the corporation, plus links to the company's home page and its investor relations department. Through those links you can access annual and quarterly reports.

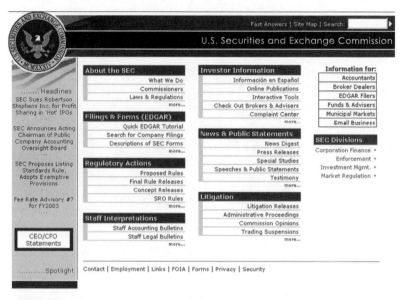

EXHIBIT 7-1 SEC Web Site Home Page

Web Sites Devoted to Investment Information

A number of Web sites are devoted to information relating to the valuation of stock. Some of the sites are free or partially free, some free sites require a viewer to register and obtain a password to use the site, and some provide information to paid subscribers only. The two completely free Web sites that we like best are MSN Investor and Yahoo Finance.

You can get to MSN Investor either through the (*www.msn.com/*) Web site by typing a stock symbol into the slot on the home page and clicking on go, or by typing the fairly long URL for the site, (*moneycentral.msn.com/investor/home.asp*), into your Internet browser. Once at the site, you can examine numerous screens of data describing a company—from a general corporate report, to SEC filings, to earnings estimates, to stock screeners and research wizards. It is a good free site and provides you with information relating to the company and with data regarding the industry in which the company operates. Information and data for the site is provided to MSN by S&P Comstock (*www.spcomstock.com/*), Zack's Investment Research (*www.zacks.com/*), Hoover's Online (*www.hoovers.com*), Thomson Financial Services (*www.thomsonfinancial.com/*), and Media General Financial Services (*www.mgfs.com/*).

Yahoo Finance provides a Web site with extensive company screens that include: market quotes and charts, historical prices, SEC filings, insider transactions, news, options quotes, earnings estimates, links to a corporation's home site and investor relations Web pages, and other information. Information and data is provided to Yahoo Finance by: Edgar Online Inc. (*www.edgar-online.com/*), Market Guide (*www.marketguide.com/*), Reuters (*www.reuters.com/*), and Commodity Systems Inc. (*www.csidata.com/*). Web sites, such as Yahoo Finance and MSN Investor, provide information that is useful for helping to estimate a company's growth rate, a corporation's beta, the 10-year Treasury rates, corporate bond yields, and preferred stock yields, as well as general business news and company-specific news.

For each of the inputs required for the FCFF approach and spreadsheet software, we point you to the Web site that will give you the best and most easily accessible information. Also heed this warning—you can burn up a lot of time without realizing it following links from one site to another in Cyberspace. On the Internet there is more information available about a corporation than almost anyone can absorb. If you enjoy cyber-surfing, have the time to spare, and have no history of carpel tunnel syndrome—great. Point, click, and be merry. If you're just looking to get information to use for a valuation, you may want to follow our suggestions to minimize Internet time.

Web Sites Devoted to Stock Valuation

Recently, several free Web sites that specialize in DCF stock valuation models have become popular with investors. Each has its strengths and weaknesses and we describe them in this section.

ValuePro. This Web site (*www.valuepro.net/*) is near and dear to our hearts. We created the site in concert with the 1999 publication of *Streetsmart Guide to Valuing a Stock,* and we have administered the site since then. The site is devoted to the DCF method of stock valuation and has links that explain the approach in great detail. In 2000, we introduced a free online valuation service that has become popular with users. Type a stock symbol into the slot on the home Web page (Exhibit 7-2), click on the Get Baseline Valuation button, and the online valuation program accesses data sources for information relating to the company that you are valuing. The program calculates 20 variables, puts them into our valuation algorithm, and calculates the intrinsic stock value—our estimate of that day's value of the shares of the company.

Announcing ValuePro 2002 Software!!

▷ Home

▷ Learn the ValuePro Approach

▷ Streetsmart Guide to Valuing a Stock

▷ Buy Streetsmart Guide

▷ Buy ValuePro 2002 Software

▷ Guide to the ValuePro 2002 Software

▷ Buy Running With the Bulls

▷ Frequently Asked Questions

▷ Message Board

▷ Contact Us

▷ Terms of Service

▷ About the Online Valuation

Thank you for your patience during our recent site downtime. We have improved not only the efficiency of our valuation scripts, but also our message board and online payment processing, which is now up and running.

ValuePro 2002 is our new easy-to-use stock valuation program that interacts with our online valuation service. Now you can download data from our web site to your computer and use ValuePro 2002 to analyze your investments. The price is only $44.95. Please see our Guide to the ValuePro 2002 Software for an in-depth description.

Try our online stock valuation service. Enter the stock symbol, click on the Get Baseline Valuation button, and we do the rest. The inputs used to value the stock are updated periodically. You can change any input and recalculate a stock value. Learn more about using the online valuation by clicking here.

Enter Stock Symbol: [   ] | Get Baseline Valuation |

We are developing a stock value/stock price screening program which will rank stocks based upon a value-to-price ratio and a portfolio valuation program.

| Value Screening | | Portfolio Valuation |

ValuePro.net was founded by three financial engineers/finance professors to develop and distribute inexpensive, easy to use and understand valuation tools.

1445712 hits since June 1, 2000

Web Site Development by (i) Intelligent Data Management.

EXHIBIT 7-2   Valuepro.net Home Web Page

The Valuepro.net Web site displays a screen (Exhibit 7-3) that shows each valuation input. You can go to any or all of the input cells, put your own estimates into the cells, hit the Recalculate button, and the online valuation program calculates the new intrinsic stock value based on the inputs that you have provided. If you want to see the detailed pro forma statement associated with the valuation, click on the Cash Flows button, and a cash flow schedule based on the underlying inputs appears. You can then click the Value Another Stock button and begin the process anew. There is no limitation to the number of valuations you may perform, and the valuations are free.

The strengths of the Web site and the online valuation program are that it is easy to use and understand, is completely interactive, and is totally transparent. Just type the symbol into the slot and the program

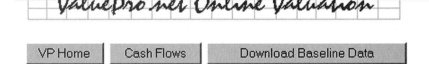

Online Valuation for CSCO - 1 / 9 / 2003

Intrinsic Stock Value	4.55	Recalculate	Value Another Stock

Excess Return Period (yrs)	10	Depreciation Rate (% of Rev)	4.6
Revenues ($mil)	19312.0	Investment Rate (% of Rev)	10.19
Growth Rate (%)	11.5	Working Capital (% of Rev)	11.24
Net Oper. Profit Margin (%)	12.28	Short-Term Assets ($mil)	15096.0
Tax Rate (%)	28.050	Short-Term Liab. ($mil)	7871
Stock Price ($)	13.7200	Equity Risk Premium (%)	3
Shares Outstanding (mil)	7233.0	Company Beta	1.5225
10-Yr Treasury Yield (%)	5	Value Debt Out. ($mil)	0
Bond Spread Treasury (%)	1.5	Value Pref. Stock Out. ($mil)	0
Preferred Stock Yield (%)	7.5	Company WACC (%)	9.57

EXHIBIT 7-3   Valuepro.net Online Valuation—Cisco

does the rest. With the exception of the WACC input, which is a calculated number, you can change any input that you desire, and the new intrinsic value based on your inputs pops up on the computer screen. You can see each input and each assumption and follow the cash flows to verify that the intrinsic value is consistent with the inputs. Another nice feature is that there (currently) is no advertising or annoying banner or pop-up ads on the site.

The weakness of the Web site is that it is a barebones site. There is no symbol-lookup feature and no ancillary information aspects to the stocks that are being valued. The singular focus is on intrinsic stock value. It is also a very low budget operation. Data is updated weekly, and there is no effort to comb the data to find inputs that are highly implausible or wrong. The online valuation service does not yet work well for some highly levered stocks, such as REITs and financials, nor does it work well for portfolio companies, such as ICGE or Berkshire Hathaway. (Sorry Warren, we did it again.)

We show the inputs associated with the Valuepro.net online valuation of Cisco on January 9, 2003. Cisco stock price closed at $14.95 per share, and the online service estimated the intrinsic stock value of Cisco to be $4.55. Several of the inputs on the online valuation service are different from the inputs that we used on August 14, 2002 when we carefully examined Cisco's financial statements and valued Cisco using the ValuePro 2002 Software.

Quicken.com. The Quicken investor Web site (*www.quicken.com/*) provides many screens and services to an investor. One of the screens is an intrinsic value calculator. If you click on Quicken's Security Evaluator link, and type CSCO into the slot, an intrinsic value screen will appear with a current price. On January 9, 2003 the stock price was $14.95, and the intrinsic value was $12.67, indicating that Cisco was overvalued. There is a small degree of interactivity—you can change the assumed earnings growth rate and the discounting rate (see Exhibit 7-4), but that's about it.

The strength of the Web site is due to all of the ancillary information that it provides. The intrinsic value program is easy to use and understand. The interactivity of the program is helpful but is limited and the algorithm that this site uses to come up with intrinsic value is opaque.

VectorVest. VectorVest (*www.vectorvest.com/*) is primarily a subscription service where you pay a monthly fee and have access to proprietary models and data for stock valuation. VectorVest has a free stock analysis service that is limited to three valuations per day per user. On January 9, 2003, we plugged CSCO into the Vector Vest free stock analysis slot and clicked. We received a dense three pages of

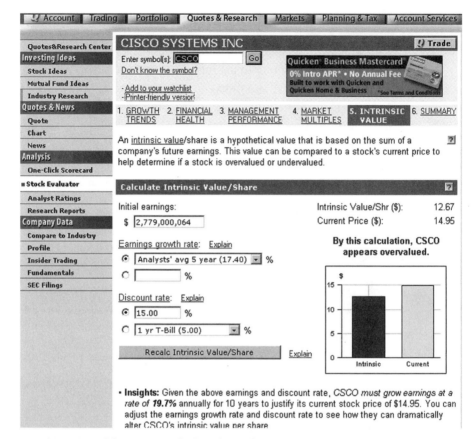

EXHIBIT 7-4 Quicken.com Intrinsic Value—Cisco

printouts listing Cisco's price—$14.95, its value—$15.57, and several other metrics, which included relative value, relative safety, relative timing, VST (value, safety, timing), along with a recommendation—which in this case was *buy*.

The strength of the VectorVest free service is that it is easy to use and you receive an intrinsic value. The bad news is that you can only use it for three valuations per day, there is no interactivity, and the valuation process is a black box. You have no idea how the intrinsic value is calculated.

In the section that follows, we segment the information that you need to run a valuation into three categories: the easy-to-find company info, the company inputs requiring estimation, and the cost of capital inputs.

Cash Flow Valuation Inputs—Easy to Find

We continue with the Cisco example valuation. The first order of business is to use our computer to tap into the Internet via our Penn State Internet connection. We use the Microsoft Internet Explorer browser to go to the Cisco Systems corporate Web site (*www.cisco.com/*).

We enter Cisco's Home Page (Exhibit 7-5), and click on the *Investor Relations* (Exhibit 7-6) link.

Another click on the *Financials/SEC Filings* link (Exhibit 7-7), gives us access to *the 2002 Financial Statements* section, which is where we want to be.

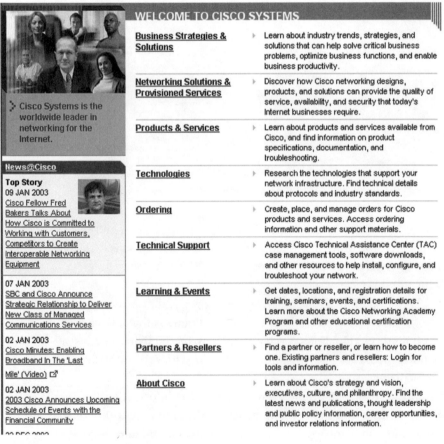

EXHIBIT 7-5   Cisco Systems Home Page

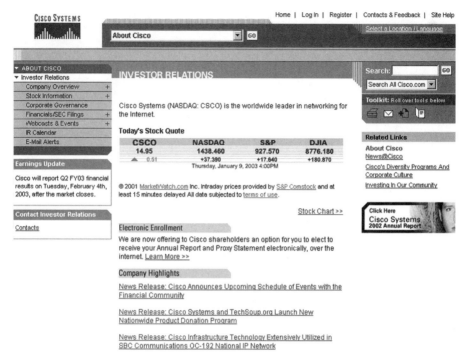

EXHIBIT 7-6 Cisco Systems Investor Relations Link

In Chapter 5, we previously printed the following sections: the consolidated statements of operations (Exhibit 5-2), the consolidated balance sheet (Exhibit 5-4), and the consolidated statements of cash flows (Exhibit 5-3). Here is how we used those reports.

Income Statement Information

To run the FCFF valuation approach, we needed to calculate ratios taken from information provided from Cisco's income statement, which it calls *consolidated statements of operations,* as shown in Exhibit 5-2, for the fiscal year ending 7/27/2002. From this statement, we took the following information: net revenues, operating costs and expenses, income before provision for taxes, provision for taxes, and weighted average shares outstanding—basic and diluted.

The income statement has information for three fiscal years—2002, 2001, and 2000. Three years of data (as opposed to one) helps us better understand the corporation, how consistently it has performed, and

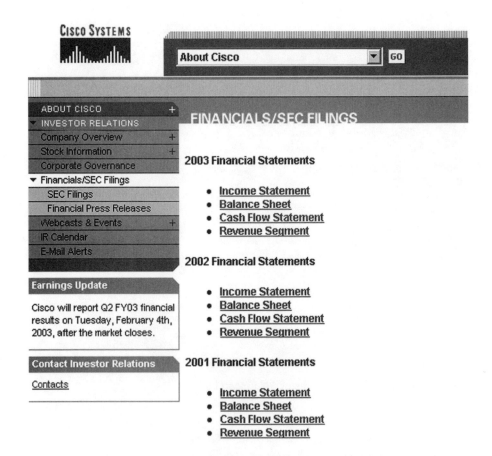

EXHIBIT 7-7 Cisco Systems Financials/SEC Filings Link

what trends in revenue growth rate or net operating margins it has experienced. The information from the income statement that we needed to value Cisco is shown in Table 7-1.

Balance Sheet Information

For the Cisco valuation, we calculated ratios based upon information from Cisco's balance sheet, as shown in Exhibit 5-4. From this statement we took the following information related to working capital: accounts receivable, inventories, accounts payable, total current assets, and total current liabilities. We also took information relating to Cisco's short-term asset/liability position balances, and the amount of debt (book value) and preferred stock (book value) outstanding.

TABLE 7-1   Cisco Systems Income Statement Information

(in millions of dollars)			
	2002	2001	2000
Total revenues	$18,915	$22,293	$18,928
Total operating costs and expenses	$15,232	$21,217	$14,209
Operating Income	$3,683	$1,076	$4,719
NOPM (%)	19.47%	4.83%	24.93%
3-year average NOPM (%)			**16.41%**
Income before provision for taxes	$2,710	−$874	$4,343
Provision for income taxes	$817	$140	$1,675
Effective income tax rate	30.15%	n.a.	38.57%
3-year average tax rate (%)			**34.36%**
Weighted average shares out–basic	7,301	7,196	6,917
Weighted average shares out–diluted	**7,447**	7,196	7,438

The balance sheet has information for two fiscal years—2002 and 2001. The balance sheet information that we used to value Cisco is shown in Table 7-2.

Cash Flow Statement Information

The final pieces of cash flow information to value Cisco's common stock came from its statement of cash flow (Exhibit 5-3). From this statement, we took the following information related to cash flow— depreciation, investment in property, plant, and equipment.

The cash flow statement has information for three fiscal years— 2002, 2001, and 2000. Cash flow statement information that we needed to value Cisco is shown in Table 7-3.

The information that we obtained from annual and quarterly reports gave us valuation inputs relating to revenue, cash flow data, short-term assets, short-term liabilities, amount of shares outstanding, and (book, not market) value of debt and preferred stock outstanding.

These reports also gave us the historic information that is helpful in estimating cash flow inputs, such as the revenue growth rate, net

TABLE 7-2   Cisco Systems Balance Sheet Information

(in millions of dollars)		
	2002	2001
Working capital data		
Accounts receivable	$1,105	$1,466
+ Inventories	$880	$1,684
− Accounts payable	$470	$644
= Net working capital	$1,515	$2,506
Net working capital/revenue	8.01%	11.24%
2-year average nwc (%)		**9.63%**
Total current assets	**$17,433**	$12,835
Total current liabilities	**$8,375**	$8,096
Long-term capital data		
Debt outstanding (book value)	0	0
Preferred stock (book value)	0	0

operating profit margin, tax rate, depreciation rate, new investment rate, and incremental working capital rate. We discuss where to find and how to interpret the information for our estimation in the next section.

TABLE 7-3   Cisco System Cash Flow Information

(in millions of dollars)			
	2002	2001	2000
Depreciation and amortization	$1,957	$2,236	$863
Depreciation/revenue (%)	10.35%	10.03%	4.56%
3-year average (%)			**8.31%**
Property and Equipment Expense	$2,641	$2,271	$1,086
Property expense/revenue (%)	13.96%	10.19%	5.74%
3-year average (%)			**9.96%**

Cash Flow Valuation Inputs Requiring Estimation

The most important cash flow inputs, the ones that drive the intrinsic stock value computation for the FCFF approach, are the estimates for the growth rate and the net operating profit margin for the company. On Wall Street, the ability to estimate these numbers is what separates the *All-American*[1] stock analysts from the also-rans. In addition, we must estimate the company's tax rate, depreciation rate, and new investment levels, and the expected change in working capital that's required to support the business.

How do we estimate these inputs? Unless a company has radically changed its operating procedures or has drastically restructured its lines of business, most analysts use a historic averaging process as a first approximation to estimate these inputs. We can estimate these inputs in one of three rational ways: use historic performance of the company as a guide to what are the likely outcomes in the future; use expectations of analysts and/or other market participants; or use a mixture of the two blended with our own common sense.

Historic performance of the company usually acts as a pretty good, although far from perfect, indicator of potential future performance. If revenues have been growing at a five-year compound growth rate of 8 percent, an estimated revenue growth rate of 25 percent may seem a tad aggressive—unless there's a new knock-em-up product (such as Viagra) or the company has undergone a massive upheaval. Recall that as a company grows in size and as the industry in which it operates becomes more competitive, the growth rate naturally drifts to the growth rate of the economy for reasons we discuss in Chapter 5.

The trend in data may highlight an area of potential concern. For example, Cisco's average NOPM for the past three years is 16.41 percent, but it has been on an erratic path—24.93 percent in 2000 to 4.83 percent in 2001 to 19.47 percent in 2002. This pattern may indicate that Cisco does not have the pricing power that it once had, and investors should be concerned about future NOPMs. The trend in revenue for Cisco is particularly disturbing. Revenue grew 17.8 percent, from $18,928 million in 2000 to $22,293 million in 2001, and then declined by 17.8 percent to $18,915 million in 2002.

Among the profusion of Web sites devoted to investment research and advice, we have found that two of the best sites having free areas that give information about revenue or earnings estimates for a company are Zacks Investment Research, and the First Call portion of the Thomson Financial Web site. Don't be overly optimistic when you value a stock, and be prepared to temper the analyst consensus numbers to estimates that you feel are attainable.

Cost of Capital Valuation Inputs

The final set of inputs we need for the FCFF valuation approach and for the ValuePro 2002 software relates to the company's weighted average cost of capital.

Current Stock Price and Shares Outstanding

The current stock price is an important input because it affects the market capitalization of the corporation and its WACC. As the stock price increases, the percentage of the company's market capitalization that is represented by stock increases. Since common stock is the cost-of-capital component with the highest yield, as the company's stock price increases its cost of capital increases.

The Internet can give you current stock prices, usually with a small delay. MSN.com has an easy-to-use stock quote service on its home page. When you plug in the company's name or stock symbol into the slot you get a current quote (20-minute delay) for the stock and you are whisked to MSN Investor where additional screens and data are available. Yahoo Finance has a similar setup and service. Numerous free Web sites offer quotes, and your choice of site depends upon your own preferences.

Both Yahoo Finance and MSN Investor list the amount of shares outstanding on the company's profile screen. Amount of shares outstanding changes over the course of a year or a quarter, sometimes significantly. Some Web sites keep tabs on this input and update it on a periodic basis. The most likely number that will be listed on the site is the actual number, not the diluted number, of shares outstanding that are reported by the company on its most recent quarterly report.

10-Year Treasury Bond Yield

With the exception of certain risk management instruments such as insurance, which usually has a negative expected rate of return, the minimum expected rate of return from any investment should be at least as great as the yield available from a risk-free investment. For common stocks, we use the yield associated with 10-year U.S. Treasury Bonds as a minimum acceptable rate of return.

The current yield on the 10-year Treasury can be found in any newspaper with a good financial section or through numerous financial Web sites of which the two easiest for us to use are Yahoo Finance and MSN Investor. The Bloomberg Web site (*www.bloomberg.com/*) is a great source for information on the U.S. Treasury market and international debt and currency markets.

The official Web site for U.S. Treasury Bond yields is that of the Federal Reserve Board of Governors which posts a daily form H15 release. The Federal Reserve Web address for the H15 release is (*www.federalreserve.gov/releases/H15/update/*).

Company Bond Yield Spread to Treasury

Also given on the Fed H15 release are the current bond yields for Moody's Aaa-rated and Baa-rated corporate bonds. The indicative yields for these two types of bonds on September 18, 2002, were 6.13 percent and 7.38 percent. Another debt-related Web site is Bonds-Online (*www.bonds-online.com/*). Through its *Treasuries* link, a current complete yield curve is displayed, along with 10 years of historic year-end data, which gives you a great perspective about what can realistically happen in the way of interest rate movement over the excess return period. Also, the *Corporates* link of Bonds-Online gives *spread to Treasuries* data by year of maturity and rating category for five classifications of corporate bonds: banks, financials, industrials, transportation, and utilities—a good source for corporate bond information.

Company Preferred Stock Yield

If the company has preferred stock outstanding that is traded on an exchange, the Internet-related quote services that we described above give you preferred stock prices for the company. To get the yield for a preferred stock that has no stated maturity, simply divide the dividend rate by the preferred stock price. For example, an issue of preferred stock of Consolidated Edison has a dividend of $5.00 per year and was trading on September 18, 2002, at a price of $77.08. Its yield is calculated by dividing $5.00 by $77.08 = ($5/$77.08) = 6.49 percent.

Equity Risk Premium

The equity risk premium is an estimate of the excess return an investor expects to earn on a *risky* stock relative to a risk-free asset. We use the yield on the 10-year U.S. Treasury Bond as a measure of the return on a risk-free asset. The equity risk premium is not an item that you stumble upon while surfing the Web. Aswath Damodaran, on his Web page (*www.stern.nyu.edu/~adamodar/*), calculates implied equity risk premiums on a yearly basis from 1960 until 2001. His most recent calculations for the year 2001 show an implied equity risk premium for the S&P 500 of 1.73 percent, using a dividend discount valuation model, and 3.62 percent, using the free cash flow to equity model of valuation. Based on the economy of early 2003, we believe that 3 percent represents a reasonable equity risk premium.

Company-Specific Beta

As we have discussed, a company's beta is the risk measure used in the CAPM, the model most frequently used by market professionals in assessing the risk of a stock. Both Yahoo Finance and MSN Investor list their estimate of a stock's beta. For example, on the date that Yahoo had a beta estimate of 1.93 for Cisco listed in the *Profiles* link, MSN Investor had a beta estimate of 1.90. Why the difference, and which beta should you use?

A company's beta is calculated by a statistical test (known as *regression analysis*) relating the price movement of the stock and the price movement of the stock market in general. Various market participants use different time periods and measurement techniques in performing these calculations, and different beta estimates may result.

When a difference arises, the most conservative approach, which results in a higher WACC and lower stock value, is to use the higher beta. Another approach is to use the average of the betas for the analysis. For the valuations in this book, we use the higher value of beta.

Value of Debt and Preferred Stock Outstanding

Book values of debt and preferred stock are listed in the balance sheet section of the corporation's annual reports. The best (and to our knowledge, only) way to get an accurate reading of total *market value* of debt and preferred stock is the old-fashioned way—price each separate issue and aggregate the values.

For some companies, like Cisco, which has no debt or preferred stock outstanding, this exercise is easy. For corporations like Consolidated Edison, which has 38 issues of various types of debt outstanding, this procedure can be tedious. What is a rational way of handling this potentially time-consuming problem?

Here's how we do it. If we're just making a quick and dirty valuation to see how a company is trading by comparing it to its rough intrinsic value, we use the book value of debt and preferred stock as reported in the company's annual or quarterly report. If we are being employed under a consulting contract on a grossly overpaid hourly basis to perform a valuation, we perform an in-depth analysis of every feature and option embedded in the debt or preferred stock so that we can value the company to the penny (and maximize our billing time).

It's fortunate that the market value of debt and preferred stock generally does not vary too much from its book value. With the exception of valuing a highly leveraged company for which debt and preferred stock make up a large percentage of the market capitalization, the use of book values does not significantly bias the analysis of the common stock's intrinsic value.

Custom Valuations—The Next Step

In Chapter 5, we discuss how to estimate the future cash flows of a company, using Cisco as an example. In Chapter 6 we see how to estimate the company's WACC, using Cisco and Consolidated Edison as examples. In this chapter, we have discussed where to get the various inputs needed to perform a valuation for Cisco, and have given you suggestions for getting the info while minimizing your online computer time.

The exercise that follows pulls together the inputs that we gathered in this chapter. In Chapter 8 we get a bit fancier and vary our assumptions regarding revenue growth rates, net operating profit margins, and WACC's. First, we finish our Cisco valuation example.

Valuation Exercise: Cisco

Let's put our Cisco valuation together using the inputs that we discuss above. On the ValuePro 2002 general input screen (see Exhibit 6-6), we plug in the different inputs, and the result is an intrinsic value of $10.87. Placing those inputs into the program, we get a cost of capital screen (see Exhibit 6-7) showing a WACC of 10.04 percent.

The general pro forma screen (see Exhibit 6-8) shows a total corporate value of $89,314 million, a total value to common equity of $80,939 million, and an intrinsic stock value per share of $10.87.

In the next chapter, we fine-tune our skills in the use of the FCFF approach in more complex, custom valuations and see how to value some difficult companies.

Notes

1. *Institutional Investor Magazine* polls institutional investors and creates an annual listing of the best analysts in different sectors of the stock market. The winners of each sector receive the title "All American" and this designation is worth an additional several hundred thousand per year in compensation to the analyst.

CHAPTER 8

Valuing a Stock—Putting It All Together

Overview

In this chapter, we value four companies—Citigroup, Merrill Lynch, and Berkshire Hathaway—all large-cap financial companies, and Washington Real Estate Investment Trust, a small-cap REIT. For each company, we make an initial *base-line* valuation, in which our cash flow and cost of capital estimates are based upon historic averages, and our growth estimates are based upon consensus analysts' expectations. This base-line valuation should give us a feel for how the market views the company's stock.

It's important to be realistic about assumptions and inputs. Too often during the high-tech bubble, analysts' expectations of growth were far too aggressive. These optimistic growth estimates generated inflated valuations and outrageous stock prices. When corporate management could not achieve the impossible goals set by Wall Street, they either cooked the books or watched their stock prices plummet and their option packages expire worthless. The excesses of the high-tech bubble have taught us to be cautious with assumptions and to use reasonable estimates!

In the valuations that follow, we vary growth rates, NOPMs, and cost of capital to see how changes in these variables affect intrinsic values. Varying inputs result in a range of value for a stock rather than a single point, and it allows us to see which cash flows and cost of capital estimates are most important to the different companies. When we value a stock, we want to use assumptions that are conservative, particularly regarding growth rates.

Based upon our valuation, we rate each stock as a buy, sell, or hold. Our rating is a *hypothetical rating*. Do not buy, sell, or hold a stock based on anyone's valuations other than your own, particularly valuations based on outdated information, as all of these will be when you read this book. You make your own decisions based upon your own analysis.

Recall that the value of any investment is the sum of its expected cash flows, discounted at a rate that takes into account the risk and timing of the cash flows. When we valued Microsoft and Cisco, the expected cash flows were the companies' net operating profit after taxes, minus net investment; and the discounting rates were each company's weighted average cost of capital. Net operating profit or operating income is simple to calculate. First, we go to the company's income statement, find its revenue from continuing operations, and subtract CGS, SG&A, and R&D. What's left over is operating income, or NOP. Operating income, for normal companies that make and sell products and services, such as Microsoft, Cisco, and McDonald's, does not include interest income, investment income, and interest expense.

The accounting statements of financial companies (*FCs*), such as commercial banks, investment banks, insurance companies, and savings banks, have a different format than the financial statements of Cisco or Microsoft. Interest income, investment income, and interest expense are included in operating income. For FCs, interest and investment income are often the largest components of revenue. Likewise, interest expense for an FC is usually its largest cost. To properly value a financial company and companies in other industries where the financial statement templates don't conform exactly to our examples, we tweak our valuation approach.

Valuing a Financial Company

An FC earns revenue by creating financial products called *secondary securities*: such as life insurance policies, savings and checking accounts, annuity products, and pension products, and by selling those products to consumers. The FC uses the revenue raised from the sale of the secondary securities to purchase higher-yielding assets called *primary securities*, such as mortgages, loans, bonds, and stocks. The interest, dividends, principal, and gains from the primary securities, along with the other assets of the FC, pay the cash flows associated with the secondary securities—the monthly pension checks, or the claims under a casualty policy, or the life insurance payment—whatever products the FC has created.

The activities underlying most FCs are based upon buying and selling claims to different streams of money. Buying and selling money is a very competitive business, which should temper assumptions of outrageous growth in these industries. Here are the adjustments that we make when we value a financial company.

1. *Calculation of Operating Income.* For financial companies, operating revenue includes all normal revenue items plus interest income, dividends received, and other investment income. Operating expense includes all normal expense items plus interest expense. The calculation of operating income is more inclusive for a financial company than for an industrial or high-tech company.

2. *The Discounting Rate.* Since interest expense for an FC is included in operating expenses, when we calculate operating income, it does not matter if the interest expense is attributable to a short-term liability or to a long-term debt. Because interest expense is included in calculating operating income, all of the cash flow of an FC after payment of taxes belongs to the preferred and common shareholders. This effectively makes the discounting rate of a financial company equal to its cost of equity capital. To accommodate this adjustment for the ValuePro 2002 software, we include the long-term debt of the company we're valuing in the short-term liability category. The placement of debt in short-term liabilities effectively makes the calculation of the WACC equal to the cost of common and preferred equity.

3. *Investment and Depreciation Rates.* Property, plant, and equipment expenditures and depreciation charges are significantly lower for financial companies than for other companies. However, capital expenditures for FCs often include the purchase of

businesses to fuel growth. If that is the case, the cost of buying businesses should be included in capital expenditures, and in the calculation of the investment rate.

4. *Balance Sheet Adjustments.* The balance sheet of most FCs does not separate assets and liabilities into current and long-term categories. Therefore, when we calculate the company's short-term assets, we take total assets and subtract goodwill and intangible assets, subtract any other asset with questionable value, and also subtract long-term assets such as PP&E from total assets.

5. *Incremental Working Capital.* Because there is no differentiation between current and long-term assets and liabilities for an FC, we adjust working capital charges to zero. A financial company generally invests all of its funds in other financial assets, most of which have the characteristics of current assets rather than PP&E. For an FC, working capital isn't a sidelight that supports a business, such as for a manufacturer or a service company. Working capital is the business of many FCs.

Let's get started by looking at one of the preeminent financial institutions in the United States and the world—Citigroup.

Valuing Citigroup—December 17, 2002

Price-$37.13, Value-$47.13 to $88.03, *Strong Buy*
General Description of Citigroup—a Global Finance
Holding Company

Incorporated in 1988, Citigroup (C: *www.citigroup.com/*) is a diversified global finance holding company that services almost 200 million customer accounts and employs 268,000 employees in over 100 countries. Citigroup is the world's largest financial institution. It conducts its activities through subsidiaries that are leaders in their respective fields: Citibank in commercial banking, Salomon Smith Barney in investment banking and brokerage activities, Travelers Property Casualty Corp. in property and casualty insurance, and the Travelers Insurance Company in life insurance and annuity products. Citigroup divides its operations and businesses into several groups: Global Consumer, Global Corporate, Global Investment Management and Private Banking, and Investment Activities.

Global Consumer provides banking, lending, investment services, and insurance to consumers and small businesses throughout the world. These products are provided by the following operating entities: Citibanking North America, Citibank Online, Mortgage Banking, North American Cards, CitiFinancial, and Primerica Financial Services.

Global Corporate provides investment advice, investment banking services, and commercial banking services to corporations, governments, and institutions in over 100 countries through its Corporate and Investment Bank (CIB). It underwrites and distributes debt and equity securities for corporations and for foreign, state, governmental, and governmental-sponsored agencies.

Global Investment Management and Private Banking offer a broad range of asset management, insurance, and annuity products. Traveler's Life and Annuity, Citigroup Asset Management, and Citigroup Private Bank provide these products to institutional, and high net worth retail clients. Investment Activities consist primarily of Citigroup's venture capital activities and special situations regarding Citigroup's lending activities to foreign entities.

Citigroup's market equity of $182 billion makes it the number-one financial services company in the world. That market value is 12.6 times earnings of $14.8 billion. Citigroup pays an annual dividend of $0.72 per share. It actively repurchases shares in the open market and repurchased 87 million shares in 2002. Its five-year price history is shown in Exhibit 8-1.

Citigroup's stock has recently been under a cloud due to concerns regarding its relationship with Enron and a series of investor suits, and state and Federal legal actions against Salomon Smith Barney relating to underwriting activities in the telecom sector. That cloud lifted on December 20, 2002, when Salomon agreed to pay $300 million in fines to the SEC and state securities regulators to settle an investigation into the behavior of some of its stock research analysts. The agreement was reached after the date of this valuation and is not reflected in the analysis, the stock price, or the intrinsic value.

Developing the Valuation Inputs—Citigroup

No valuation is timeless. A company's intrinsic value changes as its prospects, product mix, competitive position, and product market ad-

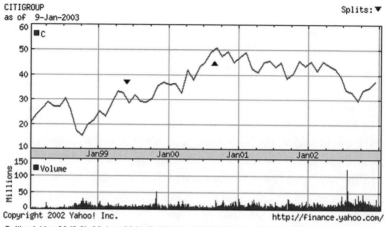

CITIGROUP
as of   9-Jan-2003   Splits: ▼

Copyright 2002 Yahoo! Inc.   http://finance.yahoo.com/

Splits: 1-Mar-93 [3:2], 30-Aug-93 [4:3], 28-May-96 [3:2], 25-Nov-96 [4:3], 20-Nov-97 [3:2], 1-Jun-
99 [3:2], 28-Aug-00 [4:3]

EXHIBIT 8-1   Citigroup Five-Year Stock Price Chart

just to new technologies, consumer needs, capital demands, and market psychology.

It's important to incorporate the most recent available information into a valuation. The fiscal year for Citigroup ends on December 31st. The latest audited information that was publicly available at the time of this valuation is for the fiscal year ending December 31, 2001, a full year stale. In this situation it is important to look at quarterly earnings releases (which are not audited) to help to assess more recent performance of the corporation. Citigroup, on October 15, 2002, posted a third-quarter earnings release for the quarter ending September 30, 2002 on its Web site.

The earnings release showed a more current picture of the corporation and was the source of much of the information incorporated in this valuation. (See Citigroup's Web site for the earnings release.)We have included Citigroup's audited 2001 income statement, balance sheet, and cash flow statement as Exhibits 8-2, 8-3, and 8-4, respectively.

We developed our valuation inputs from information provided in the third-quarter earnings release, in Citigroup's 2001 Annual Report, and on financial Web sites.

Revenues. In order of importance, the revenue sources for Citigroup are: loan interest and fees, other interest and dividends, commissions

CONSOLIDATED STATEMENT OF INCOME

Citigroup Inc. and Subsidiaries

In millions of dollars, except per share amounts	Year ended December 31,		
	2001	2000	1999
Revenues			
Loan interest, including fees	$ 39,616	$ 37,377	$33,018
Other interest and dividends	26,949	27,562	21,971
Insurance premiums	13,460	12,429	11,504
Commissions and fees	15,944	16,363	13,229
Principal transactions	5,544	5,981	5,160
Asset management and administration fees	5,389	5,338	4,164
Realized gains from sales of investments	578	806	541
Other income	4,542	5,970	4,809
Total revenues	· 112,022	111,826	94,396
Interest expense	31,965	36,638	28,674
Total revenues, net of interest expense	80,057	75,188	65,722
Benefits, claims and credit losses			
Policyholder benefits and claims	11,759	10,147	9,120
Provision for credit losses	6,800	5,339	4,760
Total benefits, claims and credit losses	18,559	15,486	13,880
Operating expenses			
Non-insurance compensation and benefits	19,449	18,633	16,169
Insurance underwriting, acquisition, and operating	3,921	3,643	3,765
Restructuring- and merger-related items	458	759	(53)
Other operating expenses	15,773	15,524	13,810
Total operating expenses	39,601	38,559	33,691
Income before income taxes, minority interest and cumulative effect of accounting changes	· 21,897	21,143	18,151
Provision for income taxes	7,526	7,525	6,530
Minority interest, net of income taxes	87	99	251
Income before cumulative effect of accounting changes	14,284	13,519	11,370
Cumulative effect of accounting changes	(158)	—	(127)
Net income	$ 14,126	$ 13,519	$11,243
Basic earnings per share			
Income before cumulative effect of accounting changes	$ 2.82	$ 2.69	$ 2.26
Cumulative effect of accounting changes	(0.03)	—	(0.03)
Net income	$ 2.79	$ 2.69	$ 2.23
Weighted average common shares outstanding	5,031.7	4,977.0	4,979.2
Diluted earnings per share			
Income before cumulative effect of accounting changes	$ 2.75	$ 2.62	$ 2.19
Cumulative effect of accounting changes	(0.03)	—	(0.02)
Net income	$ 2.72	$ 2.62	$ 2.17
Adjusted weighted average common shares outstanding	5,147.0	5,122.2	5,127.8

EXHIBIT 8-2   Citigroup 2001 Income Statement

and fees, insurance premiums, principal transactions, and asset management fees. The 2001 income statement listed *$112.022 billion* as the most recent annual revenue for Citigroup.

Revenue Growth Rate. The historic revenue growth of Citigroup has been good, growing from $80.5 billion in 1997 to $112.0 billion in 2001—a compound annual growth rate of 8.6 percent, but the growth rate has been decelerating. Revenues were flat between 2000 and 2001, and decreased by 7.8 percent in the third quarter of 2002 when compared to the third quarter of 2001. The principal reason for lower revenue growth was due to a general drop in interest rates, a two-edge sword. Lower interest rates resulted in lower interest income, but low

CONSOLIDATED STATEMENT OF FINANCIAL POSITION   *Citigroup Inc. and Subsidiaries*

In millions of dollars	December 31, 2001	December 31, 2000
Assets		
Cash and due from banks (including segregated cash and other deposits)	$ 18,515	$ 14,621
Deposits at interest with banks	19,216	16,164
Federal funds sold and securities borrowed or purchased under agreements to resell	134,809	105,877
Brokerage receivables	35,155	25,696
Trading account assets (including $36,351 and $30,502 pledged to creditors at December 31, 2001 and December 31, 2000, respectively)	144,904	132,513
Investments (including $15,475 and $3,354 pledged to creditors at December 31, 2001 and December 31, 2000, respectively)	160,837	120,122
Loans, net of unearned income		
Consumer	244,159	228,879
Commercial	147,774	138,143
Loans, net of unearned income	391,933	367,022
Allowance for credit losses	(10,088)	(8,961)
Total loans, net	381,845	358,061
Reinsurance recoverables	12,373	10,716
Separate and variable accounts	25,569	24,947
Other assets	118,227	93,493
Total assets	**$1,051,450**	**$902,210**
Liabilities		
Non-interest-bearing deposits in U.S. offices	$ 23,054	$ 21,694
Interest-bearing deposits in U.S. offices	110,388	58,913
Non-interest-bearing deposits in offices outside the U.S.	18,779	13,811
Interest-bearing deposits in offices outside the U.S.	222,304	206,168
Total deposits	374,525	300,586
Federal funds purchased and securities loaned or sold under agreements to repurchase	153,511	110,625
Brokerage payables	32,891	15,882
Trading account liabilities	80,543	85,107
Contractholder funds and separate and variable accounts	48,932	44,884
Insurance policy and claims reserves	49,294	44,666
Investment banking and brokerage borrowings	14,804	18,227
Short-term borrowings	24,461	51,675
Long-term debt	121,631	111,778
Other liabilities	62,486	47,654
Citigroup or subsidiary obligated mandatorily redeemable securities of		
subsidiary trusts holding solely junior subordinated debt securities of—Parent	4,850	2,300
—Subsidiary	2,275	2,620
Total liabilities	**970,203**	**836,004**
Stockholders' equity		
Preferred stock ($1.00 par value; authorized shares: 30 million), at aggregate liquidation value	1,525	1,745
Common stock ($.01 par value; authorized shares: 15 billion),		
issued shares: 2001—5,477,416,254 shares and 2000—5,351,143,583 shares	55	54
Additional paid-in capital	23,196	16,504
Retained earnings	69,803	58,862
Treasury stock, at cost: 2001—328,727,790 shares and 2000—328,921,189 shares	(11,099)	(10,213)
Accumulated other changes in equity from nonowner sources	(844)	123
Unearned compensation	(1,389)	(869)
Total stockholders' equity	**81,247**	**86,206**
Total liabilities and stockholders' equity	**$1,051,450**	**$902,210**

EXHIBIT 8-3   Citigroup 2001 Balance Sheet

rates also drove down interest expense. Interest costs are Citigroup's most significant expense item. Citigroup's income from continuing operations before income tax increased, growing by 16.4 percent and 3.6 percent over the last two years, and 11.6 percent over the third quarter.

As far as growth goes, let's see what the experts think. Zacks Investment Research gathers information from stock market analysts relating to earnings estimates and stock recommendations. Zacks looks

CONSOLIDATED STATEMENT OF CASH FLOWS

Citigroup Inc. and Subsidiaries

In millions of dollars	Year ended December 31,		
	2001	2000	1999
Cash flows from operating activities			
Net income	$ 14,126	$ 13,519	$ 11,243
Adjustments to reconcile net income to net cash provided by operating activities:			
Amortization of deferred policy acquisition costs and value of insurance in force	2,062	1,676	1,613
Additions to deferred policy acquisition costs	(2,592)	(2,154)	(1,961)
Depreciation and amortization	2,417	2,648	2,226
Deferred tax provision	1,014	1,537	598
Provision for credit losses	6,800	5,339	4,760
Change in trading account assets	(12,391)	(25,452)	9,928
Change in trading account liabilities	(4,564)	(5,393)	(3,848)
Change in Federal funds sold and securities borrowed or purchased under agreements to resell	(26,932)	6,778	(17,824)
Change in Federal funds purchased and securities loaned or sold under agreements to repurchase	39,834	18,034	11,566
Change in brokerage receivables net of brokerage payables	7,550	(1,033)	(4,926)
Change in insurance policy and claims reserves	4,628	824	405
Net gains on sales of investments	(578)	(806)	(541)
Venture capital activity	888	(1,044)	(863)
Restructuring-related items and merger-related costs	458	759	(53)
Cumulative effect of accounting changes, net of tax	158	—	127
Other, net	(4,300)	(12,559)	(1,227)
Total adjustments	12,452	(10,846)	(20)
Net cash provided by operating activities	26,578	2,673	11,223
Cash flows from investing activities			
Change in deposits at interest with banks	(3,052)	(3,898)	(573)
Change in loans	(34,787)	(82,985)	(120,970)
Proceeds from sales of loans	26,470	32,580	94,677
Purchases of investments	(453,504)	(103,461)	(92,495)
Proceeds from sales of investments	403,078	67,561	49,678
Proceeds from maturities of investments	31,867	34,774	35,525
Other investments, primarily short-term, net	(642)	(3,086)	2,677
Capital expenditures on premises and equipment	(1,774)	(2,249)	(1,750)
Proceeds from sales of premises and equipment, subsidiaries and affiliates, and repossessed assets	1,802	1,232	3,437
Business acquisitions	(7,067)	(8,843)	(6,321)
Net cash used in investing activities	(37,609)	(68,375)	(36,115)
Cash flows from financing activities			
Dividends paid	(3,185)	(2,654)	(2,139)
Issuance of common stock	875	968	758
Issuance of mandatorily redeemable securities of subsidiary trusts	—	—	600
Issuance of mandatorily redeemable securities of parent trusts	2,550	—	—
Redemption of mandatorily redeemable securities of subsidiary trusts	(345)	—	—
Redemption of preferred stock, net	(220)	(150)	(388)
Treasury stock acquired	(3,045)	(4,066)	(3,954)
Stock tendered for payment of withholding taxes	(506)	(593)	(496)
Issuance of long-term debt	43,735	43,527	18,537
Payments and redemptions of long-term debt	(34,796)	(22,330)	(18,835)
Change in deposits	39,398	39,013	32,160
Change in short-term borrowings including investment banking and brokerage borrowings	(32,091)	9,851	(580)
Contractholder fund deposits	8,363	6,077	5,933
Contractholder fund withdrawals	(5,486)	(4,758)	(5,028)
Net cash provided by financing activities	15,248	64,875	26,568
Effect of exchange rate changes on cash and due from banks	(323)	(530)	(98)
Change in cash and due from banks	3,894	(1,357)	1,578
Cash and due from banks at beginning of period	14,621	15,978	14,400
Cash and due from banks at end of period	$ 18,515	$ 14,621	$ 15,978

EXHIBIT 8-4 Citigroup 2001 Cash Flow Statement

at earnings-per-share growth over periods out to five years. In the DCF model, embedding growth in revenue as opposed to operating income or earnings (which are a function of revenue and NOPM), will not greatly affect a stock's intrinsic value. Zacks found consensus analyst expectations of earnings-per-share growth over the next five years for Citigroup of 14.5 percent. Of the 19 analysts who Zacks polled that cover Citigroup, 8 rated it a strong buy, 10 rated it a buy, and 1 rated it a strong sell.

In our initial valuation scenario for Citigroup, we used the 14.5-percent EPS growth assumption by the analyst's polled by Zacks. We recognize that stock analysts often are overly optimistic regarding growth rates. We understand that our initial scenario will give us a high intrinsic stock value—we do not believe that a company as large as Citigroup can grow consistently at 14.5 percent per year. The growth rate is the assumption that we vary to see its effect on intrinsic value.

We lowered our growth assumption in our next scenario. We assumed a downward trend in growth, reducing Citigroup's growth rate by 1 percent per year until it reached the 5 percent level. This is the level of long-term growth that we believe that Citigroup can maintain. This growth assumption is reasonable for Citigroup and should result in a realistic valuation. Finally, we looked at a third scenario that uses a flat growth rate of 5 percent, which we believe will give us a conservative valuation for Citigroup.

Excess Return Period. We have discussed our 1-5-7-10, boring-decent-good-great excess return period rule that we use when we approach a valuation. It would be hard to find anyone that does not consider Citigroup a well-run, great company with great brands. We used a *10-year* excess return period in our valuation.

NOPM Estimate. NOPM is the second of the five Chinese brothers. To calculate NOPMs, we need to know a company's operating expenses. In order of importance, Citigroup's expenses are: interest expense, benefits, claims and credit losses, and other operating expenses. To calculate operating income for Citigroup, we took revenue from continuing operations and subtracted total expenses. To arrive at Citigroup's NOPM, we divide operating income by revenue. Over the past three fiscal years, NOPMs have been relatively steady at 19.23 percent, 18.91 percent, and 19.55 percent, for an average of 19.23 percent. It the nine months ending September 30th, Citigroup's NOPM jumped to 24.19 percent. For our baseline valuation, we used the *19.23-percent* three-year average NOPM, and hope that Citigroup can continue to improve their operations as they have through the third quarter of 2002.

Income Tax Rates. Provision for income taxes for Citigroup averaged 35.3 percent over the three-year period from 1999 to 2001. We used that 35.3-percent rate in our baseline valuation.

New Investment and Depreciation. A typical manufacturing company, in order to grow its business, invests a significant portion of its revenues in plant, property, and equipment. Earlier in this chapter, we noted that financial companies invest very little in the way of PPE and have small depreciation charges. Financial companies do invest in software to develop proprietary trading and risk management systems, and often grow by acquiring businesses in similar fields. Citigroup has made significant investments over the past three years in business acquisitions—$6.3 billion in 1999, $8.8 billion in 2000, and $7.1 billion in 2001. On average, Citigroup spent $7.17 billion per year or an average of 6.76 percent of revenues to acquire other businesses. Citigroup also had capital expenditures over that period that averaged about $1.9 billion per year, which were more than offset from the proceeds from sales of premises and equipment and repossessed assets. For our investment rate input, we used *6.76 percent.*

Citigroup had depreciation charges of $2.2, $2.6, and $2.4 billion respectively in 1999, 2000, and 2001. The depreciation rate averaged $2.4 billion per year, or 2.26 percent of yearly revenue. We used that *2.26 percent* as our depreciation rate input.

Incremental Working Capital. As discussed previously, working capital supports the manufacturing and service activities of nonfinancial companies. Investing in working capital is a bothersome chore for manufacturing firms. For financial companies, their principal liabilities and assets are financial claims that take the place of working capital. Therefore, for financial companies, our entry for working capital was *0.*

Short-Term Assets. The third quarter balance sheet of Citigroup lists total assets of $1,031 billion. Principal assets are loans, investments, trading account assets, Federal funds sold, receivables, and cash. From that total we eliminated fixed assets and assets of questionable value, such as goodwill, $22.6 billion, and intangible assets, $7.8 billion, which gave us a short-term asset entry of *$1,000.6 billion.*

Short-Term Liabilities. Citigroup's principal liabilities are deposits, Federal funds purchased, trading account liabilities, insurance policy and claims reserves, contract holder funds, and short-term borrowings. As discussed previously, to be consistent with the treatment of interest as an operating expense for financial companies, we included

Citigroup's long-term debt in the short-term liability category. When we value financial companies, we use a 0 entry as the debt outstanding input in the ValuePro 2002 software. Our entry for short-term liabilities for Citigroup was *$950.8 billion*—the total amount of liabilities, which included $109 billion of long-term debt, shown on its third-quarter balance sheet.

Stock Price. Citigroup's closing stock price on December 17, 2002 was *$37.13*.

Shares Outstanding. The third-quarter balance sheet notes that 5.062 billion shares are outstanding on September 30, 2002, and there are 5.168 billion adjusted weighted average common shares outstanding on September 30, 2002. We discuss our concerns regarding dilution in Chapter 6, and we use the highest number of shares outstanding when we value a stock. In this case our input is *5.168 billion*.

Debt Outstanding. As we discussed previously, in the entry for short-term liabilities we include debt outstanding for financial companies. Our entry for debt outstanding was *0*.

Preferred Stock Outstanding. According to Citigroup's third-quarter 2002 balance sheet, it has *$1.4 billion* of preferred stock outstanding.

Preferred Stock Yield. We used *6.5 percent* in this example—a rate that is between the cost of Citigroup's debt and its cost of common equity.

Risk-Free Rate. We used the 10-year Treasury yield on December 17, 2002 of 4.11 percent.

Bond Spread to Treasury. Since we have a 0 entry for debt outstanding, our entry was *0*.

Beta. According to Yahoo Finance, Citigroup's beta was *1.48*, and that was our entry for the ValuePro 2002 software.

Equity Risk Premium. We used 3 percent for this input for our valuation examples.

Citigroup Valuation—Baseline Scenario: 14.5 percent Growth Rate, Value—$88.03

We plugged all of these figures into the ValuePro general input screen, which we show as Exhibit 8-5. The resulting cost of capital showed Citigroup to have a cost of equity of 8.54 percent, and the general input

ValuePro 2002
General Input Screen
Intrinsic Stock Value $88.03
General Inputs

Company Ticker.....	Citigroup		
Excess Return Period (years)	10	Depreciation Rate (% of Rev.)	2.26
Revenues ($mil)	112022	Investment Rate (% of Rev.)	6.76
Growth Rate (%)	14.50	Working Capital (% of Rev.)	0.00
Net Operating Profit Margin (%)	19.23	Short-Term Assets ($mil)	1000600
Tax Rate (%)	34.34	Short-Term Liabilities($mil)	950800
Stock Price($)	37.13	Equity Risk Premium (%)	3.00
Shares Outstanding (mil)	5168.7	Company Beta	1.48
10-year Treasury Yield (%)	4.11	Value of Debt Out. ($mil)	0
Bond Spread to Treasury (%)	0.00	Value of Pref. Stock Out. ($mil)	1400
Preferred Stock Yield (%)	6.50	Company WACC (%)	8.54

EXHIBIT 8-5   Citigroup General Input Screen—Baseline Scenario

screen showed Citigroup's stock to have an intrinsic value of $88.03—more than double its closing price of $37.13 on December 17th. Why was the difference between market price and our calculation of value so large?

Citigroup Valuation—Multistage Growth Scenario: Growth Rate Declining from 14.5 percent to 5 percent, Value—$66.13

It is our belief that the 14.5 percent consensus analyst expectation of earnings growth for Citigroup is too high. It is unreasonable to expect that a company with revenues of over $100 billion can continue to grow consistently at double-digit rates. Let's look at what happens to the intrinsic value of Citigroup when its growth rate decreases. Assume that Citigroup's growth rate lives up to the 14.5-percent growth expectation this year, and then declines by 1 percent per year over the excess return period.

How do we handle this type of multistage growth rate? The Value-Pro 2002 custom valuation input screen (Exhibit 8-6) permits an investor to change assumptions on a yearly basis for growth rates, NOPMs, new investment and depreciation rates, income tax rates, incremental working capital rates, and WACC rates. When we reduced the 14.5 percent growth assumption by 1 percent per year in the growth rate column for years 2–9, and to 5 percent for the growth rate in year

ValuePro 2002
Custom Valuation Input Screen
Citigroup
Intrinsic Stock Value $66.13

Period	12 Months Ending	Growth Rate	Net Operating Margin	Tax Rate	Invest. Rate	Dep. Rate	Increm. Working Capital	WACC
0	01/12/2003							
1	01/12/2004	14.50	19.23	34.34	6.76	2.26	0.00	8.54
2	01/12/2005	13.50	19.23	34.34	6.76	2.26	0.00	8.54
3	01/12/2006	12.50	19.23	34.34	6.76	2.26	0.00	8.54
4	01/12/2007	11.50	19.23	34.34	6.76	2.26	0.00	8.54
5	01/12/2008	10.50	19.23	34.34	6.76	2.26	0.00	8.54
6	01/12/2009	9.50	19.23	34.34	6.76	2.26	0.00	8.54
7	01/12/2010	8.50	19.23	34.34	6.76	2.26	0.00	8.54
8	01/12/2011	7.50	19.23	34.34	6.76	2.26	0.00	8.54
9	01/12/2012	6.50	19.23	34.34	6.76	2.26	0.00	8.54
10	01/12/2013	5.00	19.23	34.34	6.76	2.26	0.00	8.54
Residual								8.54

EXHIBIT 8-6 Citigroup Custom Input Screen—Multistage Growth Scenario

10, the intrinsic value dropped by 25 percent—from $88.03 to $66.13. The cash flows associated with this decreasing growth rate scenario are shown in the custom pro forma screen (Exhibit 8-7).

Citigroup Valuation—Low-Growth Scenario: 5-percent Growth Rate, Value—$47.13

What if the growth in earnings at Citigroup only matches the upper end of the growth rate of the economy—5 percent? If we keep other inputs constant and plug 5 percent into the growth rate window of the general input screen (Exhibit 8-8), we see that Citigroup's intrinsic value is $47.13.

Citigroup Stock—Buy? Sell? Hold?

When you use conservative assumptions in valuation, and the intrinsic value of a stock exceeds its price, then it's worthy of serious consideration to add to your portfolio. Based on its current price level of $37.13 and a reasonable growth rate of 5 percent, Citigroup's valuation ratio is ($47.13/$37.13) equal to 1.27.

The price of Citigroup stock is low enough to warrant a purchase. The stock price is depressed because of investor concerns about how corporate defaults and bankruptcies, such as Enron, WorldCom, and United Airlines, will affect Citigroup's profits. The market is also wary of shareholder lawsuits and state and Federal fines and legal proceedings relating to Citigroup's investment banking activities for the

ValuePro 2002
Custom Pro Forma Screen
10-year Excess Return Period
Citigroup

Disc. Excess Return Period FCFF	$105,478
Discounted Residual Value	$187,953
Short-Term Assets	$1,000,600
Total Corporate Value	$1,294,031

Total Corporate Value	$1,294,031
Less Debt	$0
Less Preferred Stock	($1,400)
Less Short-Term Liabilities	($950,800)
Total Value to Common Equity	$341,831
Intrinsic Stock Value	$66.13

(1)	(2)	(3)	(4)	(5)	(6)	(7)	(8)	(9)	(10)	(11)	(12)	(13)
	12 Months			Adj.				Change in	Change in Working		Discount	Discounted
Period	Ending	Revenues	NOP	Taxes	NOPAT	Invest.	Deprec.	Invest.	Capital	FCFF	Factor	FCFF
0	01/13/03	112,022										
1	01/13/04	128,265	24,665	8,470	16,195	8,671	2,899	5,772	0	10,423	0.9214	9,604
2	01/13/05	145,581	27,995	9,614	18,382	9,841	3,290	6,551	0	11,831	0.8489	10,043
3	01/13/06	163,779	31,495	10,815	20,679	11,071	3,701	7,370	0	13,309	0.7821	10,410
4	01/13/07	182,613	35,117	12,059	23,058	12,345	4,127	8,218	0	14,840	0.7206	10,694
5	01/13/08	201,788	38,804	13,325	25,479	13,641	4,560	9,080	0	16,398	0.6640	10,888
6	01/13/09	220,957	42,490	14,591	27,899	14,937	4,994	9,943	0	17,956	0.6118	10,985
7	01/13/10	239,739	46,102	15,831	30,270	16,206	5,418	10,788	0	19,482	0.5636	10,981
8	01/13/11	257,719	49,559	17,019	32,541	17,422	5,824	11,597	0	20,943	0.5193	10,876
9	01/13/12	274,471	52,781	18,125	34,656	18,554	6,203	12,351	0	22,305	0.4785	10,672
10	01/13/13	288,194	55,420	19,031	36,389	19,482	6,513	12,969	0	23,420	0.4409	10,325
Residual		288,194	55,420	19,031	36,389	6,513	6,513	0	0	426,338	0.4409	187,953

EXHIBIT 8-7   Citigroup Custom Pro Forma Screen—Multistage Growth Scenario

telecom industry. We think those actions and concerns will be a temporary drag on profits, and the financial penalties that Citigroup eventually may pay will not significantly harm the company. At that price level, and based on our valuation assumptions at the time we valued it, Citigroup stock appeared to be a *strong buy*.

ValuePro 2002
General Input Screen
Intrinsic Stock Value $47.13
General Inputs

Company Ticker.....	Citigroup		
Excess Return Period (years)	10	Depreciation Rate (% of Rev.)	2.26
Revenues ($mil)	112022	Investment Rate (% of Rev.)	6.76
Growth Rate (%)	5.00	Working Capital (% of Rev.)	0.00
Net Operating Profit Margin (%)	19.23	Short-Term Assets ($mil)	1000600
Tax Rate (%)	34.34	Short-Term Liabilities($mil)	950800
Stock Price($)	37.13	Equity Risk Premium (%)	3.00
Shares Outstanding (mil)	5168.7	Company Beta	1.48
10-year Treasury Yield (%)	4.11	Value of Debt Out. ($mil)	0
Bond Spread to Treasury (%)	0.00	Value of Pref. Stock Out. ($mil)	1400
Preferred Stock Yield (%)	6.50	Company WACC (%)	8.54

EXHIBIT 8-8   Citigroup General Input Screen—Low-Growth Scenario

Valuing Merrill Lynch—December 18, 2002

Price—$40.13, Value—$43.83 to $72.50, *Buy*

General Description of Merrill Lynch—a Great Securities Firm

Merrill Lynch & Co., Inc. (MER: *www.ml.com/*) is a holding company that provides securities brokerage, financing, investment, insurance, banking and advisory services, and related products in 37 countries throughout the world. It has 53,400 employees and 14,600 financial advisors that serve clients with assets of over $1.3 trillion. Merrill Lynch is comprised of three business segments: the Global Markets and Investment Banking (GMI), Private Banking, and Merrill Lynch Investment Managers.

GMI provides investment banking and financing services to corporate and institutional clients and governments in the United States and throughout the world. GMI activities include: underwriting, M&A advisory services, investment banking, trading, and corporate lending services.

The Private Client Group provides services and products related to the management of wealth, including broker/dealer activities, banking, retirement planning, insurance and trust services, and mortgage lending. Brokerage activities are provided by two subsidiaries: Merrill Lynch, Pierce, Fenner and Smith; and Merrill Lynch International. Insurance activities consist of underwriting and marketing life insurance and annuity products written by Merrill Lynch Life Insurance Company and ML Life Insurance Company of NY.

Merrill Lynch Investment Managers (MLIM) has approximately $529 billion in assets under management. MLIM manufactures and offers tax-exempt and taxable fixed-income mutual funds, and equity and balanced funds.

Merrill's market equity is $35.4 billion. That market value is 73 times a depressed 2001 earnings amount of $0.56 per share, but only 1.61 times book value of $25.37 per share. Merrill pays an annual dividend of $0.64 per share. Its five-year price history is shown in Exhibit 8-9.

The high-tech stock market crash and the events of September 11th have negatively and significantly affected Merrill Lynch's revenues, earnings, and stock price. For the third quarter of 2002, revenues fell by almost 30 percent when compared to the third quarter of 2001. Ad-

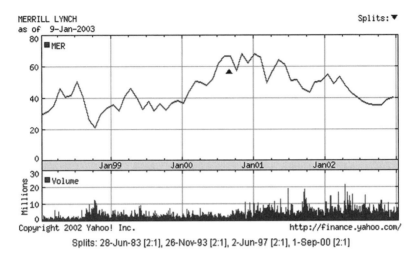

EXHIBIT 8-9   Merrill Lynch Five-Year Stock Price Chart

ditionally, Merrill Lynch has suffered from activities relating to biased stock research, having recently settled a regulatory action for $100 million.

Developing the Valuation Inputs for Merrill Lynch

The fiscal year for Merrill Lynch ends on the last Friday in December. On October 16, 2002, Merrill posted a third-quarter earnings release on its Web site for the quarter ending September 27, 2002. We have included the audited 2001 income statement, balance sheet, and cash flow statement of Merrill as Exhibits 8-10, 8-11, and 8-12, respectively.

We used information provided in the third-quarter earnings release, in Merrill Lynch's 2001 Annual Report, and on financial Web sites to develop our valuation inputs.

Revenues. In order of importance, the revenue sources for Merrill are: interest and dividend revenues, commissions, asset management and portfolio service fees, principal transactions, and investment banking fees. According to the 2001 income statement, the most recent annual revenue for Merrill was *$38.757 million.*

Revenue Growth Rate. The historic revenue growth of Merrill has been erratic, growing by 27 percent from $35.3 billion in 1999 to $44.8 billion in 2000, and then dropping 13.6 percent in 2001. Total revenues were down 30 percent in the third quarter of 2002 when compared to

	Year Ended Last Friday in December		
	2001	2000	1999
REVENUES			
Interest (principally from affiliates)	$ 3,397	$ 5,314	$ 3,693
Management service fees (from affiliates)	448	448	336
Other	14	16	20
Total Revenues	3,859	5,778	4,049
Interest Expense	3,694	5,401	4,094
Net Revenues	165	377	(45)
NON-INTEREST EXPENSES			
Compensation and benefits	316	435	323
Restructuring charge	239	-	-
September 11th-related	71	-	-
Other	375	605	358
Total Non-Interest Expenses	1,001	1,040	681
EQUITY IN EARNINGS OF AFFILIATES	1,095	4,127	3,179
EARNINGS BEFORE INCOME TAXES	259	3,464	2,453
Income Tax Benefit	314	320	240
NET EARNINGS	$ 573	$ 3,784	$ 2,693
OTHER COMPREHENSIVE INCOME (LOSS), NET OF TAX	(23)	45	(268)
COMPREHENSIVE INCOME	$ 550	$ 3,829	$ 2,425
NET EARNINGS APPLICABLE TO COMMON STOCKHOLDERS	$ 535	$ 3,745	$ 2,654

EXHIBIT 8-10   Merrill Lynch 2001 Income Statement

	December 28, 2001	December 29, 2000
ASSETS		
Cash and cash equivalents	$ 822	$ 5
Marketable investment securities	2,392	7,394
Loans to, receivables from and preference securities of affiliates	80,621	80,845
Investments in affiliates, at equity	22,238	21,435
Equipment and facilities (net of accumulated depreciation and amortization of $201 in 2001 and $377 in 2000)	120	175
Other receivables and assets	3,232	2,473
TOTAL ASSETS	$ 109,425	$ 112,327
LIABILITIES AND STOCKHOLDERS' EQUITY		
LIABILITIES		
Commercial paper and other short-term borrowings	$ 1,909	$ 12,978
Loans from and payables to affiliates	10,237	7,409
Other liabilities and accrued interest	4,666	6,299
Long-term borrowings	72,605	67,337
Total Liabilities	89,417	94,023
STOCKHOLDERS' EQUITY		
Preferred Stockholders' Equity	425	425
Common Stockholders' Equity:		
Shares exchangeable into common stock	62	68
Common stock, par value $1.33 1/3 per share; authorized: 3,000,000,000 shares; issued: 2001 – 962,533,498 shares; 2000 – 962,533,498 shares	1,283	1,283
Paid-in capital	4,209	2,843
Accumulated other comprehensive loss (net of tax)	(368)	(345)
Retained earnings	16,150	16,156
	21,336	20,005
Less: Treasury stock, at cost: 2001 – 119,059,651 shares; 2000 – 154,578,945 shares	977	1,273
Unamortized employee stock grants	776	853
Total Common Stockholders' Equity	19,583	17,879
Total Stockholders' Equity	20,008	18,304
TOTAL LIABILITIES AND STOCKHOLDERS' EQUITY	$ 109,425	$ 112,327

EXHIBIT 8-11   Merrill Lynch 2001 Balance Sheet

CONDENSED FINANCIAL INFORMATION OF REGISTRANT
MERRILL LYNCH & CO., INC.
(Parent Company Only)
CONDENSED STATEMENTS OF CASH FLOWS
(dollars in millions)

	Year Ended Last Friday in December		
	2001	2000	1999
Cash Flows from Operating Activities:			
Net Earnings	$ 573	$ 3,784	$ 2,693
Noncash items included in earnings:			
Equity in earnings of affiliates	(1,095)	(4,127)	(3,179)
Depreciation and amortization	65	53	45
Amortization of stock-based compensation	84	23	17
Restructuring charge	144	-	-
Other	(303)	(98)	20
(Increase) decrease in			
Operating assets, net of operating liabilities	(316)	956	(287)
Dividends and partnerships distributions from affiliates	1,113	1,332	1,764
Cash Provided by Operating Activities	265	1,923	1,073
Cash Flows from Investing Activities:			
Proceeds from (payments for):			
Loans to affiliates, net of payments	3,162	5,121	(2,106)
Sales of available-for-sale securities	7,447	124	12
Purchases of available-for-sale securities	(2,449)	(6,315)	(1,198)
Investments in affiliates, net of dispositions	(886)	(7,178)	(4)
Equipment and facilities	(104)	(18)	(95)
Cash Provided by (Used for) Investing Activities	7,170	(8,266)	(3,391)
Cash Flows from Financing Activities:			
Proceeds from (payments for):			
Commercial paper and other short-term borrowings	(11,069)	(11,079)	7,071
Issuance and resale of long-term borrowings	35,380	25,888	11,685
Settlement and repurchase of long-term borrowings	(31,211)	(9,507)	(16,092)
Common stock transactions	861	1,182	459
Dividends to shareholders	(579)	(515)	(426)
Cash (Used for) Provided by Financing Activities	(6,618)	5,969	2,697
Increase (Decrease) in Cash and Cash Equivalents	817	(374)	379
Cash and Cash Equivalents, beginning of year	5	379	-
Cash and Cash Equivalents, end of year	$ 822	$ 5	$ 379

EXHIBIT 8-12   Merrill Lynch 2001 Cash Flow Statement

the third quarter of 2001. Two principal reasons for the decline in revenue are a general drop in interest rates and the terrorist attacks of 9/11, which greatly disrupted operations. Merrill's corporate headquarters are in a building that is located only two hundred yards from the twin towers of the World Trade Center. Merrill Lynch's earnings before income taxes grew 36 percent from 1999 to 2000, and then dropped 75 percent between 2000 and 2001—a very difficult year. During the third quarter of 2002, earnings before income taxes were about the same level as in the third quarter of 2001.

Let's examine Merrill's growth potential. Of the 19 analysts whom Zacks polls that cover Merrill, 3 rated it a strong buy, 8 rated it a buy, and 8 rated it a hold. A consensus analyst expectation of earnings-per-share growth over the next five years for Merrill was 13 percent.

For our base-line valuation of Merrill Lynch, we used a 13-percent growth rate. The growth rate is the assumption that we vary to see its affect on intrinsic value. For our low growth scenario, we used a growth rate of 5 percent, which produced a conservative valuation for Merrill.

Excess Return Period. We consider Merrill a well-managed, great securities firm and we used a *10-year* excess return period in our valuation.

NOPM Estimate. In order of importance, Merrill's expenses are: interest expense, compensation and benefits, communications and technology, occupancy and related depreciation, advertising and market development, and brokerage, clearing and exchange fees. To calculate operating income for Merrill, we subtracted total expenses from total revenue. To arrive at Merrill's NOPM, we divided operating income by revenue. Over the past three fiscal years, NOPMs were 3.55 percent, 12.75 percent, and 11.9 percent, for an average of 9.4-percent. It the nine months ending September 27th, Merrill Lynch's NOPM jumped to 12.96 percent. We used the 9.4 percent three-year average NOPM in the baseline valuation, with the hope that Merrill will continue to improve their operations, as they have through 2002.

Income Tax Rates. Income tax expense for Merrill Lynch averaged 35.33 percent over the three-year period from 1999 to 2001. We used that 35.33-percent rate in our valuations.

New Investment and Depreciation. To grow their business, financial companies make investments in equipment and facilities, and often acquire other businesses or investments. Merrill Lynch has made investments in equipment and facilities and other investments that over the past three years have averaged *4.4 percent* of revenue, which we used for the investment rate input. Merrill had depreciation charges that averaged *2.08 percent* of yearly revenue over the past three years, which we used as our depreciation rate input.

Incremental Working Capital. Our entry for working capital was *0.*

Short-Term Assets. The annual report of Merrill lists total assets of $419.4 billion. Principal assets are: securities financing transactions, receivables, trading assets, marketable investment securities, and cash and equivalents. From that total, we eliminated long term assets, such as equipment and facilities—$2.8 billion, assets of questionable value, such as goodwill—$4.0 billion, and other assets—$2.5 billion, which gave us a short-term asset entry of *$409.997 billion.*

Short-Term Liabilities. Merrill's principal liabilities are: securities financing transactions, deposits, trading liabilities, other payables, commercial paper, and liabilities of insurance subsidiaries. We included Merrill Lynch's long-term debt of $76.575 billion in the short-term liability asset category. When we value financial companies, we use a zero entry for the debt outstanding input in the ValuePro 2002 software. Our entry for short-term liabilities for Merrill was *$396.7 billion*—the total amount of liabilities.

Stock Price. Merrill's closing stock price on December 18, 2002 was *$40.13.*

Shares Outstanding. The third-quarter balance sheet notes that *942 million* average shares diluted were outstanding on September 27, 2002.

Debt Outstanding. As we discussed previously, we included debt outstanding for financial companies in the entry for short-term liabilities. Our entry for debt outstanding was *0.*

Preferred Stock Outstanding. According to Merrill's third-quarter 2002 balance sheet, it had *$1.4 billion* outstanding of preferred stock.

Preferred Stock Yield. We used 7.6 percent in this example.

Risk-Free Rate. We used the 10-year Treasury yield on December 18, 2002 of *4.06 percent.*

Bond Spread to Treasury. Since we had a 0 entry for debt outstanding, our entry was 0.

Beta. According to Yahoo Finance, Merrill's beta was *1.52,* and that was our entry for the ValuePro 2002 software.

Equity Risk Premium. We used 3 percent for this input for our valuation examples.

Merrill Lynch Valuation—Baseline Scenario: 13-Percent Growth Rate, Value—$72.50

The results of the baseline valuation are shown in ValuePro general input screen (Exhibit 8-13), which shows Merrill to have an 8.53-percent cost of equity, and Merrill's stock to have an intrinsic value of $72.50—significantly higher than its closing price on December 17th, of $40.13.

Merrill Lynch Valuation—Low-Growth Scenario: 5 percent Growth Rate, Value—$43.83

It is our belief that the 13-percent consensus analyst expectation of earnings growth is too high for Merrill. What if the growth in earnings at Merrill follows a more reasonable 5 percent? If we keep other inputs

ValuePro 2002
General Input Screen
Intrinsic Stock Value $72.50
General Inputs

Company Ticker.....	Merrill		
Excess Return Period (years)	10	Depreciation Rate (% of Rev.)	2.08
Revenues ($mil)	38757	Investment Rate (% of Rev.)	4.40
Growth Rate (%)	13.00	Working Capital (% of Rev.)	0.00
Net Operating Profit Margin (%)	9.40	Short-Term Assets ($mil)	409997
Tax Rate (%)	35.33	Short-Term Liabilities($mil)	396716
Stock Price($)	40.13	Equity Risk Premium (%)	3.00
Shares Outstanding (mil)	962.5	Company Beta	1.52
10-year Treasury Yield (%)	4.05	Value of Debt Out. ($mil)	0
Bond Spread to Treasury (%)	0.00	Value of Pref. Stock Out. ($mil)	3120
Preferred Stock Yield (%)	7.60	Company WACC (%)	8.53

EXHIBIT 8-13   Merrill Lynch General Input Screen—Baseline Scenario

constant and plug 5 percent into the growth rate window of the general input screen (Exhibit 8-14), we see that Merrill's intrinsic value is $43.83.

Merrill Lynch Valuation—Low-Growth, Increasing NOPM Scenario: 5-percent Growth Rate, 12-percent NOPM, Value—$55.19

Let's keep our growth rate assumption at 5 percent. Merrill's 2001 fiscal year was a debacle due in large part to 9/11 and a depressed stock market. In that environment, Merrill's NOPM dropped to 3.55 percent, bringing the 3-year average NOPM to 9.4 percent. Merrill's NOPM averaged 12.3 percent during 1999 and 2000, and was running at 12.96 percent through the first three quarters of 2002. What happens to intrinsic value if the NOPMs at Merrill return to an average of 12 percent or higher? If we keep other inputs constant and plug 12 percent into the NOPM window of the general input screen (Exhibit 8-15), we see that Merrill's intrinsic value is $55.19.

Merrill Lynch Stock—Buy? Sell? Hold?

Based upon the 5-percent growth rate, lower NOPM value of $43.83 for Merrill Lynch, the stock is worth a second look. Based on its price level of $40.13, Merrill Lynch's valuation ratio is ($43.83/$40.13) equal to 1.09. The real upside to this stock occurs if Merrill's NOPM increases to its pre-2001 levels of greater than 12 percent. At a 5-percent growth

ValuePro 2002
General Input Screen
Intrinsic Stock Value $43.83
General Inputs

Company Ticker.....	Merrill		
Excess Return Period (years)	10	Depreciation Rate (% of Rev.)	2.08
Revenues ($mil)	38757	Investment Rate (% of Rev.)	4.40
Growth Rate (%)	5.00	Working Capital (% of Rev.)	0.00
Net Operating Profit Margin (%)	9.40	Short-Term Assets ($mil)	409997
Tax Rate (%)	35.33	Short-Term Liabilities($mil)	396716
Stock Price($)	40.13	Equity Risk Premium (%)	3.00
Shares Outstanding (mil)	962.5	Company Beta	1.52
10-year Treasury Yield (%)	4.05	Value of Debt Out. ($mil)	0
Bond Spread to Treasury (%)	0.00	Value of Pref. Stock Out. ($mil)	3120
Preferred Stock Yield (%)	7.60	Company WACC (%)	8.53

EXHIBIT 8-14   Merrill Lynch General Input Screen—Low-Growth Scenario

rate and 12-percent NOPM, Merrill Lynch's intrinsic stock value is $55.19, and its valuation ratio is ($55.19/$40.13) equal to 1.375, and a very definite buy.

If you believe that Merrill Lynch will improve its NOPMs after a very difficult 2001, Merrill's a buy. This is a bet on an operating turnaround. At the time of this valuation, we believed that at a price level of $40 or below, Merrill Lynch stock was a *buy*.

ValuePro 2002
General Input Screen
Intrinsic Stock Value $55.19
General Inputs

Company Ticker.....	Merrill		
Excess Return Period (years)	10	Depreciation Rate (% of Rev.)	2.08
Revenues ($mil)	38757	Investment Rate (% of Rev.)	4.40
Growth Rate (%)	5.00	Working Capital (% of Rev.)	0.00
Net Operating Profit Margin (%)	12.00	Short-Term Assets ($mil)	409997
Tax Rate (%)	35.33	Short-Term Liabilities($mil)	396716
Stock Price($)	40.13	Equity Risk Premium (%)	3.00
Shares Outstanding (mil)	962.5	Company Beta	1.52
10-year Treasury Yield (%)	4.05	Value of Debt Out. ($mil)	0
Bond Spread to Treasury (%)	0.00	Value of Pref. Stock Out. ($mil)	3120
Preferred Stock Yield (%)	7.60	Company WACC (%)	8.53

EXHIBIT 8-15   Merrill Lynch General Input Screen—Increasing NOPM Scenario

Valuing Berkshire Hathaway—December 18, 2002

Price—$72,000, Value—$63,028 to $80,627, *Hold*

General Description of Berkshire Hathaway—Warren's Baby

Berkshire Hathaway Inc. (BRKa: *www.berkshirehathaway.com/*) is a holding company that owns subsidiaries that are engaged in the property and casualty insurance and reinsurance business, finance and financial products, building products, flight services, retail businesses, and manufacturing companies. Berkshire also can be viewed in part as a portfolio company that owns stock in other companies, similar to an investment trust. Berkshire Hathaway's chairman is Warren Buffett, the legendary value investor. Rather than pay dividends or repurchase shares in the open market, Berkshire invests a significant portion of its free cash flows in stocks of other companies that Mr. Buffett believes are undervalued. Berkshire and its subsidiaries have approximately 110,000 employees and assets worth over $167 billion.

The insurance group contributes about one-half of the revenue of Berkshire's operating businesses. The insurance group consists of GEICO, which provides low-cost auto insurance throughout the United States, General Re, which conducts a global reinsurance business in the property and casualty area, and Berkshire Hathaway Primary Insurance Group and Reinsurance Group.

In order of importance after the insurance group, the businesses that generate revenue for Berkshire are: Shaw Industries (carpet manufacturing), building products, flight services, financial products, and retail companies. As of September 30, 2002, Berkshire owned multibillion-dollar equity positions in four companies: The Coca-Cola Company–$9.6 billion, American Express Company—$4.7 billion, The Gillette Company-$2.8 billion, and Wells Fargo & Company—$2.5 billion, and held equity investments of over $8.1 billion in other companies. The current value of these investments are reflected in Berkshire's balance sheet, which is very important in determining the value of a portfolio company.

Berkshire Hathaway's market equity is $108.7 billion. That market value is 34 times earnings of $2085 per share, but only 1.74 times book value of $40,926 per share. Berkshire pays no annual dividend. The events of September 11th significantly affected the expenses and earnings of the insurance group and negatively affected Berkshire's stock

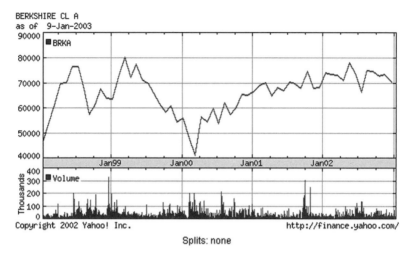

EXHIBIT 8-16   Berkshire Hathaway Stock Price Chart

price. From fiscal year 2000 to 2001, earnings fell over 75 percent. Earnings have recovered during fiscal year 2002. Berkshire's stock price history is shown in Exhibit 8-16.

Developing Valuation Inputs for Berkshire Hathaway

The fiscal year for Berkshire Hathaway ends on December 31st. On November 8, 2002, Berkshire issued a third-quarter report to shareholders for the quarter ending September 30, 2002, and posted it on its Web site. We included the audited 2001 income statement, balance sheet, and cash flow statement of Berkshire as Exhibits 8-17, 8-18, and 8-19, respectively.

We used information provided in the third-quarter earnings release, in Berkshire Hathaway's 2001 Annual Report, and on financial Web sites to develop our valuation inputs.

Revenues. In order of importance, the revenue sources for Berkshire are: insurance premiums earned; sales and service revenues; interest, dividend, and other investment income; realized investment gains; and income from financial products. According to the 2001 income statement, the most recent annual revenue for Berkshire was *$37.668 billion.*

Revenue Growth Rate. The historic revenue growth of Berkshire has been significant, growing by 41 percent—from $24 billion in 1999 to

BERKSHIRE HATHAWAY INC.
and Subsidiaries
CONSOLIDATED STATEMENTS OF EARNINGS
(dollars in millions except per share amounts)

	Year Ended December 31,		
	2001	**2000**	**1999**
Revenues:			
Insurance premiums earned	$17,905	$19,343	$14,306
Sales and service revenues	14,902	7,361	5,918
Interest, dividend and other investment income	2,765	2,686	2,314
Income from MidAmerican Energy Holdings Company	165	105	—
Income from finance and financial products businesses	568	556	125
Realized investment gain	1,363	3,955	1,365
	37,668	34,006	24,028
Cost and expenses:			
Insurance losses and loss adjustment expenses	18,398	17,332	12,518
Insurance underwriting expenses	3,574	3,632	3,220
Cost of products and services sold	10,446	4,893	4,065
Selling, general and administrative expenses	3,000	1,703	1,164
Goodwill amortization	572	715	477
Interest expense	209	144	134
	36,199	28,419	21,578
Earnings before income taxes and minority interest	1,469	5,587	2,450
Income taxes	620	2,018	852
Minority interest	54	241	41
Net earnings	$ 795	$3,328	$1,557
Average common shares outstanding *	1,527,234	1,522,933	1,519,703
Net earnings per common share *	$ 521	$2,185	$1,025

* *Average shares outstanding include average Class A Common shares and average Class B Common shares determined on an equivalent Class A Common Stock basis. Net earnings per common share shown above represents net earnings per equivalent Class A Common share. Net earnings per Class B Common share is equal to one-thirtieth (1/30) of such amount or $17 per share for 2001, $73 per share for 2000 and $34 per share for 1999.*

EXHIBIT 8-17   Berkshire Hathaway 2001 Income Statement

$34 billion in 2000, and then increasing by 11 percent in 2001 to $37.7 billion. Total revenues were up 5.1 percent in the third quarter of 2002 when compared to the third quarter of 2001. Berkshire's earnings before income taxes grew 228 percent from 1999 to 2000, and then dropped 74 percent between 2000 and 2001. Again, a large portion of the blame was due to 9/11 considerations. During the third quarter of 2002, earnings before income taxes increased 390 percent above the level of the third quarter of 2001.

What is Berkshire's growth potential? A consensus analyst expectation of earnings-per-share growth over the next five years for Berk-

BERKSHIRE HATHAWAY INC.
and Subsidiaries
CONSOLIDATED BALANCE SHEETS
(dollars in millions except per share amounts)

	December 31, 2001	December 31, 2000
ASSETS		
Cash and cash equivalents	$ 5,313	$ 5,263
Investments:		
Securities with fixed maturities	36,509	32,567
Equity securities	28,675	37,619
Other	1,974	1,637
Receivables	11,926	11,764
Inventories	2,213	1,275
Investments in MidAmerican Energy Holdings Company	1,826	1,719
Assets of finance and financial products businesses	41,591	16,829
Property, plant and equipment	4,776	2,699
Goodwill of acquired businesses	21,407	18,875
Other assets	6,542	5,545
	$162,752	$135,792
LIABILITIES AND SHAREHOLDERS' EQUITY		
Losses and loss adjustment expenses	$ 40,716	$ 33,022
Unearned premiums	4,814	3,885
Accounts payable, accruals and other liabilities	9,626	8,374
Income taxes	7,021	10,125
Borrowings under investment agreements and other debt	3,485	2,663
Liabilities of finance and financial products businesses	37,791	14,730
	103,453	72,799
Minority shareholders' interests	1,349	1,269
Shareholders' equity:		
Common Stock:*		
Class A Common Stock, $5 par value		
and Class B Common Stock, $0.1667 par value	8	8
Capital in excess of par value	25,607	25,524
Accumulated other comprehensive income	12,891	17,543
Retained earnings	19,444	18,649
Total shareholders' equity	57,950	61,724
	$162,752	$135,792

> * *Class B Common Stock has economic rights equal to one-thirtieth (1/30) of the economic rights of Class A Common Stock. Accordingly, on an equivalent Class A Common Stock basis, there are 1,528,217 shares outstanding at December 31, 2001 versus 1,526,230 shares outstanding at December 31, 2000.*

EXHIBIT 8-18   Berkshire Hathaway 2001 Balance Sheet

shire was 11 percent. Zacks polled the three analysts that covered Berkshire. All rated it a buy.

For our initial valuation of Berkshire, we used an 11-percent growth rate. We also used a growth rate of 7 percent in a lower growth scenario, which gave us a more conservative valuation for Berkshire.

BERKSHIRE HATHAWAY INC.
and Subsidiaries
CONSOLIDATED STATEMENTS OF CASH FLOWS
(dollars in millions)

	Year Ended December 31,		
	2001	**2000**	**1999**
Cash flows from operating activities:			
Net earnings	$ 795	$3,328	$1,557
Adjustments to reconcile net earnings to cash flows from operating activities:			
Realized investment gain	(1,363)	(3,955)	(1,365)
Depreciation and amortization	1,076	997	688
Changes in assets and liabilities before effects from business acquisitions:			
Losses and loss adjustment expenses	7,571	5,976	3,790
Deferred charges – reinsurance assumed	(498)	(1,075)	(958)
Unearned premiums	929	97	394
Receivables	219	(3,062)	(834)
Accounts payable, accruals and other liabilities	(339)	660	(5)
Finance businesses trading activities	(1,083)	(1,126)	473
Income taxes	(329)	757	(1,395)
Other	(404)	350	(145)
Net cash flows from operating activities	6,574	2,947	2,200
Cash flows from investing activities:			
Purchases of securities with fixed maturities	(16,475)	(16,550)	(18,380)
Purchases of equity securities	(1,075)	(4,145)	(3,664)
Proceeds from sales of securities with fixed maturities	8,470	13,119	4,509
Proceeds from redemptions and maturities of securities with fixed maturities	4,305	2,530	2,833
Proceeds from sales of equity securities	3,881	6,870	4,355
Loans and investments originated in finance businesses	(9,502)	(857)	(2,526)
Principal collection on loans and investments originated in finance businesses	4,126	1,142	845
Acquisitions of businesses, net of cash acquired	(4,697)	(3,798)	(153)
Other	(727)	(582)	(417)
Net cash flows from investing activities	(11,694)	(2,271)	(12,598)
Cash flows from financing activities:			
Proceeds from borrowings of finance businesses	6,288	120	736
Proceeds from other borrowings	824	681	1,118
Repayments of borrowings of finance businesses	(865)	(274)	(46)
Repayments of other borrowings	(798)	(806)	(1,333)
Change in short term borrowings of finance businesses	826	500	(311)
Changes in other short term borrowings	(377)	324	340
Other	116	(75)	(137)
Net cash flows from financing activities	6,014	470	367
Increase (decrease) in cash and cash equivalents	894	1,146	(10,031)
Cash and cash equivalents at beginning of year	5,604	4,458	14,489
Cash and cash equivalents at end of year *	$ 6,498	$ 5,604	$ 4,458
* Cash and cash equivalents at end of year are comprised of the following:			
Finance and financial products businesses	$ 1,185	$ 341	$ 623
Other	5,313	5,263	3,835
	$ 6,498	$ 5,604	$ 4,458

EXHIBIT 8-19   Berkshire Hathaway 2001 Cash Flow Statement

Excess Return Period. We consider Berkshire a well-managed, great financial/diversified firm, and we used a *10-year* excess return period in our valuations.

NOPM Estimate. In order of importance, Berkshire's expenses are: insurance losses and loss adjustment expenses, cost of products and services sold, insurance underwriting expenses, and SG&A. To calculate operating income for Berkshire, we subtracted total expenses from total revenue. To arrive at Berkshire's NOPM, we divided operating income by revenue. Over the past three fiscal years, NOPMs were 10.2 percent in 1999, 16.4 percent in 2000, and 3.9 percent in 2001, for an average of 10.2 percent. It the nine months ending September 30th, Berkshire Hathaway's NOPM jumped to 14.41 percent. We used the *10.2-percent* three-year average NOPM in the base-line valuation, and adjusted the NOPM upward in a subsequent valuation.

Income Tax Rates. Income tax expense for Berkshire averaged 37.7 percent over the three-year period from 1999 to 2001. We used that *37.7 percent* rate in our baseline valuation.

New Investment and Depreciation. To fuel its growth, Berkshire Hathaway actively purchases other businesses. Berkshire's business acquisitions, net of cash acquired, has averaged *8.09 percent* of revenue over the past three years, which we used for the investment rate input. Berkshire had depreciation charges that averaged *2.88 percent* of yearly revenue over the past three years, which we used as our depreciation rate input.

Incremental Working Capital. Our entry for working capital was *0*.

Short-Term Assets. Like other financial firms, Berkshire's balance sheet does not differentiate between current assets and long-term assets. The third-quarter balance sheet of Berkshire lists total assets of $167.7 billion. Principal assets are: investments, loans and receivables, cash and cash equivalents, trading account assets, inventories, goodwill, PP&E, and other assets. From that total, we eliminated long-term fixed assets of PP&E—$5.2 billion, and assets of questionable value, such as goodwill—$22.2 billion, and other assets—$6.6 billion, which gave us a short-term asset entry of *$133.682 billion*.

Short-Term Liabilities. Berkshire's principal liabilities are: losses and loss adjustment expenses, unearned premiums, accounts payable, repurchase and investment agreements, and trading account liabilities. Our entry for short-term liabilities for Berkshire was *$105.132 billion*—the total amount of liabilities, plus minority shareholders' interests, as shown on Berkshire's third-quarter balance sheet.

Stock Price. Berkshire's closing stock price for its Class A shares on December 18, 2002 was *$72,000.*

Shares Outstanding. The third-quarter balance sheet noted that *1,527,234* average common shares were outstanding on September 30, 2002.

Debt Outstanding. As we discussed previously, we include debt outstanding for financial companies in the entry for short-term liabilities. Our entry for debt outstanding was *0.*

Preferred Stock Outstanding. Berkshire had no preferred stock outstanding, *0.*

Preferred Stock Yield. 0.

Risk-Free Rate. We used the 10-year Treasury yield on December 18, 2002 of *4.06 percent.*

Bond Spread to Treasury. Since we had a 0 entry for debt outstanding, our entry was *0.*

Beta. According to Yahoo Finance, Berkshire's beta was *0.54,* and that was our entry for the ValuePro 2002 software.

Equity Risk Premium. We used *3 percent* for this input for our valuation examples.

Berkshire Hathaway Valuation—Baseline Scenario:
11-Percent Growth Rate, 10.2-Percent NOPM, Value—$70,330

The results of the base-line valuation are shown in ValuePro general input screen (Exhibit 8-20), which shows Berkshire to have cost of equity of 5.68 percent. In this scenario, Berkshire's stock has an intrinsic value of $70,330—2 percent lower than its closing price on December 18th of $72,000.

Berkshire Hathaway Valuation—Higher NOPM, Higher Rate Scenario:
14-Percent NOPM, 5.06-Percent Treasury Rate, Value—$80,627

It was our belief that the three-year average NOPM of 10.2 percent that we used in the base-line valuation was too low for Berkshire. The 2001 NOPM of 3.9 percent was due in large part to the losses suffered by the insurance subsidiaries for claims relating to the 9/11 terrorist at-

ValuePro 2002
General Input Screen
Intrinsic Stock Value $70330.17
General Inputs

Company Ticker.....	Berk Hath		
Excess Return Period (years)	10	Depreciation Rate (% of Rev.)	2.88
Revenues ($mil)	37668	Investment Rate (% of Rev.)	8.09
Growth Rate (%)	11.00	Working Capital (% of Rev.)	0.00
Net Operating Profit Margin (%)	10.20	Short-Term Assets ($mil)	133682
Tax Rate (%)	35.00	Short-Term Liabilities($mil)	105132
Stock Price($)	72000.00	Equity Risk Premium (%)	3.00
Shares Outstanding (mil)	1.528217	Company Beta	0.54
10-year Treasury Yield (%)	4.06	Value of Debt Out. ($mil)	0
Bond Spread to Treasury (%)	0.00	Value of Pref. Stock Out. ($mil)	0
Preferred Stock Yield (%)	0.00	Company WACC (%)	5.68

EXHIBIT 8-20 Berkshire Hathaway General Input Screen—Baseline Scenario

tack. In 2000, the NOPM for Berkshire was 16.4 percent and it was running at 14.4 percent through the third quarter of 2002. Let's assume that Berkshire operates at an NOPM level of 14 percent. This positively affects Berkshire's intrinsic value.

Conversely, interest rates on the date of the valuation were at historically low levels. The 10-year Treasury rate was 4.06 percent. We believe that interest rates will rise to a more normal level. Let's assume that rise will average 1 percent, increasing the 10-year Treasury rate to 5.06 percent.

When we keep other inputs constant, and plug 5.06 percent into the 10-year Treasury rate window, and 14 percent into the net operating profit margin window of the general input screen (Exhibit 8-21), we see that Berkshire's intrinsic value is $80,627.

Berkshire Valuation—Lower Growth, Higher NOPM, Higher Rate Scenario: 7-Percent Growth Rate, 14-Percent NOPM, 5.06 Treasury Rate, Value—$63,028

Excessive growth rates always concern us when we value a company. It may be difficult for management, even as astute as Warren Buffett and Charlie Munger, to keep a company as large as Berkshire Hathaway growing at an 11-percent rate. Let's keep everything else the same from our last scenario, but reduce the growth rate assumption to 7 per-

ValuePro 2002
General Input Screen
Intrinsic Stock Value $80627.71
General Inputs

Company Ticker.....	Berk Hath		
Excess Return Period (years)	10	Depreciation Rate (% of Rev.)	2.88
Revenues ($mil)	37668	Investment Rate (% of Rev.)	8.09
Growth Rate (%)	11.00	Working Capital (% of Rev.)	0.00
Net Operating Profit Margin (%)	14.00	Short-Term Assets ($mil)	133682
Tax Rate (%)	35.00	Short-Term Liabilities($mil)	105132
Stock Price($)	72000.00	Equity Risk Premium (%)	3.00
Shares Outstanding (mil)	1.528217	Company Beta	0.54
10-year Treasury Yield (%)	5.06	Value of Debt Out. ($mil)	0
Bond Spread to Treasury (%)	0.00	Value of Pref. Stock Out. ($mil)	0
Preferred Stock Yield (%)	0.00	Company WACC (%)	6.68

EXHIBIT 8-21   Berkshire Hathaway General Input Screen—Higher NOPM Scenario

cent. This is a rate with which we feel more comfortable, and one that will produce a more conservative valuation.

What happens to intrinsic value if Berkshire's growth rate in the future averages 7 percent? If we keep other inputs constant and plug 7 percent into the growth rate window of the general input screen (Exhibit 8-22), we see that Berkshire's intrinsic value is $63,028. This is 10 percent below the current price for Berkshire stock.

ValuePro 2002
General Input Screen
Intrinsic Stock Value $63028.45
General Inputs

Company Ticker.....	Berk Hath		
Excess Return Period (years)	10	Depreciation Rate (% of Rev.)	2.88
Revenues ($mil)	37668	Investment Rate (% of Rev.)	8.09
Growth Rate (%)	7.00	Working Capital (% of Rev.)	0.00
Net Operating Profit Margin (%)	14.00	Short-Term Assets ($mil)	133682
Tax Rate (%)	35.00	Short-Term Liabilities($mil)	105132
Stock Price($)	72000.00	Equity Risk Premium (%)	3.00
Shares Outstanding (mil)	1.528217	Company Beta	0.54
10-year Treasury Yield (%)	5.06	Value of Debt Out. ($mil)	0
Bond Spread to Treasury (%)	0.00	Value of Pref. Stock Out. ($mil)	0
Preferred Stock Yield (%)	0.00	Company WACC (%)	6.68

EXHIBIT 8-22   Berkshire Hathaway General Input Screen—Lower Growth Scenario

Berkshire Hathaway Stock—Buy? Sell? Hold?

In valuing Berkshire Hathaway, we looked at three scenarios: a baseline scenario with an 11-percent growth rate and a 10.2-percent NOPM that resulted in an intrinsic value of $70,330; an 11-percent growth, 14-percent NOPM, 1-percent higher Treasury rate scenario, which had a value of $80,627; and a 7 percent growth, 14 percent NOPM, 1 percent higher rate scenario that gave a value of $63,038. Berkshire Hathaway is a great company with terrific management. However, at the price of $72,000 per share, it was not a bargain. The price was midway between our low valuation of $63,038 and our high valuation of $80,627. At that level, we viewed Berkshire Hathaway as a *hold*.

Valuing Washington REIT—December 20, 2002

Price—$25.55, Value—$24.81 to $17.38, *Sell*

General Description of Washington REIT—a Real Estate Investment Trust

Washington Real Estate Investment Trust (WRE: *www.writ.com/*) is an equity real estate investment trust that owns and operates 59 properties in the Baltimore-Washington corridor. Their properties consist of 24 office buildings, 15 industrial buildings, 11 retail centers, and 9 multifamily properties. WRE's objective is to invest in real properties in prime locations, to improve the properties, and to manage, develop, and lease the projects to improve their economic performance.

WRE's market equity is only $1 billion—a small cap stock. That market value is 20 times earnings and 3 times book value of $8.38 per share. WRE pays an annual dividend of $1.41 per share and has a dividend yield of 5.52 percent. From third quarter of 2001 to third quarter of 2002, income from real estate was flat, and earnings have declined. WRE's stock price history is shown in Exhibit 8-23.

Valuing a Real Estate Investment Trust

REITs essentially act as mutual funds for real estate, and shareholders own a proportionate interest in a portfolio of real estate properties. The market value of an REIT is directly related to the value of the underlying real estate and properties, and inversely related to interest rates. REITs are an easy way for investors to diversify their portfolio

WASHINGTON REIT
as of 9-Jan-2003   Splits: ▼

Copyright 2002 Yahoo! Inc.   http://finance.yahoo.com/
Splits: 1-Apr-81 [3:1], 15-Jul-85 [3:2], 19-Dec-88 [3:2], 1-Jun-92 [3:2]

EXHIBIT 8-23   Washington REIT's Stock Price Chart

with real estate. Often, the price of real estate and the price of stocks move in opposite directions. We've seen that happen with the bursting of the high-tech bubble. As stock prices plummeted, investors withdrew funds from the equity markets and shifted them into the real estate market—and real estate prices increased significantly.

There are over 200 REITs that are traded in the stock market. Trading REITs provides the attractive feature of instant liquidity for an investment in real estate. Many REITs have a particular specialty, such as apartments or office buildings or industrial buildings, and many may invest in a certain geographic location, such as WRE in Washington and Baltimore. An important investment consideration is that REITs, if they meet certain requirements, are not taxed at the corporate level. So all of the income from an REIT flows through to shareholders without being taxed. Shareholders must pay taxes on the dividend income. Because of high dividend yields, many investors hold REITs in a tax-advantaged account.

The businesses underlying most REITs are based on building, buying, and operating properties and owning real estate. Real estate, absent certain manias such as the real estate bubble that occurred in Japan in the early 1990s, is a less volatile investment than stock. Growth in an REIT's stock price generally follows the growth in the underlying property values. We keep that in mind when we estimate growth rates. Here are the adjustments that we make when we value a real estate investment trust.

1. *Calculation of Operating Income.* For REITs, we take income from real estate, which includes depreciation and amortization, and subtract general and administrative expenses. We exclude other income, gains on sale of real estate, and interest expense.

2. *Tax Rate.* The tax rate for REITs, if they meet certain requirements, is 0.

3. *Depreciation and Capital Expenditures.* Depreciation charges and capital expenditures—to acquire additional real estate and properties and to make improvements to existing properties—are significantly higher for REITs than for other companies.

4. *Adjustment to Beta.* Often, a beta associated with an REIT will be extremely low. For instance, Yahoo Finance lists a beta of 0.01 for WRE. This is because the beta of the stock price of the REIT is calculated by regressing it against the S&P 500, which generates an artificially low result. Some academicians have argued that the risk of an REIT should be regressed against asset returns that also contain real estate indices or interest rates. Aswath Damodaran, in *Investment Valuation,*[1] cites a study that calculates a beta estimate of 0.8 when regressing the returns of office buildings against a market portfolio that includes real estate. We believe that a return associated with a typical real estate investment should fall somewhere near the upper level of the difference between the return for a risk-free asset and the return for a stock that has a beta of 1.0. Therefore, we use a beta of 0.80 when we value WRE.

So let's get started by looking at a typical small cap real estate investment trust—Washington Real Estate Investment Trust.

Developing Valuation Inputs for Washington REIT

The fiscal year for Washington REIT ends on December 31st. The results for the quarter ending September 30, 2002 for WRE are available on its Web site. We have included the audited 2001 income statement, balance sheet, and cash flow statement of WRE, as Exhibits 8-24, 8-25, and 8-26, respectively.

CONSOLIDATED STATEMENTS OF INCOME

	For the Years Ended December 31.		
	2001	2000	1999
(In thousands, except per share data)			
Real estate rental revenue	**$148,424**	$134,732	$118,975
Real estate expenses			
Utilities	**8,351**	7,682	7,298
Real estate taxes	**10,307**	9,347	8,496
Repairs and maintenance	**6,148**	5,580	4,765
Administrative	**3,068**	2,753	2,520
Management fees	**4,669**	4,195	3,693
Operating services and supplies	**5,864**	5,459	4,856
Common area maintenance	**2,074**	1,961	1,850
Other expenses	**1,666**	1,339	1,803
Total real estate expenses	**42,147**	38,316	35,281
Operating income	**106,277**	96,416	83,694
Depreciation and amortization	**26,735**	22,723	19,590
Income from real estate	**79,542**	73,693	64,104
Other income	**1,686**	943	732
Interest expense	**(27,071)**	(25,531)	(22,271)
General and administrative expenses	**(6,100)**	(7,533)	(6,173)
Income before gain on sale of real estate	**48,057**	41,572	36,392
Gain on sale of real estate	**4,296**	3,567	7,909
Net Income	**$ 52,353**	$ 45,139	$ 44,301
Basic earnings per share	**$ 1.39**	$ 1.26	$ 1.24
Diluted earnings per share	**$ 1.38**	$ 1.26	$ 1.24
Weighted Average Shares Outstanding—Basic	**37,674**	35,735	35,714
Weighted Average Shares Outstanding—Diluted	**37,951**	35,872	35,723

EXHIBIT 8-24 Washington REIT 2001 Income Statement

We used information provided in the third-quarter earnings release, in Washington REIT's 2001 Annual Report, and on financial Web sites to develop our valuation inputs.

Revenues. The principal operating revenue source for WRE is real estate rental revenue. Other nonoperating revenue sources are other income and gains on sale of real estate. According to the 2001 income statement, the most recent annual revenue for WRE was *$148.4 million.*

Revenue Growth Rate. The historic revenue growth of WRE has been good, growing by 13 percent from $119 million in 1999 to $135 million in 2000, and then increasing by 10 percent in 2001 to $148 million. Total revenues were up 2 percent in the third quarter of 2002 when compared to the third quarter of 2001. WRE's adjusted income from real estate grew 14 percent from 1999 to 2000, and by 11 percent between 2000 and 2001. During the third quarter of 2002, adjusted in-

CONSOLIDATED BALANCE SHEETS

	As of December 31,	
	2001	2000
(in thousands)		
ASSETS		
Land	**$ 151,782**	$ 142,811
Building	**622,804**	555,702
Total real estate, at cost	**774,586**	698,513
Accumulated depreciation	**(122,625)**	(100,906)
Total investment in real estate, net	**651,961**	597,607
Cash and cash equivalents	**26,441**	6,426
Rents and other receivables, net of allowance for doubtful accounts of $1,993 and $1,743, respectively	**10,523**	9,795
Prepaid expenses and other assets	**19,010**	19,587
Total assets	**$ 707,935**	$ 633,415
LIABILITIES AND SHAREHOLDERS' EQUITY		
Accounts payable and other liabilities	**$ 13,239**	$ 13,048
Advance rents	**3,604**	3,269
Tenant security deposits	**6,148**	5,624
Mortgage notes payable	**94,726**	86,260
Notes payable	**265,000**	265,000
Total liabilities	**382,717**	373,201
Minority interest	**1,611**	1,558
Shareholders' equity		
Shares of beneficial interest, $.01 par value; 100,000 shares authorized: 38,829 and 35,740 shares issued and outstanding, respectively	**388**	357
Additional paid in capital	**323,257**	261,004
Retained earnings (deficit)	**(38)**	(2,705)
Total shareholders' equity	**323,607**	258,656
Total liabilities and shareholders' equity	**$ 707,935**	$ 633,415

EXHIBIT 8-25   Washington REIT 2001 Balance Sheet

come from real estate was down 1 percent from the level in the third quarter of 2001.

What is WRE's growth potential? We compared information from two Web sites, Multex Investor and Yahoo Finance, to find analyst consensus growth estimates. Multex polled four analysts and found an average growth rate of 5.5 percent, with a high rate of 8 percent and a low of 3 percent. Yahoo Finance had a consensus analyst expectation of EPS growth of 8 percent over the next five years. Zacks polled the eight analysts that cover WRE. One rated it a buy, six rated it a hold, and one rated it a strong sell.

For our valuation of WRE, we used a *5.5-percent* growth rate. The growth rate of WRE has been decelerating, particularly in 2002. We think that a 5.5-percent rate is in line with the probable growth in the

CONSOLIDATED STATEMENTS OF CASH FLOWS

	For the Years Ended December 31,		
	2001	2000	1999
(in thousands)			
CASH FLOW FROM OPERATING ACTIVITIES			
Net income	**$ 52,353**	$ 45,139	$ 44,301
Adjustments to reconcile net income to cash provided by operating activities:			
Gain on sale of real estate	**(4,296)**	(3,567)	(7,909)
Depreciation and amortization	**26,735**	22,723	19,590
Increases in other assets	**(1,949)**	(3,382)	(1,954)
Increases (decreases) in other liabilities	**1,810**	834	(985)
Share grants	**219**	227	177
Cash provided by operating activities	**74,672**	61,974	53,220
CASH FLOWS FROM INVESTING ACTIVITIES			
Real estate acquisitions, net*	**(59,250)**	(26,581)	(53,197)
Improvements to real estate	**(14,015)**	(16,268)	(18,371)
Nonreal estate capital improvements	**(538)**	(267)	(350)
Net proceeds from sale of real estate	**8,115**	5,732	22,033
Cash used in investing activities	**(65,688)**	(37,384)	(49,885)
CASH FLOWS FROM FINANCING ACTIVITIES			
Net proceeds from share offering	**53,083**	—	—
Dividends paid	**(49,886)**	(43,955)	(41,341)
Line of credit advances	**43,000**	21,000	33,000
Repayments of lines of credit	**(43,000)**	(54,000)	(44,000)
Proceeds from mortgage note payable	**—**	—	49,225
Mortgage principal payments	**(843)**	(778)	(594)
Net proceeds from debt offering	**—**	54,753	—
Net proceeds from the exercise of share options	**8,477**	100	496
Cash provided by (used in) financing activities	**11,031**	(22,880)	(3,214)
Net increase in cash and cash equivalents	**20,015**	1,710	121
Cash and cash equivalents, beginning of year	**6,426**	4,716	4,595
Cash and cash equivalents, end of year	**$ 26,441**	$ 6,426	$ 4,716
Supplemental disclosure of cash flow information:			
Cash paid for interest	**$ 25,866**	$ 24,001	$ 18,968

EXHIBIT 8-26   Washington REIT 2001 Cash Flow Statement

real estate markets, and would give us a realistic and conservative valuation for WRE.

Excess Return Period. We consider WRE a well-managed real estate investment trust and we used a 10-year excess return period in our valuation.

NOPM Estimate. In order of magnitude, WRE's operating expenses are: real estate taxes, utilities, repairs and maintenance, operating services and supplies, management fees, and administrative. To calculate operating income or adjusted income from real estate for WRE, we took total real estate rental revenue and subtracted total real estate expenses and general and administrative expenses. To arrive at WRE's NOPM, we divided adjusted income from real estate by real estate rental revenue. Over the past three fiscal years, NOPMs were 48.7 percent in 1999, 49.1 percent in 2000, and 49.5 percent in 2001, for an average of 49.09 percent. During the third quarter ending September 30th, WRE's NOPM slipped slightly to 48.4 percent. We used the *49.09-percent* three-year average for our NOPM estimate.

Income Tax Rates. As previously discussed, the income tax rate for most REITs, including WRE, is *0*.

New Investment and Depreciation. To fuel growth, WRE actively purchases, renovates, and sells properties. Net real estate acquisitions and improvements totaled $71.5 million, $42.8 million, and $73.2 million in 1999, 2000, and 2001 respectively, for an average new investment of 47.11 percent of real estate rental revenue. We used *47.11 percent* for the investment rate input. WRE had depreciation charges that average *17.11 percent* of yearly real estate rental revenue over the past three years, which we used as our depreciation rate input.

Incremental Working Capital. Real estate investment trusts often benefit from a positive working capital basis. Typically, security deposits and advance rental payments may be required. Accounts payable, advance rents, and security deposits exceeded rents and other receivables by $12.1 million in 2000 and $12.5 million in 2001 for an average of −8.05 percent of real estate rental revenues. Our entry for working capital was *−8.05 percent.*

Short-Term Assets. The third-quarter balance sheet of WRE lists short-term assets—cash, rents, and other receivables, and prepaid expenses—totaling *$49.5 million,* which was our short-term asset entry.

Short-Term Liabilities. The third-quarter balance sheet of WRE lists short-term liabilities—accounts payable, advance rents, and security deposits—totaling *$22.5 million,* which was our short-term liability entry.

Stock Price. WRE's closing stock price for its shares on December 20, 2002 was *$25.55.*

Shares Outstanding. The third-quarter balance sheet notes that *39.358* million fully diluted average shares were outstanding on September 30, 2002.

Debt Outstanding. The third-quarter balance sheet for WRE shows $265 million in notes payable, $87.2 million of mortgage notes payable, and $53.7 million in line of credit payable. We assume that all three of these categories either are payable over the long term or will be converted to long-term debt by WRE. Our entry for debt outstanding was *$405.9 million.*

Preferred Stock Outstanding. WRE had no preferred stock outstanding, *0.*

Preferred Stock Yield. 0.

Risk-Free Rate. We used the 10-year Treasury yield on December 20, 2002 of *3.96 percent.*

Bond Spread to Treasury. Interest expense of $27.071 million was about 7.54 percent on the debt outstanding in 2001. The 10-term Treasury rate averaged close to 5 percent during 2001, so we estimate that WRE's Bond Spread to Treasury was about *2.5 percent,* which was our entry.

Beta. In accordance with our previous discussion relating to beta for an REIT, our beta entry was *0.80* for WRE.

Equity Risk Premium. We used *3 percent* for this input for our valuation examples.

Washington REIT Valuation—Baseline Scenario:
5.5-Percent Growth Rate, 3.96-Percent Interest Rate, Value—$24.04

The results of the baseline valuation are shown in ValuePro general input screen (Exhibit 8-27), which shows WRE to have a WACC of 6.39 percent. In this scenario, WRE's stock has an intrinsic value of $24.04— 6 percent lower than its closing price on December 20th of $25.55.

Washington REIT Valuation—Higher Interest Rate Scenario:
5.5-Percent Growth Rate, 0.25 Percent per Year Increasing Interest Rate, Value—$16.85

We felt comfortable with the growth rate and NOPMs of Washington REIT. What concerned us most about this scenario was the effect of increasing interest rates on WRE's stock price. At the time of this valuation, interest rates were at historically low levels. Absent a general and prolonged deflation, which occurred in Japan during the 1990s

ValuePro 2002
General Input Screen
Intrinsic Stock Value $24.04
General Inputs

Company Ticker.....	WashREIT		
Excess Return Period (years)	10	Depreciation Rate (% of Rev.)	17.11
Revenues ($mil)	148.4	Investment Rate (% of Rev.)	47.11
Growth Rate (%)	5.50	Working Capital (% of Rev.)	-8.05
Net Operating Profit Margin (%)	49.09	Short-Term Assets ($mil)	49.5
Tax Rate (%)	0.00	Short-Term Liabilities($mil)	22.5
Stock Price($)	25.55	Equity Risk Premium (%)	3.00
Shares Outstanding (mil)	39.358	Company Beta	0.80
10-year Treasury Yield (%)	3.96	Value of Debt Out. ($mil)	405.9
Bond Spread to Treasury (%)	2.50	Value of Pref. Stock Out. ($mil)	0
Preferred Stock Yield (%)	0.00	Company WACC (%)	6.39

EXHIBIT 8-27   Washington REIT General Input Screen—Baseline Scenario

through 2000, it was our belief that interest rates would rise significantly from their current levels.

Let's assume that long-term interest rates increase one-quarter percent per year over the next five years. How does this interest rate movement affect WRE's intrinsic stock value? We use the custom input screen to handle this type of what-if scenario. In the WACC column of the custom input screen (Exhibit 8-28), we increased the WACC one-quarter percent per year over a 5-year period—from 6.39 percent in year 1, to 6.64 percent in year 2, . . . to 7.64 percent in years 6 to 10—a total interest rate increase of 1.25 percent.

Keeping all other inputs constant, displayed at the top of the custom input screen is the new intrinsic value—$16.85. The cash flows associated with this scenario are shown in the custom pro forma screen, Exhibit 8-29.

Washington REIT Stock—Buy? Sell? Hold?

In valuing Washington REIT, we looked at two scenarios. The baseline scenario had a 5.5-percent growth rate, a 10-year Treasury rate of 3.96 percent, and a WACC of 6.39 percent, and resulted in an intrinsic value of $24.04. The second scenario assumed all of the inputs of the baseline scenario, and an increase in interest rates of one-quarter percent per year over a 5-year period. WRE's weighted average cost of capital

ValuePro 2002
Custom Valuation Input Screen
WashREIT
Intrinsic Stock Value $16.85

Period	12 Months Ending	Growth Rate	Net Operating Margin	Tax Rate	Invest. Rate	Dep. Rate	Increm. Working Capital	WACC
0	01/12/2003							
1	01/12/2004	5.50	49.09	0.00	47.11	17.11	-8.05	6.39
2	01/12/2005	5.50	49.09	0.00	47.11	17.11	-8.05	6.64
3	01/12/2006	5.50	49.09	0.00	47.11	17.11	-8.05	6.89
4	01/12/2007	5.50	49.09	0.00	47.11	17.11	-8.05	7.14
5	01/12/2008	5.50	49.09	0.00	47.11	17.11	-8.05	7.39
6	01/12/2009	5.50	49.09	0.00	47.11	17.11	-8.05	7.64
7	01/12/2010	5.50	49.09	0.00	47.11	17.11	-8.05	7.64
8	01/12/2011	5.50	49.09	0.00	47.11	17.11	-8.05	7.64
9	01/12/2012	5.50	49.09	0.00	47.11	17.11	-8.05	7.64
10	01/12/2013	5.50	49.09	0.00	47.11	17.11	-8.05	7.64
Residual								7.64

EXHIBIT 8-28 Washington REIT Custom Input Screen—Higher Rate Scenario

increased from 6.39 percent in year 1 to 7.64 percent in years 6 to 10. WRE's intrinsic stock value slipped to $16.85 percent. A relatively small movement in interest rates dropped WRE's intrinsic stock price $7.43, or −30 percent.

Washington REIT is a very well-run real estate investment trust with steady NOPMs and decent growth. However, it was our belief that the downside risk of the stock was greater than the upside potential. Although it was not greatly overpriced at $25.55, at this level at the time of the valuation, we viewed Washington REIT as a weak *sell*.

ValuePro 2002
Custom Pro Forma Screen
10-year Excess Return Period
WashREIT

Disc. Excess Return Period FCFF	$262		Total Corporate Value	$1,091
Discounted Residual Value	$780		Less Debt	($406)
Short-Term Assets	$49.5		Less Preferred Stock	$0
Total Corporate Value	$1,091		Less Short-Term Liabilities	($22)
			Total Value to Common Equity	$663
			Intrinsic Stock Value	$16.85

(2) 12 Months Ending	(3) Revenues	(4) NOP	(5) Adj. Taxes	(6) NOPAT	(7) Invest.	(8) Deprec.	(9) Change in Invest.	(10) Change in Working Capital	(11) FCFF	(12) Discount Factor	(13) Discounted FCFF
01/12/2003	148										
01/12/2004	157	77	0	77	74	27	47	-1	31	0.9399	29
01/12/2005	165	81	0	81	78	28	50	-1	32	0.8793	28
01/12/2006	174	86	0	86	82	30	52	-1	34	0.8188	28
01/12/2007	184	90	0	90	87	31	55	-1	36	0.7589	27
01/12/2008	194	95	0	95	91	33	58	-1	38	0.7001	26
01/12/2009	205	100	0	100	96	35	61	-1	40	0.6429	26
01/12/2010	216	106	0	106	102	37	65	-1	42	0.5973	25
01/12/2011	228	112	0	112	107	39	68	-1	44	0.5549	25
01/12/2012	240	118	0	118	113	41	72	-1	47	0.5155	24
01/12/2013	253	124	0	124	119	43	76	-1	49	0.4789	24
	253	124	0	124	43	43	0	0	1,629	0.4789	780

EXHIBIT 8-29 Washington REIT Custom Pro Forma Screen—Higher Rate Scenario

Summary

In this chapter, we put the 10 principles and all of the valuation pieces together to value the stocks of three financial companies and a real estate investment trust. When we valued Citigroup, we looked closely at the relationship between growth rates and stock value. We noted that Wall Street analysts tend to be an optimistic group and suggested that their growth estimates would be difficult to maintain over the long run. When we reduced the growth rate from the 14.5 percent predicted by analysts to 5 percent, our more conservative estimate, the intrinsic value of Citigroup was still significantly above its current market price. The value/price ratio of 1.27 was our rationale for a strong buy recommendation.

When we valued Merrill Lynch, we focused on two areas of concern. At an estimated 13 percent, we believed growth estimates were too high. We also believed that the recent NOPMs of Merrill Lynch were too low, primarily due to the terrorist attacks and the bursting of the high-tech bubble. We looked at a second scenario with low growth, and a third scenario with low growth and an increased NOPM and in each case found intrinsic values for Merrill Lynch that exceeded its current $40.13 price. We believed that buying Merrill's stock was a bet on an operating turnaround, and we rated Merrill Lynch as a buy.

Led by Warren Buffett, Berkshire Hathaway is a great company. We valued it based on analysts' expected growth rates of 11 percent, and found a value of $70,330. In our second scenario, when NOPMs increased to preterrorist attack levels and interest rates increased by 1 percent, Berskshire's value grew to over $80,000. And when we lowered the growth rate to 7 percent, Berkshire's value dropped to $63,000. We believed that at the current market price of $72,000, Berkshire Hathaway was properly valued, and we rated it a hold.

Our final valuation was for a small-cap REIT, Washington Real Estate Investment Trust. Growth estimates for WRE were reasonable at 5.5 percent and its NOPMs have been steady. The baseline valuation for WRE had an intrinsic value of $24.04, and the stock's price was $25.55, resulting in a valuation ratio of 0.94. A valuation ratio of less than 1.0 indicates that a stock is overvalued. If interest rates rose, what would happen to WRE's stock value? When we examined a scenario in which interest rates increased by one-quarter percent per year over a five-year period, WRE's intrinsic stock value dropped 30 percent to $16.85. Although WRE is a well-run REIT, we believed that it was overpriced at $25.55, and that its downside risk outweighed its upside potential. Therefore, we rated it a weak sell.

We hope that you enjoyed this book and find it helpful in developing your own investment approach. Good luck!

Notes

1. Aswath Damodaran, *Investment Valuation*, John Wiley & Sons, 1996, page 476.

Glossary

accounts payable The amount owed to suppliers for goods and services purchased on credit; payment obligations usually range between 30 and 90 days.

accounts receivable The amount due from customers for goods and service sold on credit; discounts are often given for timely payment (e.g., within 10 days).

alpha The rate of return on an investment in excess of the expected rate of return as forecast by a pricing model (e.g., CAPM).

after-tax cost of debt The tax-adjusted cost of debt; the nominal interest rate adjusted for tax benefits of interest payments. The equation is (1 − tax rate) * (nominal interest rate).

arbitrage pricing model (APM) An asset pricing model that predicts expected returns on a security on the basis of a correlation between the security and multiple input variables.

average-risk stock A stock with a beta equal to 1; an issue that moves with the market.

bear market A long-term downward trend in security prices. Recently, this has been defined as a decline of 20 percent or more over an extended time period. The worst bear market in the last 50 years occurred between 2000 and 2002.

beta   The measure of *systematic risk* of a security. The beta of the market is defined as 1. If a security's beta is greater than 1, it is expected to exceed market changes (e.g., when the market increases by 5 percent, the security increases by 10 percent). If a security's beta is less than 1, it is expected to lag behind market changes (e.g., when the market increases by 10 percent, the security increases by 5 percent).

bonds   A security issued by a borrower that establishes a contractual obligation to repay a specified amount at a future date, usually with periodic interest payment.

book value   The accounting value of a corporate security.

book value per share (BVPS)   Common stockholder equity divided by the number of shares outstanding. This is an estimate of the equity stake in an organization that each share represents.

bottom-line growth   A company's growth in net income.

bull market   An extended period of increasing security prices.

capital asset pricing model (CAPM)   An asset pricing model that determines the required rate of return on securities on the basis of a *market risk premium* and a *risk-free rate.*

cash flow   An exchange of cash, either inflow or outflow, as a result of a transaction.

cash inflow   The net cash amount flowing into a firm (e.g., revenues) as a result of the ongoing operations of a business.

cash outflow   The net cash amount flowing out of a firm (e.g., expenses) from the ongoing operations of a business.

clientele effect   The tendency of investors to purchase stock of a company based on its dividend policy. Investors who desire predictable current income buy stocks with higher dividends (e.g., ConEd), while those who desire growth buy stocks that pay little or no dividends (e.g., Intel).

common stock   Equity ownership in a corporation. Two important characteristics of common stock are that its owners have a residual claim on corporate assets (behind bondholders and preferred stockholders) and are subject to limited liability.

common stock equivalents   Common stock plus securities convertible into common stock of a company.

compound   The process of accumulating the time value of money over time. For example, compounding interest payments means that an investor who earns interest in one period will earn additional interest in the following period because of the reinvestment of interest in each period.

compound annual growth rate (CAGR)   A rate that assumes annual compounding of growth.

contingent claim   A claim whose value is based on the value of another asset or the outcome of a specific event.

corporate value   The estimated total dollar value of an enterprise, usually determined by models and appraisals.

current stock price   The most recent price level at which an equity investment traded, as determined by the financial market where that security trades.

cyclical stocks   Companies or industries whose financial performance (revenues and earnings) is tied to business cycle fluctuations. The automotive, steel, and cement industries are examples.

debt/equity ratio   The total amount of debt financing that the firm has in its capital structure, divided by the dollar amount invested by shareholders.

defensive stocks   Stocks that provide necessary services, such as electric utilities and gas; essentials, such as food; or staples, such as soft drinks. Because of the nature of these products, the stocks provide a degree of stability during periods of economic decline.

depreciation   The periodic allocation of the cost of property, plant, and equipment over the useful revenue-generating life of the asset. Depreciation is a noncash expense and is not a cash outflow.

depreciation rate   Annual depreciation divided by annual revenues.

diluted earnings per share   Earnings per share adjusted for all potential equity claims on earnings. Diluted EPS is lower than basic EPS because it accounts for potential dilutive common shares from complex securities like convertible bonds and stock options.

discount   The process of calculating the present value of expected cash flows. To discount means to multiply a number by less than 1.0.

discount factor   The multiplier used to convert an expected future cash flow into current dollars.

discount rate   The rate of return used to measure the time value of money. The discount rate varies with risk of the cash flows being discounted.

discounted cash flow approach   A valuation model based on the present value of expected cash flows.

dividend   A payment of cash or stock by the company to its stockholders.

diversification   Spreading investment holdings across multiple industries, strategies, or firms to reduce the company-specific risk associated with an investment portfolio.

Dow Jones Industrial Average (DJIA)   A price-weighted equity index of 30 blue-chip New York Stock exchange companies.

earnings   Net income.

earnings before interest and taxes (EBIT)   Income generated by the company before the payment of interest on debt and income taxes.

earnings before interest but after taxes (EBIAT)   Same as EBIT minus the payment of income taxes.

earnings per share (EPS)   Corporate earnings divided by shares outstanding.

efficient capital market   A market in which information asymmetries do not provide profit opportunities, and new information is quickly interpreted and reflected in the value of shares.

excess marketable securities   Marketable securities held by the firm for investment purposes. Marketable securities do not include treasury stock of the issuing firm.

excess return period   The number of years that a company is expected to earn a return on incremental investment in excess of its weighted average cost of capital.

expected return   The return an investor expects to earn at a specific level of risk.

expected return of the market (Rm)   The expected return on a market benchmark index (e.g., S&P 500) for a specific period. Historic data are often used to estimate this variable.

fairly valued stock   A stock's price that is equal to its intrinsic stock value.

Financial Accounting Standards Board (FASB)   The primary rule-making body that establishes, interprets, and publishes financial accounting principles for public and private firms.

fiscal year (FY)   The accounting year consistent with the operating cycle for which a firm reports its periodic financial statements.

free cash flow (FCF)   Equal to cash inflows minus cash outflows.

free cash flow to equity (FCFE)   Equal to free cash flow minus interest expense.

free cash flow to firm (FCFF)   The free cash flow available to all shareholders and stakeholders after capital expenditure obligations are fulfilled.

fully valued stock   A stock with a price that is generally considered to be at the high end of its intrinsic value. High-growth firms eventually become fully valued when all future growth expectations and opportunities are priced into the shares and there is a limited additional upside.

fundamental analysis   Security analysis that incorporates all available public information relating to a particular company, including historic prices, industry data, and overall market performance.

greater fool theory   A theory based on the belief that anyone who makes an investment will be able to sell it to a less informed investor for a profit in the future.

growth stocks   Stocks of companies in expanding industries where the growth in earnings on revenues is expected to be significantly greater (e.g., 15 percent or more)

hedge fund   A hedge fund is a sophisticated investment partnership that borrows money, purchases financial assets, and simultaneously hedges the risks associated with owning the assets by selling offsetting hedge liabilities.

incremental working capital expenditure   The change in *working capital* from period to period.

initial public offering (IPO)   The first publicly traded issue of a corporation's common stock.

intrinsic stock value   The firm's raw material, work in process, and finished goods surplus that has not been used or sold in the normal operating process.

investment rate   Investment in property, plant, and equipment, divided by annual revenues.

leverage   The use of debt financing in a firm's capital structure.

leveraged buyout (LBO)   The purchase that is financed with a large percentage of debt and is secured by the firm's assets.

long Treasury rate   The yield on long-term U.S. Treasury securities—typically the benchmark 10-year Treasury Bond.

market capitalization   The total market value of the outstanding debt and equity of a firm.

market risk premium   The difference between the expected return on the market portfolio (usually the historic return on the S&P 500) and the *risk-free rate of return.*

merger   A combination of two firms in which one firm absorbs the assets and liabilities of the other firm in their entirety.

momentum trading strategy   A technical trading technique that involves buying a stock because the trend in a stock's price has been up, and selling a stock because its stock price trend has been down.

net change in working capital   The difference in working capital from one period to another.

net investment   New investment minus depreciation.

net operating income (NOI)   Earnings from continuing operations before paying interest on debt or income taxes.

net operating profit (NOP)   See *net operating income.*

net operating profit after taxes (NOPAT)   Operating income before interest payments on debt and income taxes. Used to calculate cash flows to the firm, the measurement seeks to exclude the tax benefits of debt financing in the profit measurement.

net operating profit margin (NOPM)   Net operating profit per dollar of sales (NOP divided by revenues).

net present value (NPV)   The present value of future cash flows, minus the initial cost of the venture or project.

operating income   Income from continuing operations before paying income tax and interest expense.

overvalued stock   A stock whose price is greater than its intrinsic value.

par value   The nominal dollar amount assigned to a security by the issuing firm. Par value for stock is generally 1 cent or $1 and has nothing to do with the ultimate market price or book value of the issue. Par value for bonds is generally $1000.

period of competitive advantage   See *excess return period.*

pretax cost of debt   The nominal rate of interest on a debt issue; the figure does not incorporate the tax benefits of debt interest expense.

preferred stock An ownership claim on corporate assets senior to that of common stock but junior to debt. It is technically an equity security, but has features similar to both debt and equity. Preferred stock pays shareholders a periodic dividend payment. However, unlike bond payments, preferred dividend payments are not legally binding, and the board of directors can withhold dividends during the hard times.

premium The amount by which a security sells above its *par value.*

present value (PV) The value of future payments discounted to today's value to incorporate risk and the time value of money.

price/book value (P/BV) ratio The market price per share of stock, divided by the book value per share.

price/cash flow (P/CF) ratio The market price of stock per share, divided by the cash flow per share. Cash flow per share is roughly estimated by using earnings before interest, taxes, depreciation, and amortization on a per-share basis.

price/earnings (P/E) ratio The relationship between earnings per share and the market price of common stock. Generally speaking, a high P/E multiple relative to other companies in the same industry implies that investors have confidence in a company's ability to generate higher future profits.

price/earnings/growth (PEG) ratio The P/E ratio divided by the projected earnings growth rate. It measures the price that one pays for expected future growth. This measurement was popularized by the Motley Fool.

price/sales (P/S) ratio The market value of a firm divided by its annual revenues. Companies with high profit margins usually have higher P/S ratios.

price volatility The relative rate at which the price of a security moves up or down, as determined by the annualized standard deviation of daily changes in price.

pro forma Projections of what a company's financial performance will be in the future.

random walk hypothesis The theory that investment price movements do not follow any pattern or trend over time, and that past price movements have no impact on future price movements.

relative value approach Valuing a firm relative to other firms in the industry on the basis of size, earnings, and similar characteristics. Common relative value measurements include market/ book, price/earnings, price/cash flow, and price/sales.

residual value   The terminal value of a company beyond the *excess return period*. Calculated by dividing NOPAT by WACC.

return to stockholder   A shareholder-realized return in the form of capital appreciation and dividends over the holding period.

revenues   Net sales generated by firm operations.

revenue growth rate   An annualized growth rate of sales over a specified time period, usually 5–10 years.

risk   Unanticipated change in investment returns over an extended period of time, as measured by the volatility of returns.

risk-free rate of return (Rf)   The rate of return on the 30-year U.S. Treasury bond.

secondary market   The markets in which securities are traded after their initial issuance. The NYSE, AMEX, and NASDAQ are secondary markets.

senior claims   The highest level of financial claims issued by a company. The level of seniority is used to determine claims on assets upon liquidation. Senior debt claims are paid prior to any payments of junior claims. Debt and preferred stock have claims that are senior to common stock.

share repurchase program   A program under which a firm purchases shares of its own stock via the secondary market.

shares outstanding   The total number of shares issued by a firm that has not been retired or repurchased.

short sale   Borrowing a security from a broker and selling it at the current market price, with the understanding that it must later be bought back (hopefully at a lower price) and returned to the lending agent.

short squeeze   A situation where a rise in stock prices forces investors who sold stock short to purchase shares to cover their short position and cut their losses. As the price of the shares continues to rise, more short sellers feel compelled to cover their positions.

spread to Treasuries   The difference between security yields and the yield on 30-year Treasury Bonds. High yield, emerging debt, corporate debt, and dividend yield are often measured as a spread to Treasury bonds.

standard deviation   A statistical measurement equal to the square root of the variance; a measurement of dispersion of a data sample around the average. A security with a high standard deviation of returns is risky because of the large range of potential returns that the investor can expect.

Standard & Poor's 500 A market value weighted index of 500 stocks that represents more than $8 trillion in *market capitalization* in the U.S. equity markets.

systematic risk Risk that cannot be diversified away by holding a portfolio of securities. Measured by a stock's beta.

takeover The act of acquiring control of an organization through a cash or stock bid.

tax rate The ratio equal to the corporation's provision for income taxes divided by income before taxes.

technical analysis Analysis of market data (stock prices, volume, correlations, etc.) in an attempt to predict future price movements of a security on the basis of historic market trends. Technical analysis includes chart analysis, moving averages, support and resistance measurement, and numerous other measures of historic relationships.

top-line growth Revenue growth of a company.

undervalued stock A stock whose market price is below its intrinsic value.

unsystematic risk Any risk attached to a security that can be diversified away by holding a portfolio of securities.

value to common equity Equal to total corporate value minus senior claims. The current market value of all common stock.

ValuePro 2002 Easy-to-use stock valuation software that applies the *discounted cash flow approach.*

volatility The relative rate at which the price of a security or index moves up or down, as determined by the annualized *standard deviation* of daily change in price.

weighted average cost of capital (WACC) The weighted average cost of financing for a firm.

working capital Accounts receivable, plus the inventories minus accounts payable. Working capital is required to support the revenue-generating activities of a firm.

yield The annual percentage rate earned on a particular security of investment asset.

Acronyms

APM	Arbitrage Pricing Model
BV	Book Value
BVPS	Book Value Per Share
CAPM	Capital Asset Pricing Model
CAGR	Compound Annual Growth Rate
CGS	Cost of Goods Sold
CEO	Chief Executive Officer
CFO	Chief Financial Officer
DCF	Discounted Cash Flow
DJIA	Dow Jones Industrial Average
EBIAT	Earnings before Interest and After Taxes
EBIT	Earnings before Interest and Taxes
EPS	Earnings Per Share
FCF	Free Cash Flow
FCFE	Free Cash Flow to Equity
FCFF	Free Cash Flow to the Firm
IPO	Initial Public Offering
LBO	Leveraged Buy Out

M&A	Mergers and Acquisition
MBA	Master's of Business Administration
MV	Market Value
NASDAQ	National Association of Securities Dealers Quotation System
NOI	Net Operating Income
NOP	Net Operating Profit
NOPAT	Net Operating Profit after Taxes
NOPM	Net Operating Profit Margin
NPV	Net Present Value
P/BV	Price/Book Value Ratio
P/E	Price/Earnings Ratio
PEG	Price/Earnings/Growth Ratio
P/S	Price/Sales Ratio
PV	Present Value
R&D	Research and Development costs
SEC	Securities and Exchange Commission
SGA	Sales, General, and Administrative expenses
S&P500	Standard & Poor's 500 Index
URL	Uniform Resource Locator
WACC	Weighted Average Cost of Capital

Bibliography

Banz, Rolf, "The Relationship Between Return and Market Value of Common Stocks." *Journal of Financial Economics*, March 1981.

Basu, S., "The Relationship Between Earnings Yield, Market Value, and Return for NYSE Common Stocks." *Journal of Financial Economics*. June 1983.

Bernstein, Peter L., *Against the Gods*. Wiley, 1996.

Bernstein, Peter L., *Capital Ideas*. Macmillan, 1992.

Bernstein, William J., *The Four Pillars of Investing*. McGraw-Hill, 2002.

Bodie, Zvi, and Robert C. Merton, *Finance*. Prentice Hall, 1997.

Brinson, Gary P., Randolph L. Hood, and Gilbert L. Beebower, "Determinants of Portfolio Performance." *Financial Analysts Journal*, July/August 1986.

Brinson, Gary P., Brian D. Singer and Gilbert L. Beebower, "Determinants of Portfolio Performance II: An Update." *Financial Analysts Journal*, May/June 1991.

Copeland, Tom, Tim Koller, and Jack Murrin, *Valuation—Measuring and Managing the Value of Companies*. Wiley 1996.

Damodaran, Aswath, *Investment Valuation*. Wiley, 1996.

Damodaran, Aswath, *The Dark Side of Valuation*. Prentice Hall, 2001.

DeBondt, Werner, and Richard H. Thaler, "Does the Stock Market Overreact." *Journal of Finance,* 40 (3) 1985.

Dunbar, Nicholas, *Inventing Money*. Wiley, 2001.

English, James R., *Applied Equity Analysis*. McGraw-Hill, 2001.

Fama, Eugene F., *Foundations of Finance*. Basic Books, 1976.

Fama, Eugene F., "The Behavior of Stock Prices." *The Journal of Business,* January 1965.

Eugene Fama, "Random Walks in Stock Market Prices." *Financial Analyst Journal,* September–October 1965.

Fama, Eugene F., and Kenneth R. French, "The Cross-Section of Expected Stock Returns." *Journal of Finance,* June 1992.

Fama, Eugene F., and Kenneth R. French, "Value versus Growth: The International Evidence." *Journal of Finance,* December 1998.

Gray, Gary, Patrick J. Cusatis, and J. Randall Woolridge, *Streetsmart Guide to Valuing a Stock*. McGraw-Hill, 1999.

Haugen, Robert A., *The New Finance, The Case Against Efficient Markets*. Prentice Hall, 1999.

Ibbotson Associates, *Stocks, Bonds, Bills and Inflation*. Ibbotson Associates, annual.

Jaffe, Jeffrey, "Special Information and Insider Trading." *Journal of Business,* April 1974.

Levitt, Arthur, and Paula Dwyer, *Take on the Street*. Pantheon Books, 2002.

Malkiel, Burton G., *A Random Walk Down Wall Street*. W.W. Norton, 1999.

McKelvey, Edward F., "The Brave New Business Cycle: Its Implications for Corporate Profitability." U.S. Economic Research, Goldman, Sachs & Co, 1998.

Modigliani, Franco, and Merton H., "Dividend Policy, Growth and the Valuation of Shares." *Journal of Business,* 1961.

O'Shaugnessy, James P., *What Works on Wall Street*. McGraw-Hill, 1996.

Rappaport, Alfred, and Michael J. Mauboussin, *Expectations Investing*. Harvard Business School Press, 2001.

Reilly, Frank K., and Keith C. Brown, *Investment Analysis Portfolio Management*. Thomson South-Western, 2003.

Reinganum, Marc, "Misspecification of Capital Asset Pricing: Empirical Anomalies Based on Earnings Yield and Market Value." *Journal of Financial Economics,* March 1981.

Rosenburg, Barr, Kenneth Reid, and Ronald Lanstein, "Persuasive Evidence of Market Efficiency." *Journal of Portfolio Management,* Spring 1985.

Sharpe, Stephen, "Stock Prices, Expected Returns and Inflation," unpublished paper, Federal Reserve Board, Washington, D.C., 1999.

Shiller, Robert J., *Irrational Exuberance.* Broadway Books, 2000.

Siegel, Jeremy J., *Stocks for the Long Run.* McGraw-Hill, 1998.

Womack, Kevin, "Do Brokerage Analysts' Recommendations Have Investment Value." *Journal of Finance,* March 1996.

Index

Note: Boldface numbers indicate illustrations.

About the Authors

Gary Gray, Ph.D. is a Visiting Professor of Finance at The Pennsylvania State University and is a consultant to investment and commercial banks. Previously he was a Managing Director with Lehman Brothers and was with Shearson Lehman Brothers and E.F. Hutton prior to the Shearson merger. Dr. Gray has been an investment banker/financial engineer since 1972, specializing in new product development in municipal bonds and preferred stock. He has been responsible for a number of innovative financial products including: tax-exempt zero coupon bonds and capital appreciation bonds; tender option crossover refunding bonds; RIBs/SAVRs; Municipal Call Hedging Option Program (Muni CHOPs); Bond Payment Obligations (BPOs); agricultural revenue bonds; secondary market programs for tax-exempts and preferred stock, including Multiple Option Municipal Securities, and a variety of Unit Investment Trust products and leveraged limited partnership structures.

Dr. Gray attended Penn State on a football scholarship and played inside linebacker and was a graduate assistant coach under Joe Paterno. He has articles published in numerous periodicals including *Harvard Business Review* and *Municipal Finance Journal*. He is the author of *Running with the Bulls*, Lyons Press, 2001, and coauthor, along with Pat Cusatis, of *Municipal Derivative Securities: Uses and Valuation*, which was published by Irwin Professional Publishing in October, 1994. He is an avid fly fisherman and runs the encierro each July in Pamplona, Spain.

Patrick J. Cusatis, Ph.D. is an Assistant Professor of Finance at The Pennsylvania State University at Harrisburg and is a consultant to financial institutions. Previously Dr. Cusatis was with Lehman Brothers, First Union Capital Markets, and Tucker Anthony Sutro and specialized in new product development, quantitative techniques, and hedging strategies. He was responsible for the financial modeling and implementation of Muni CHOPs, BPOs, Residual Interest Bonds (RIBs)/Select Auction Rate Variable Securities (SAVRs) Program; and a secondary market program using levered RIBs/SAVRs. Dr. Cusatis also was responsible for developing a call-valuation strategy model for issuers with multiple series of municipal bonds outstanding.

Dr. Cusatis has published articles in the *Journal of Financial Economics*, the *Journal of Applied Corporate Finance*, and the *Municipal Finance Journal*. He is coauthor, along with Gary Gray, of *Municipal Derivative Securities: Uses and Valuation*. He is an avid fly fisherman, hunter, and antique collector.

J. Randall Woolridge, Ph.D. is the Goldman, Sachs & Co. and Frank P. Smeal Endowed University Professor of Finance at The Pennsylvania State University. His teaching and research interests are in corporate finance with an emphasis on the valuation consequences of corporate strategic investment and financial decisions. He has won the Excellence in Teaching Award at the Penn State MBA Program. Dr. Woolridge has also participated in over 300 executive development programs in more than 20 countries in North and South America, Europe, Asia and Africa. His specialty areas in executive programs include: corporate financial management and strategy, financial engineering, security analysis, and creating shareholder value. He has consulted for numerous corporate clients including: AT&T, Merrill Lynch, Goldman Sachs, Morgan Stanley, Bankers Trust, Paine Webber, Bank of Boston, and Knight Ridder, among others.

Dr. Woolridge has published over 25 articles in leading academic and professional journals including: the *Journal of Finance*, the *Journal of Financial Economics*, and the *Journal of Applied Corporate Finance*. His research has been highlighted extensively in the financial press, including: *The New York Times*, *The Wall Street Journal*, *Barron's*, *Fortune*, *Forbes*, and *Business Week*. He has appeared on CNN's *Money Line* and CNBC's *Business Today*. Dr. Woolridge is an avid marathon runner and soccer player.